# THE LESSONS OF THE VIETNAM WAR ARE TOO VALUABLE TO IGNORE....

"This a book about values. We who remember invite you to look back with us, behind the veil of myth and rhetoric. Though at times we must swallow our pride and examine tragic mistakes, the common humanity of the forty-eight people here is a shared triumph of the human spirit.

"In no way do we claim to represent the whole story. But we hope to bring to light some of the complicated realities that have often been overlooked. Please allow our truths to be a part of the larger discussion and debate."

from the introduction by
**AL SANTOLI**

"WHAT SANTOLI HAS UNCOVERED MUST ALTER THE MANNER IN WHICH MANY AMERICANS VIEW OUR INVOLVEMENT IN SOUTHEAST ASIA."

John Del Vecchio, author of
*The Thirteenth Valley*

(more)

"Santoli traveled throughout the United States, Europe and Asia for three years to obtain these interviews....What he offers us is Vietnam through the eyes of Southeast Asians. It is a unique and needed view....a powerful book, the first oral history to look at war in Southeast Asia within a broader frame of time."

*The Dallas Times Herald*

"The eighty or so interview excerpts making up this book are not, and weren't intended to be, a comprehensive history; they are fragments of lives that were themselves fragments of a colossal and complicated tragedy. Santoli's achievement was to make those fragments into a mosaic that shows, unforgettably, how many different views of the war there were—and how many different kinds of pain."

*Chicago Tribune Book World*

"THIS BOOK IS NECESSARY TO UNDERSTAND THE MOST SIGNIFICANT ASPECT OF THE INDOCHINA WARS: THE HUMAN ONE."

Tran Van Dinh, author of
*Blue Dragon White Tiger: A Tet Story*

"Santoli has done his homework, spending time in the refugee camps and wherever else his research took him. He knows these people, whose stories are so compelling and consistent that to dismiss them would be like ignoring the trains that carried Jews to death camps."

*The Denver Post*

"The voices in this book raise disturbing questions and provide insights into both the American and Vietnamese attitudes and beliefs about the war. They leave a trail of clues about that most elusive of subjects—what really happened in Vietnam. Al Santoli weaves a fabric both illuminating and frustrating, frustrating because a reader, at least this reader, would like to spend hours if not days talking to each of the people within these pages."

Jack Reynolds
Network Correspondent
NBC

"A VIVID COLLECTION OF HISTORICAL REMINISCENCES...RIVETING AND WELL-TOLD."

*The Washington Post*

Also by Al Santoli
*Published by Ballantine Books:*

EVERYTHING WE HAD

# TO BEAR ANY BURDEN

The Vietnam War and Its Aftermath
in the Words of Americans
and Southeast Asians

## Al Santoli

BALLANTINE BOOKS • NEW YORK

*For the Vietnam Generation,
American and Southeast Asian.*

*In memory of Penn Nhach,
who sacrificed the best years of his life
so that others might have freedom.*

Library of Congress Catalog Card Number: 84-28690

ISBN 0-345-33188-5

This edition published by arrangement with E. P. Dutton, Inc.

Manufactured in the United States of America

First Ballantine Books Edition: June 1986

We are forced to intervene in many directions simply because we have to be on our guard in many directions; now, as previously, we have come as allies to those of you here who are being oppressed; our help was asked for, and we have not arrived uninvited.

—THUCYDIDES
*The Peloponnesian War*


Let every nation know, whether it wishes us well or ill, that we shall pay any price, bear any burden, meet any hardship, support any friend, oppose any foe to assure the survival and success of liberty.

—JOHN F. KENNEDY
*Inaugural Address, 1960*


People, more than terrain, are the objectives in this war.

—GENERAL WILLIAM WESTMORELAND
*August 26, 1966*


For the fifth time we have declared clearly that the DRV government [Hanoi] and the PRG [Viet Cong] have never wished to force a Communist government on South Vietnam.

—LE DUC THO
*Paris peace talks, 1972*


We do not say Vietnam is the center of world conflict, but it is the place where the big contradictions of our era are converging. Maybe in ten years it will be somewhere else. . . . We don't speak of the Vietnam example, but the Vietnam experience.

—NGUYEN KHAC VIEN
*Vietnam, 1972*

# CONTENTS

SECTION IV    NO WAR, NO PEACE

SECTION V   VALUES

# INTRODUCTION

I returned home from Vietnam in March 1969. Ten years later, in 1979, as if coming out of a shock-induced trance, I stopped running from my experiences there. I began interviewing and soul-searching with fellow veterans for an oral history of the war, *Everything We Had*. This was the soldiers' story. It showed us to be ordinary human beings caught in an awesome nightmare not of our making.

The widespread appeal of *Everything We Had* put me in touch with a large number of Americans on all sides of the Vietnam debate. I found that a division still exists between those who believed in the war and those who opposed it. At the same time, I began meeting and corresponding with a number of Vietnamese and Cambodian refugees, who began to unfold their stories of what happened in Southeast Asia after April 30, 1975. I was amazed by how much I didn't know or understand. And I recognized in myself—as well as in the people I talked to, American and Southeast Asian alike—the need to explore more deeply our memories and the meaning of Vietnam.

My experiences as a nineteen-year-old infantry sergeant during heavy fighting on the Cambodian border were similar to the experiences of many other American soldiers. Though we went to Vietnam committed to winning the war, we became frustrated and disillusioned by factors never mentioned in our pre-Vietnam training. Political restrictions gave privileged sanctuary to very tough enemy forces. Ill-conceived military tactics and callous irresponsibility by some of our senior officers created needless American and

Vietnamese casualties. And unreliable South Vietnamese soldiers in my area were too often content to watch gung-ho Americans carry on the fight.

But in spite of these handicaps, our soldiers were successful in turning back every large-scale North Vietnamese advance from the Ho Chi Minh Trail. By post-Tet 1968 we had cleaned out the main-force Viet Cong units. And in fierce fighting we pushed the North Vietnamese back to their Cambodian jungle bases.

This, however, was not done without painful sacrifice and the loss of valuable American and Vietnamese lives. All of us who were engaged in the ambushes, firefights, and battles in obscure little places like Duc Hoa, My Tho, Katum, Dong Ha, and Khe Sanh have an honor roll of lost friends forever inscribed in our hearts. While negotiators argued in Paris over the shape of the bargaining table, I was wounded on three different occasions during the post-Tet period.

The third time, a gangrene infection set into a shrapnel wound in my back and I was evacuated to Japan. While undergoing treatment I was further exposed to the price of the war. Working full time as an on-the-job trained assistant in the physical therapy clinic, I tended to scores of severely wounded soldiers and battlefield amputees. We were young men who had grown old long before our time.

I remember sitting in the hospital movie theater, among a crowd of hardened veterans in blue pajamas, roaring with laughter. The movie was John Wayne's *The Green Berets*. Our Vietnam experience had taught us special appreciation for patriotic clichés.

Though not a war-lover, I agreed to return to Vietnam. After our Tet and post-Tet successes, I believed that we could end the war decisively, in spite of the political chaos and less-than-inspiring military leadership. I could not walk away from the conflict while my friends were still in the field. And having witnessed the massacre of an entire village near Cu Chi by black-pajama–clad Communist soldiers, I had no illusions about the enemy we were up against.

Many mornings, while mine-sweeping farm roads and Highway 13, we found the bodies of victims of the terrorists who haunted the peasants' nights. And I was sickened by the vicious disregard with which the North Vietnamese Army (NVA) and the Viet Cong (VC) purposely turned vil-

lages and towns into battlegrounds. I had no doubt about
the fate of South Vietnam if the wrong side prevailed.

Instead of returning to the blood-and-guts infantry, I volunteered to join my former platoon leader, Mike Andrews,
who was forming an experimental American and Vietnamese reconnaissance platoon. We operated independently of
American forces in villages and the jungle near the Cambodian border. It was an area notorious for Communist activity. My experience living among the villagers in this
dangerous area gave me a unique view of the war and valuable insight into human nature.

These people had known only war for the better part of
three generations. Because of their precarious geographical location near the NVA and VC sanctuaries, they had no
choice but to honor the stronger force. But in discussions
with many of these peasants, we learned that they had no
interest in politics, taxes, or armies. They only wished to
continue their ancestral heritage and farm their land in
peace. They viewed the American army as just another
deadly force that threatened their existence.

I was struck by what little understanding my friends and
I had of the people we were supposed to be protecting. Mike
Andrews and I began to realize that, though our soldiers
were performing valiantly in combat, the key to winning the
war was to respect and learn to coexist within the traditions
and needs of these "little people."

Discreetly, the villagers confided to us their distrust and fear
of the North Vietnamese soldiers who took their rice and
impounded their sons. I remember a fearless old woman in
a border village who had gone beyond cowering to the
threats of VC cadre. She told us defiantly about a North
Vietnamese unit that had passed through the village the night
before: "They are not like us. They do not act our way."

With the passive support of the local people, our platoon
was quite successful at beating the North Vietnamese and
VC on their own turf. We ran small patrols deep into the
jungle to locate NVA base camps. And through our Vietnamese members, local villagers kept us abreast of enemy
activities in populated areas. A mystique developed about
us; we were regarded as friends.

This was not taken very kindly by COSVN (the Central
Office of South Vietnam—the North Vietnamese/Viet Cong

Command headquarters), which was based in the area. Years later, while I was working on this book, a former chief of COSVN security who is now living in Europe told me that the VC had teams hunting for us. As a small group of soldiers far away from friendly forces, we could not have survived without the support of the local villagers. On one occasion, which I thank God I did not witness, Communist forces executed every living man, woman, and child in a village for refusing to tell where we had gone.

While our friendships with the local people were growing, the feeling of some American officers toward us was little more than contempt. We had "gone native." In an operation where our platoon led a battalion thrust into a North Vietnamese stronghold in the Michelin rubber plantation, we were left to die by a cowardly captain. It took a revolt by some of the enlisted men in the captain's company, who disobeyed a direct order, to rescue us. By this time, near the end of my tour of duty, I was becoming cynical and embittered by the senseless conduct of the war.

I did not want to see the Communists succeed or the lives of my friends wasted. But with no mandate for victory, and a senseless obsession with body counts, I felt that our lives and ideals meant nothing. We were just cold statistics in Washington's political computers. Everything I ever believed in was turned upside down.

I came home from Vietnam torn between two realities. I felt pride in my service and the people with whom I had served, but bitter contempt for the powers who were arrogantly prolonging the war without reason.

I did not feel like a movie hero or a baby killer. And I was deeply hurt by the horrible misconceptions of the situation in Vietnam by both supporters and opponents of the war. But I was still an inarticulate teenager, confused and exhausted by my year in combat. There was no way that I could express what I had seen and knew to be true. So for ten years I said nothing.

After the publication of *Everything We Had*, I realized that the recognition given to it and to Vietnam veterans in general is only one step in our coming to terms with the Vietnam trauma. The larger story is more than one of combat by American soldiers in Vietnam, or one that ends with America's direct involvement there. It seemed also necessary to take a look at the revolution that preceded America's involvement, as well as the effects of the Communist victory in Vietnam, Cambodia, and Laos.

This book presents the voices and experience of forty-eight Americans and Southeast Asians. They represent not only the military, but a larger community of veterans: soldiers, revolutionaries, foreign aid advisors, journalists, diplomats, relief workers, and refugees. I have chosen these people because I was deeply touched by the depth of their experience on the front lines of the Indochina conflict. Even though some were on the opposing side of the war, they share a common humanity that transcends their differences. All of them bear the scars of battle or betrayed idealism. However, they have not only survived but have become more committed to realizing those lost ideals. They have journeyed through the dark night of memory to present their stories here. With some tears and laughter, they have looked back, with courage, so that we might learn from the trials they have endured.

For three years I traveled throughout the United States, Europe, and Asia. In the spring of 1983, while visiting the Thailand-Cambodia border, the ongoing conflict in Southeast Asia became all too real to me. I was caught in the midst of a ruthless Vietnamese Army artillery bombardment of 20,000 defenseless refugees, mostly women and children. I was deeply shaken to learn that among the North Vietnamese army units participating in the attack was the 271st Regiment, one of the same regiments I had fought against on the Vietnam-Cambodia border fifteen years earlier. I learned firsthand that the war, for the Indochinese people, has never ended. Through the first half of 1984, nearly ten years after the Americans departed, a monthly average of 4,000 Vietnamese (by boat, overland, and orderly departure) and more than 1,500 Laotian refugees continued to flee the tyranny in their homelands. More than 250,000 Cambodians, facing ongoing Vietnamese attacks, live in makeshift refugee encampments along the Thai border.

At the sprawling bamboo-and-thatch-hut refugee camp of Nong Samet live more than 65,000 survivors of the Khmer Rouge holocaust and the current terror of Vietnamese occupation. As a Vietnamese and Thai artillery duel raged nearby and the camp faced imminent attack, I spoke with the commander of the undersupplied non-Communist

Cambodian defense forces. With admirable courage and determination he told me, "We will wait, we will fight. If we die, it will not be as refugees in a foreign country, but in our own country, on our own soil. I say this not only for myself, but for all people who love freedom. Some of my people and I may die, but we will not be defeated." These impoverished "little people," most of whom have no formal education, taught me that the struggle for liberty and basic human dignity will persevere.

This is a book about values. We who remember invite you to look back with us, behind the veil of myth and rhetoric. Though at times we must swallow our pride and examine tragic mistakes, the common humanity of the forty-eight people here is a shared triumph of the human spirit. In no way do we claim to represent the whole story. But we hope to bring to light some of the complicated realities that have often been overlooked. Please allow our truths to be a part of the larger discussion and debate.

The Vietnam War shook the foundation of American self-assurance and basic beliefs. There are those who still claim it was the beginning of an American decline. At this time in history, to embrace the disillusionment of the Vietnam era can mean an end to our evolution and survival as a nation. But the experience of Vietnam can also be a watershed of wisdom that teaches us how to apply more skillfully our power—political, economic, and military—in an increasingly interdependent and volatile world.

Those of us who speak here, though representing very different cultures, believe that the ongoing struggle in Southeast Asia should be a reminder to us all that the values and dedication to freedom that John F. Kennedy spoke of in his 1960 Inaugural Address remain universally valid, whatever our disagreements about how best to realize them.

We who have experienced the war, struggled in its aftermath, and learned valuable lessons from our survival now present our story.

—AL SANTOLI
*New York City*
*September 1984*

# ACKNOWLEDGMENTS

The process of researching and conducting the interviews for this book involved more than three years of travel. Throughout the United States, Europe, and Asia, the hospitality and guidance of friends and strangers were invaluable. Though their stories do not appear here, they are very much a part of this work. I would like to thank some of my hosts and translators:

Bill Laurie, Linda Andrews, Bob Owen, Bill and Huong Bach, Geraldine Moorefield, Nguyen Quang Chon, Sichan Siv, Jim Henderson, Don Bailey, Rusty and Penny Brown, Birabhongse Kasemsri, Chan Heng Wing, Kobsak Chutikul, Carole Bates, Karl Jackson, Sean Randolph, Dao Van Mon, Harry and Sasa Hayes, Pham Xuan Canh and family, Phan Thanh Son and family, Lai The Hung and family, Mr. and Mrs. Lee Van Ran, Thai Quang Trung, Thach Yen, Dennis Grace, John Crowley, Mike and Chan Eiland, Andrea Crossland, Dr. Amos Townsend, Prasart Mansuwan, Miss Souwanna, Pipop Boonrawd, Col. Prasith, Gen. Sak Sutsakan, Gen. Dien Del, Penn Thula, Soubert Sann, Dr. Tran Ngoc Hop, Nguyen Bay, Suthep Chungcharatrat, Col. Thou Thipp, Col. Kao Vibol, Mrs. Ung Thiem, Prasong Sunsiri, Arsa Sarasin, Don and Xuan Colin, Bill and Nam Xuan Bell, Vaughn Forrest, Michelle Van Cleave, Billie Shaddix, Joseph and Lan Langlois, and Penn Nhach.

Jack Bloomfield and his valiant staff of typists transcribed countless hours of interview tapes. And Joan Siegel and Gabriela Kaufman arranged for much of my travel.

I would especially like to thank:

Jeri Engle at Dutton for her commitment to this project from the beginning. Paul DeAngelis, my editor, for his challenging insight and understanding. Anne Sibbald and Mort Janklow, my literary agents, for their guidance and taking care of business. Walter Anderson, at *Parade*, for his encouragement and kindness. And my family and my wife, Phuong, for their faith and support.

# TO BEAR ANY BURDEN

*The Vietnam War and Its Aftermath in the Words of Americans and Southeast Asians*

Eddie Adams
Chuck Allen
Lt. Col. Michael Andrews
Mark Berent
Kay Bosiljevac
Edward Brady
Peter Braestrup
Eve Burton
Chhang Song
Doan Van Toai
Janis Dodge (Otis)
Ha Thuc Ky
Hoang Van Chi
Kassie Neou
Mrs. Keo Vey
Col. Dennison Lane
Gen. Edward Lansdale
Mrs. Le Thi Anh
Lu Mong Lan
Mrs. Lu Thi Duc
Frank McCarthy
Anne Miller
Ken Moorefield
Nguyen Cong Hoan

Nguyen Tuong Lai (alias)
Jim Noonan
Ron Norris
Oung Chumnet
Dr. Erwin Parson
Penn Nouth
Rufus Phillips
Dan Pitzer
Jonathan Polansky
Prak Savath
Prasith Sayaphon
Berta Romero
Ginetta Sagan
Al Santoli
David Sciacchitano
Adolphus Stuart
Col. Harry Summers
Tran Thanh Son
Tran Tri Vu (alias)
Tran Van Luu
Truong Mealy
Truong Nhu Tang
Dr. Yang Dao
Stephen Young

# PRELUDE

# GIVE US TV

--------

## Rufus Phillips

*Assistant Director of Rural Affairs*
*U.S. AID*
*South Vietnam*

*September 1962 – November 1963*

*President Ngo Dinh Diem of South Vietnam was over-*
*thrown and assassinated on November 1 and 2, 1963.*
*Three weeks later, President John F. Kennedy was as-*
*sassinated in Dallas.*

After the Diem coup, General Big Minh, the new leader
of South Vietnam, was asking for a lot of political advice
from the Americans in Saigon. Some of his officers got
in touch with me, and I gave them some suggestions. I
didn't want to see them wipe out certain hamlet programs,
because there were a lot of good things under Diem. And
the North Vietnamese were sending political and military
units south to exploit the chaos.

Word got back to Ambassador Henry Cabot Lodge that
I was giving this new government political advice. And
Lodge started raising hell about that. He decided to personally talk with Big Minh. And the kind of advice he
gave was very interesting.

Big Minh asked Lodge, "What should I do politically?"
And Lodge said, "Well, it's a little bit like after Kennedy
was assassinated. The American people were very upset
and concerned about the future. So President Johnson
went on television and explained that he was going to
carry on. And this reassured the American people. You
need to reassure the Vietnamese people."

Big Minh said, "Fine. Give us TV."

# SECTION I

# APRIL 1975

# CITY OF PHANTOMS

## Kassie Neou

*Cambodian Survivor*

*1975—1981*

On April 17, 1975, when the Khmer Rouge marched into
Phnom Penh, I was at my school office. The first time I
actually saw them was around 9:00 A.M. The first troops
were teenagers. Young girls, young boys, some under
fourteen years old, bearing very heavy portable rocket
launchers. The girls wore hand grenades around their
waists and across their chests like necklaces.

Then came the regular troops, all dressed in black. They
shouted, "Put out white flags. It's peace. Peace." So we
put a flag in front of my office, just a white piece of cloth.
Looking down the boulevard, we saw white pieces of
cloth everywhere. The Khmer Rouge marched in, shouting, "Peace, peace," while they shot through the air.

In the past months in Phnom Penh thousand of refugees
came in from other provinces. They said, "The Khmer
Rouge are killing people. They cut their throats using
pieces of palm stems." We didn't believe that: "This is
too exaggerated. Khmer would not kill other Khmer. Because we are all Buddhists."

And now as the Khmer Rouge marched in, we cheered
for peace together. They behaved in a friendly manner.
And being so tired of the destructive war for five years,
when we heard the word "peace" we thought, "Oh, that's
nice. We might be able to go back home and join our
relatives." I had lost my father since 1973. So I hoped my
family would be reunited.

Two and a half hours later, the situation changed. The
Khmer Rouge announced, "Please. Brothers and sisters,

7

mothers and fathers, out of Phnom Penh as soon as possible. The American airplanes will bomb the city. For your own safety, you have to be out." The first announcement was very protective, very nice. Not many of us seemed to be listening to that.

The second announcement, the next hour: "You have to be out only for three days. We are here to protect you. You have to be out." I began to see more and more people moving—by foot, by car, any means. The KR said to anyone who had a military uniform, "Put down your gun and take off this imperialist uniform."

The third announcement, they didn't use "fathers and mothers." They didn't use any nice language: "You guys must be out . . . or else." And the killing began. In front of my office, they used a B-40 rocket through the third floor because some families tried to hide and refused to to go out. They had hoped after three or four days it would be okay. The KR found them because of a barking dog. BANG—a lot of people killed. Relatives and families who managed to escape the war had come to Phnom Penh and lived together. So in one house there were four or five families. Many of them were killed by Khmer Rouge grenades. And they began to shoot people in the streets. I saw it through my eyes. "Out, or else." People were too afraid to talk.

The Khmer Rouge speech was very rural dialects. Even their appearance—they looked dark. And the way they behaved was not our way. One block behind my office, my brother-in-law was in a military hospital. He had been wounded while guarding the airport. So, I sent my sister to be with him, hoping that no one would harm people in the hospital. But I was wrong: "Everyone must be out." Those who were not able—that's it. The Khmer Rouge stabbed them with knives, right in the hospital beds.

So the one-legged, just cut off the night before, had to crawl on their bellies, like earthworms, out of the hospital. It looked funny, but terrible. Terrible. My brother-in-law could not walk on his own. So my sister, with a newborn baby in one arm and her husband on her other shoulder, walked one and a half blocks to my office.

Most of the Khmer Rouge that were doing the killing were young. Pol Pot was smart in choosing the young to behave in a very fierce and cruel manner. They refused to talk with us. They only said, "Out. Out." If we tried to say something, they immediately shouted, "No questions. Out. The Americans will bomb." But there were no airplanes. All we heard were AK-47 rifles and grenades from the KR.

My daughter was two years old and my son still an infant. We joined a long procession—you can't imagine— millions of people moving out of the city. The Khmer Rouge used the big Central Market as the dividing point. People gathered at the French Embassy, the Hotel Royale, and other places north of Central Market must move north. My office, my house, were south of Central Market, so we must move out of the city southward. We moved toward Katum, South Vietnam. My home village was north, but I saw people try to move across the market—they were shot dead. Anyone, even children. But they shot the father first. For family members it was more than shock. But we were not allowed to cry. If you cried, they'd shoot you. "No crying. Move. Move."

Still, we had hope. We heard on the radio that Sihanouk would come, and our peaceful time would be back. Some people had faith in Sihanouk when he said on the radio from Peking, "The Father wants you to stay here and support the Liberation Soldiers [the KR]. They are trying to liberate Cambodia, which has been slapped by the imperialist Americans and Lon Nol, the dog of the Americans. Stay in your homes, you'll be safe. Your Father will be back." Because of these broadcasts, the Khmer Rouge gained popular support. We kept hoping.

I carried my two children and helped my mother. My wife was not with us. As the Communists came to power, she was visiting her mother in the western part of the city. So the KR sent her westward, toward Battambang. As we started moving out of the city, we heard another announcement. "Those of you who used to serve the government are invited back to Phnom Penh, to help rebuild the new society." We heard this several times a day.

But as we continued moving south, we started seeing many dead bodies lying around the road. Hands tied behind their backs and blindfolded. The majority of them had military uniforms on. So it was clear what was happening. The KR continued many different announcements—nice, tricky. We heard "brothers and sisters" again.

Being an educated person, I hid my identity. I had gone to the University of Phnom Penh, specializing in psychology and sociology. I became a teacher in 1968. We were told to fill out biographical forms: "Don't worry, brother. Just tell the truth. Our *Angka* [Organization] will take good care of you, now that you are liberated."

After seven days, ten days, the elderly, the sick, patients out of the hospital—no way they can survive. They were just left alongside the road. We stepped over the dead bodies. We heard the loudspeakers: "Move on. Move on."

Moving south, I kept hoping that I could cross the border into Vietnam. I might be able to go to the U.S. Embassy in Saigon and tell them that my sister worked in the U.S. Embassy in Phnom Penh. We might be rescued.

On April 30, after walking thirteen days, we reached a village of fishermen, eleven kilometers from Vietnam. I began to see big airplanes flying from south to north. I thought, "Uh oh, something else has happened."

That evening we heard the announcement on the loudspeaker: "We have ousted the imperialist Americans in South Vietnam, too."

# THE RIVER
--------
## David Sciacchitano

*Political Officer*
*U.S. Consulate,*
*Can Tho*

*1975*

The Friday before Vietnam collapsed, nobody had any
illusions. I had been assigned to the enormous consulate
in the Delta town of Can Tho since January 1975. Can
Tho was a trading center on the Bassac River, eighty miles
south of Saigon. Around a couple hundred thousand people lived in the immediate area.

I was a political officer, and was responsible for trying
to evacuate American citizens and Vietnamese dependents. The consul general, Francis McNamara, began
planning early for a complete failure in the system. He
managed to acquire two LCMs [naval landing crafts] and
a big old rice barge that looked like a miniature Noah's
Ark. He began preparing to evacuate by river.

The embassy in Saigon for some reason sent a man to
speak to us who had been through the collapse of the
northern provinces and the Danang evacuation. He was
supposed to review things and help us out. But he was a
raving lunatic who had cracked under the strain. All he
could talk about in a high-pitched voice was, "How horrible it was! People clinging to helicopter skids ... and
being knocked off of airplanes!"

Why the embassy would send out anybody like that, I
don't know. But it showed a lack of judgment in Saigon.
Here was a guy that was panicked around people who
were calm. And of course, that sowed the seeds of panic.

We were already having problems. A couple of weeks
earlier we started shipping a couple Vietnamese at a time
to Saigon by bus. But we couldn't get a clear idea of what

11

was happening to them. On that last Thursday—the collapse was on the following Tuesday—Averill Christian, the administration officer, and I decided to go to Saigon to see how it was working. And we were shocked.

We got off the airplane at Tan Son Nhut Airport. It was absolute chaos. The terminal where they were doing the departure processing was a big hangar. We saw a mass of desperate people pushing and shoving. One of the embassy officers was so frustrated, he picked up a Coke bottle, started screaming, and threw it across the room. Exploding against the wall. One officer was stamping hundreds of documents at a time, passing them out to the Vietnamese.

We discovered that the only way that any of our people were going to get on an airplane was to have a mimeographed sheet, which is just a piece of paper with the consulate stamp. Which neither they nor we had access to. It became evident in the first couple of minutes that the system we were feeding people into was no system at all.

We drove along the hangars. Groups of people were roped off like herds of cattle, marching onto military planes to Bangkok. We heard shouts. We looked over and there were a bunch of bar girls from Can Tho that we hadn't sent up. They waved and shouted, "Hey, hey, hooray." We also found there were employees of the U.S. government taking huge groups of Vietnamese posing as relatives. They would go to Bangkok, then come back to Saigon for another group, two, three, four times. We were shaken by this.

We went to the embassy to see a guy in AID [Agency for International Development]. It was like talking with a zombie. He was in his office at the time. All the people who worked for him were constantly in meetings, eight hours a day. We couldn't see any of them because they were all locked up in a big conference room. And I understand from people who were there later, that as things got worse the meetings got longer and longer.

The AID man was sitting in his chair, sort of emotionlessly leaning back: "Hi, how are ya? Oh, everything will be all right. Nothing to worry about, the Communists aren't going to hurt anybody. It's all a bunch of nonsense."

He was going on and on. We asked him some hard questions and never got answers. Like, "How do we get our people out?" His attitude was, "Everything's going to be easy. Go back down to the Delta. The big transport planes and the helicopters will come and get you out."

After we saw this absolute mess, we hurried back down to Can Tho to get as many people out as we could. I made up some transit sheets and stamped them myself. I also had a conference with some of the CIA people in the consulate. They were shocked. Because their bosses were telling them that the Vietnamese who worked for them were being taken care of. The consul general had a meeting with the CIA base chief, who said we didn't know what we were talking about. The consul general believed the CIA had responsibility to their agents in the field. Some of whom would be in a precarious position after the Communist takeover.

Seeing what was about to happen, a couple of agency people took my packets. I made about fifty or a hundred sheets for them. And they started moving some of their people effectively. The CIA never showed any signs that things were going badly. They behaved toward their employees in the Delta the way they behaved toward them everywhere else—they were ready to abandon them.

An AID man and a marine sergeant went back to the consulate one last time to make sure everything was in order. In the back area where we destroyed documents, they found the CIA radio man calmly breaking up his equipment. Of all the CIA people, this is the one guy who has a lot of top secret information. The radio man, the communicator, the guy who's got all the codes. And they forgot him. The helicopters were gone by then. He didn't know because the base chief had not informed him.

On the twenty-ninth of April we received an obscure telephone call from Saigon which went dead in the middle of the conversation: "Get out." No further communication. Up until that point we were working under the assumption that we had some days to go. We shut down the consulate, cleaned everything out. Burned the rest of the classified materials. I got in my jeep and went around trying to find people.

Noon was a terrible time to have to do this. I couldn't

find a lot of people. And in addition, Saigon didn't tell us
how much time we had left. Did we have another day?
Did we have a couple hours? What was the threat? We
didn't know. We were completely cut off. So the decision
had to be to leave.

I didn't have time to wait for some Vietnamese that I
felt we had a responsibility to get out. I just couldn't find
them. One American Catholic brother drove me crazy.
I'd already gotten him out once. Just before the roads
closed, this guy walks back to Can Tho. He's got a baseball cap on, looking ridiculous. I said, "What are you
doing here?" He said, "I'm going back to my flock to say
goodbye." He didn't like what they told him in Saigon,
so he came back. And he didn't get out until 'seventy-
six.

There were a lot of Americans' kids and a few wives—
Vietnamese—eligible for passports, whom I couldn't get
out. I had some of them in my office every goddamned
day. They just weren't going to leave their mother or
relatives. I'd say, "You've got to go. If you want your
mother to go with you, I'll take your mother out. But
you've got to go. Your husband can't come and get you."
One woman, who was the most stubborn, wasn't going
to leave unless he came to get her. She was furious. And
I was cabling him and calling him on the phone. But I had
other people to take care of.

A Vietnamese interpreter we had working for us was
a fine fellow. He understood the danger to himself. But
he couldn't convince his wife to leave. And he wouldn't
leave his family. I went to visit him at home, talked to
his wife. We did everything but kidnap the guy to get him
out. But, knowing he faced a difficult future, he decided
to stay with his family. There were lots of people like that.

A woman had an American citizen's kid. She had been
married and divorced. I tried to get the husband to come
and get them, because that was the official way. I couldn't
reach him. And that woman never got out. On the last
day, I drove around and around. I was one of the last
people on the boat, because I couldn't find her. I knocked
on her door, I asked her neighbors where she was. She'd
gone out for lunch someplace. And the saddest thing about
it is, if we'd just had a little more information from Saigon,

we could have waited. We could have gotten out the next day.

The Vietnamese were not panicking. A lot of them were nervous and worried, but Can Tho was really removed from all the chaos in Saigon. Throughout the Delta, the South Vietnamese army continued successfully advancing until the middle of the thirtieth. They had been really successful the past couple years, suffering no serious setbacks. They were pressing the Communist forces all the way until they were ordered to surrender by Saigon.

I remember a terrible phone call I received at the last minute. I was cleaning up and a Vietnamese down in Soc Trang asked, "Can you tell us what's happening? When should we leave? Should we come up to Can Tho?" And I was thinking, "Jesus Christ. We're all leaving. What can I tell this guy?" So I told him to call back later. I didn't have the heart, but I should have told him, "We're leaving now. Get out." But all I could think of was, "We've got all these guys in the field depending on us. And we've failed them."

So we gathered all the people we could find and went down to the docks. We loaded more than 200 Vietnamese on one LCM and the rice barge. The other LCM was up the river, around a bend. In addition we had a little makeshift gunboat. We threw a machine gun on it. And we had a defense attaché civilian who didn't know how to shoot and a CIA man who were going to provide us a little escort.

They said, "Just a minute, we're going to check things out up the river." And we never saw them again. Because the CIA helicopters came in and they fled on them, and left us with the boats and their Vietnamese employees. We had 375 to 400 Vietnamese. More than half were women and kids. The rice barge began leaking. We had to offload all the people onto the two LCMs. We had room because the LCMs are about eighty feet long.

We didn't know what we were supposed to do. Saigon didn't tell us anything. All they said was "Get out." We couldn't find out whom we were supposed to meet with. The CIA radio man remained with us. A stroke of luck, we thought, because he brought all five of his portable radios. But he could not raise anybody because our navy was ordered not to answer international frequencies. And guess what . . . Saigon never gave us the classified frequencies for the evacuation.

The rest of the Delta had been abandoned. We didn't know where the hell we were going. We just floated down the river. We were out just maybe an hour when we were stopped by the Vietnamese navy. They fired across our bow because they were under orders not to let any active-duty military go. The Vietnamese military in the Delta kept fighting until the order to surrender. The commander down there was a realistic man, a good general. He committed suicide shortly after the surrender.

Active-duty people stayed at their positions, with a couple exceptions. Two people jumped to our boat. One was a military dentist, and some other guy with him. We didn't really want them because they jeopardized our leaving. We had to hide them under a tarpaulin when the navy stopped us. And we had some military interpreters. Although we had an agreement with the commander not to do this, we knew the military people who had been attached to us were in danger becaused they were known by the Communists. Now, if the navy had wanted to board the two ships, that would have been the end.

We talked to the commodore, who knew our consul general. He said, "Mr. Consul General, I want your word that there is nobody on these ships that's not supposed to be going out." And of course, everyone knew that we were lying. I almost cried when we said goodbye to the navy. They were good men. We knew the officers and some of the enlisted men. It was like a formal leavetaking. The consul general and all of our people stood up. And then the navy stood up, saluted, and said goodbye.

Further up the river, the communists opened fire on us with rockets. A B-40 went right across the rear of the ship and exploded on the other bank. And we blasted away at them. As day turned to night, it began to rain. We just kept drifting on the river, constantly calling on the radio and never getting an answer.

All the Vietnamese were seasick. We didn't have any food. We had water, but it wasn't adequate for very long. We got to the mouth of the river near dark, still not knowing what to do. So we decided to head out to sea and hoped somebody would find us.

In the darkness and rain, our two boats had a hell of a time seeing each other. The lights didn't work on one of the LCMs. In the middle of the storm, we decided to strap the boats together. We were all inexperienced sailors. The consul general had been in the navy, but he was a submariner. So he didn't know what the hell he was doing. But he heroically stood at the wheel of the boat for twelve to fourteen hours. Never sat down. Got a drink of water once or twice. I think he ducked when the rocket went over, but that was it.

One guy, an AID employee, was heroic throughout the whole thing. Of course, AID fired him right after that, when they were trying to get their numbers down. But after the storm, on the open sea, he lashed the boats together, almost single-handedly. But once they were lashed, they started to destroy each other. In the rough water, the two multiton boats started smashing each other to pieces. So he had to go through this heroic task again, to untie them. It was wet, dark, and slippery. No starlight, no moonlight. We only had tiny little lights on one LCM.

Around eleven o'clock that night we saw a glow in the distance. We tried to hold a straight course in the rough water to reach the horizon. And around 2:00 A.M. we reached a freighter. It was an old liberty ship, the *Pioneer Contender*. It had been used to evacuate refugees out of Danang. And now carried new refugees.

Leaning over one of its rails was one of the CIA men who had fled Can Tho by helicopter. He got out on the stern and was looking down at us and laughing. He was making a joke about it, "Hey, too bad you had to get wet."

# THE VICTORY PARADE

## Truong Nhu Tang

*Minister of Justice*
*National Liberation Front (Viet Cong)*
*South Vietnam*

*1960–1976*

On Victory Day, May 15, 1975, as a founder of the National Liberation Front I stood on the official podium of honor in Saigon, now called Ho Chi Minh City. I listened to the victorious speeches of the Communist Politburo leaders and reviewed the liberation troops in the parade. But I did not notice any PRG or NLF [Viet Cong] uniforms or flags flying. I turned to General Van Tien Dung, commander of the North Vietnamese Army, and asked, "Where are the National Liberation Front flags?" He replied coldly, "The armed forces are now unified."

Two weeks earlier, the war had finally ended. After so many years of living in the jungle, I believed that we must continue our revolution by rebuilding the nation. I had argued in NLF councils for the policy of National Reconciliation and Concord, which was one of the centerpieces of the Paris peace accords in 1973. And for the gradual democratic reunification of the country. This policy had been publicly supported by the Hanoi regime and guaranteed by Le Duan, the head of the Party.

We had promised the South's population that families would be reunited and there would be no bloodshed or revenge. But the Hanoi Communist Party concentrated power into the hands of corrupt and incompetent bureaucrats and brutal security forces. They fought among themselves to confiscate the best houses, the richest plantations and black market luxuries.

As Justice Minister, I assembled a staff of legal experts. But those not approved by the northern cadre were sent to reeducation camps. When the Communist government asked most of the officers of the army and middle- and upper-level civil servants of the former republic to go for thirty days' reeducation, I asked my brother, who had been a doctor in the South Vietnamese army, to go. After one month, when I saw that no one was coming back from these camps, I went to see top government officials. I said, "Why did you ask people to go for just thirty days and now you retain them? This is treason. It goes against the policy of reconciliation." They said, "We only told people to bring clothes for thirty days. We never specified how long we would keep them."

I told them, "Now we are strong. We have all the power in our hands. Why do we behave like conquerors?" They gave me no answers.

People would stop me on the street and demand to know what I was doing about their relatives whose property was being seized, who were disappearing in reeducation camps or being forced to move to New Economic Zones. I felt helpless. There was nothing I could do.

# GIAI PHONG (LIBERATION)

## Tran Van Luu

*Vietnamese Boat Refugee*
*Escaped from Ho Chi Minh City*

*May 1978*

On April 30, 1975, as the Communists took over Saigon, my neighbors were just wandering in the streets, very shocked. Crowds mutely stared at tanks rolling by, carrying militia wearing red armbands and shooting into the air. We did not know what to do. Many people were still trying to find the rendezvous point for American helicopters. And rumors were spreading around the city that ships would leave from one place or another.

At first people came into the streets to watch the North Vietnamese fighters out of curiosity. There was no voluntary demonstration to support the new government. We regarded the Communists as strangers, not heroes. But after a few weeks, when the Communists organized demonstrations, a lot of people came because we were scared.

After the collapse, I chose to remain in Saigon. My wife was teaching school and I had enough money saved to buy and sell things. But I became more and more afraid for my family because there were public executions. The Communists appointed a very tough major to maintain order. I saw with my own eyes people being executed near the theater on Truong Minh Giang Street, where I lived. In front of a crowd of people, including children, they shot a young boy, just twelve or thirteen years old.

Many Catholics or Buddhists could not hold gatherings or ceremonies in churches or temples. Communist puppet monks from the North began to arrive to take over. Our Buddhist monks began some resistance after May 1975, because of arrests and desecration of temples.

For my wife and children, the school system changed drastically. Teachers identified as having commitment to the former republic were arrested. The Communist Party sent in new teachers from the North to take over the schools in Saigon. They created Party cells for teachers and among the students. Ho Chi Minh Youth Movements were created to denounce teachers.

My children at the time were five and six years old. We continued to send them to kindergarten and primary school. But their teachers only taught them militaristic and ideological songs and drawing weapons like the AK-47 rifle. Pupils could no longer learn how to show faithful respect toward their parents. They learned instead the story of a youngster who was killed while working as a Communist liaison agent. Arithmetic was formed around such destructive themes as: "There are eighty enemy helicopters in the sky; our victorious soldiers brought down six. How many are left?"

The Communists made an announcement for registration of former military and civil servants for reeducation. As a former press department employee, I went to register for the reeducation section on June 20, 1975.

We entered an auditorium in single file, watched by northern soldiers, armed with various types of automatic weapons. The Communist cadre started the session by telling us to remain calm and receptive. Then they began reading charges against us nonstop for four days. We were urged and then threatened to tell "the truth." To confess our "crimes" and denounce our friends.

At that time, my family was trying to find a way to get out. We learned from leaflets of dangerous escape routes in certain areas or the killing of people in other regions.

# SECTION II

# DEMOCRATS
# AND
# REVOLUTIONARIES
# 1954–1963

# LAND OF THE OPEN FLY

--------

## Anne Miller

*Writer*
*U.S. Information Service*
*Indochina*

*1954–1960*

In October 1954, I flew into Saigon with General John O'Daniel. I had been doing movies in the Philippines for USIS. They had run out of writers for Saigon movies, so I went to Charlie Mertz and said, "I'd be glad to go, it would be fun."

For the next six years I was in Vietnam, Cambodia, Laos, and Thailand, documenting our AID program with movies. I took notes on everything that had happened in Indochina since the late forties.

President Eisenhower had no illusions about the French. In the First World War, the French put very high ranks on their officers, so the Yanks were never allowed any input in command. This enraged our young officers like Eisenhower, Omar Bradley, and George Marshall. And the French had not distinguished themselves in the Second World War.

Eisenhower, as European commander, was very aware of all the postwar issues in Europe. Both Italy and France had very strong Communist movements. Their economy was dead. So, Ike saw it in terms of not only holding firm in Asia, where we had just had a standoff with the Chinese in Korea, but Europe had to be somehow strengthened. We could not send troops into Vietnam and relieve France in an open, ugly manner. France would have instantly gone Communist. They were already full of hatred for Americans.

Even though we had saved them in World War II, they had lost face, lost dignity, their troops were never accountable for any triumph. And they were obviously losing their overseas empire. The French turned indignantly on America because we were strong, we had been so outstanding in the war, and we had such a great country. And the first little misstep that keyed everybody that we were not the strongest country in the world was Korea.

Both Eisenhower and Dulles believed implicitly in the domino theory. They were convinced that if Vietnam went, so would the whole of Southeast Asia. India was not very strong. And China was already Communist.

This world situation made Eisenhower have a very firm policy in Vietnam. We were going to try to help the French troops, but simultaneously try to peacefully bring Vietnam up to some kind of strength. So Vietnam could stand by itself as a free nation.

The AID programs we were doing at the outset in 'fifty-four were tremendous ones. In North Vietnam we were getting water for villages, wells put in. The Black River Valley [north of Hanoi] was a teeming, productive part of the country—many industries, many mines. This is where we were putting the bulk of our aid. The Communists had to go in there with military infiltration to stop it. We were teaching people to read, opening schools, doing all the necessary programs to help an underdeveloped country. And they were succeeding.

Saigon at that time was one of the wickedest cities in the world: prostitutes, gambling, drugs, every kind of vicious circumstance. You couldn't walk down any street without smelling opium. The smell dominated the whole downtown area. They had two main brothels. One of them, for soldiers and poor men, covered a whole city block. The other was called "The Hall of Mirrors"—reputedly managed by Emperor Bao Dai from abroad. It had a thousand women: every color, every race, every language.

For gambling, the top place was the Grand Monde, which was a block of gambling houses. The place was jammed every night. I went there once. It was just hair-raising. I was sure that I was in the middle of the most sin in all the world.

This was all run by Binh Xuyen river pirates. And very well organized. They allegedly shared it with Emperor Bao Dai. It was cut three ways: the gambling, the prostitution, and the drugs. They gave the French a share of the profit they were making from the brothels and the opium. I watched one French general get on a ship. Followed by three truckloads of processed opium. That was his retirement.

Among the ordinary people, the hatred of the French was frightening to see. The Vietnamese didn't care much about the common soldier who brought in money. But the French colonials after World War II still owned every industry in Vietnam, ninety percent. No Vietnamese were allowed to buy stocks and bonds, have any share in the rubber plantations, or in anything going on in their country.

Because they were surrounded by ugliness and criminality, the people stretched out their hands for anything that promised to be decent. For example, the Cao Dai is a religious sect with over one and a half million followers in southern Vietnam. The first Cao Dai pope invented the movement as a coverup for a political movement against the French. He wanted to draw together people who were patriots. And nobody was more horrified than he was when the people took the religious aspect seriously.

The way the Vietnamese hated the French was just pathological. You'd sit at a dinner party and hear a pistol shot outside. We'd know that a Frenchman was lying in the street, shot in the stomach. Because it's a long slow death. It incapacitates a man and he just has to lie there and die.

In the countryside, people were more secure because they were not as surrounded by this corruption. I was in Dalat, Tay Ninh. And Hue, for instance, was a divine town. Beautiful and old, it was loaded with charm. The Perfume River was absolutely gorgeous.

What Eisenhower was trying to do in Vietnam was give enough aid to turn the economic tide. The French had lost billions. And yet they wouldn't allow the native people to move in and try to develop. The only thing we could do was give an enormous amount of economic aid, and try to build a nationalist army out of a nonexistent army. Because the villagers in the countryside were not safe from terror.

In Saigon, our film office was right across the street

from the Department of Defense. I used to call it "The Land of the Open Fly." Because any office you went into, there sat a man with his feet on the desk, his belt unbuckled, and his fly open. It was gross. There was no discipline or knowledge of how a soldier behaved until General O'Daniel got there.

Ed Lansdale had been picked by Eisenhower to come in. Because the only place in Asia where we had great success after World War II was the Philippines. And Ed was very much a part of that. Before President Magsaysay was elected, Ed started all kinds of development programs in the Philippine countryside. Wells were dug. People from the government helped with the villages' needs.

It was wonderful to drive past the President's Palace in Manila at sunset. During the changing of the guard, the whole palace yard was filled with people from villages and from Manila. The door was open. And President Magsaysay tried to see everyone.

# THE WHITE HOUSE MISSION

## Gen. Edward Lansdale

*Intelligence Officer*
*White House Mission to Vietnam*

1953

*Edward Lansdale was a major implementer of U.S.
policy in the Philippines after World War II.*

In June 1953, I was stationed in the Philippines, helping
to establish an independent government after the Huk
rebellion. A White House mission was enroute to Indochina to check on the French. They had been putting a
lot of pressure on Washington, trying to get some help.
President Eisenhower appointed General John O'Daniel
as head of the mission. He stopped off in the Philippines
and started talking to me about the fighting.

I was a colonel in the air force at the time. During World
War II I had served in army intelligence in the Pacific.
And I'd just been through fighting the Communist Huks—
while the U.S. was fighting the Communist forces in Korea. It had become very set in concrete who our enemies
were.

We drove to Clark Air Force Base that evening, and
O'Daniel said, "Why don't you come with us to see Indochina? They're up against guerillas and Communists,
too." I thought he said it would be about a ten-day trip.
I wasn't listening well, I guess. I figured if I could get my
laundry done, I could last ten days. But we stayed about
six weeks.

When we arrived in Saigon, the French really screamed
at my being part of it. They were very aware of what I
was doing for Philippine independence. And they were
losing a colony. But General Navarre had just taken com-

29

mand, and he was happy that I was there. He wrote a letter to his generals in the field, introducing me. It gave me a chance to see a great deal of not only Vietnam, but Laos and Cambodia also. I even got into Dien Bien Phu.

As an American, the French didn't want me anywhere near them. I'd be trying to talk with the Vietnamese to see what their commands were like. And the French would come and say, "Take a look over here, we have this problem with barbed wire."

President Roosevelt had been against French rule coming back. If the Brits hadn't given it back to them, things would have come out far differently. We weren't on the French side wholeheartedly. We didn't like their colonial policies, so we went in very gingerly. We did help them very generously. But we did not want to get into a colonial war or help them to colonize Vietnam.

A guy with our mission had a movie camera. General O'Daniel wanted pictures taken when he inspected French equipment. One day we went into the MAAG [Military Assistance Advisory Group] housing place for lunch. I saw a big French building next to it. And I asked one of the MAAG officers what it was. He said, "The French run a whorehouse there, it's a big one. Go up to my room and look out the window. You can see the courtyard with a big pink wall along the street."

I grabbed the movie camera and went up to his room. I could see the French coming in. And all the girls running up to the black troops from Africa—they're bigger guys than the French. I started yelling at them to look up. And they're all waving. I said, "Hollywood, Hollywood." They began acting out and calling to us. The girls were all smiling. The French unzipped their pants to show how big their dongs were. I took dirty movies of them. And I was waiting for the general's group to go back home and show it in the Pentagon.

The U.S. MAAG mission was there to help the French with supplies. But the French took a lot of it back to France or to North Africa. I didn't think much of the French after having seen them up close that way.

# REVOLUTION

--------

## Mrs. Le Thi Anh

*Resistance Operative*
*Advance Guard Youth*
*Mekong Delta*

*1945–1952*


In 1945, when I was nineteen years old, the war against the French erupted. I left school and joined the anti-French underground. My grandfather had been chief of Lai Vung subdistrict in the 1940s. But he was against the French and had joined a clandestine nationalist movement, Thien-Bia-Hoi. My father was one of the earliest graduates of the French Catholic Tabert school in Saigon. He worked briefly as secretary for the French governor in Saigon. But he was unhappy that the French ruled our country. So he resigned and became a tangerine farmer in Long Hau village in Sadec Province, about ninety miles south of Saigon.

I was born after he went back to Sadec. Until the age of twelve, I went to a small elementary school in Long Hau village. My father then bought my place in a French boarding school, Lycée Marie Curie, in Saigon. During World War II, when the Japanese occupied Vietnam, the Allies bombed Saigon and my school was moved to Can Tho in the Mekong Delta. And when the Japanese surrendered in 1945, I went straight into the anti-French underground.

Like thousands of other students, I saw an opportunity to recover our national independence. I loved my French teachers and I owe much of what I am today to the French culture. It was the writings of the great French philosophers Rousseau and Voltaire that taught me the ideals of freedom and democracy, for which I later took arms against French colonial rule. I adored my French literature teacher.

31

But after I left her classroom to join the underground, I was ready to shoot her should she stand in the way of our struggle for national independence, which was sacred to me—the very freedom and democratic liberties she had taught me to love. I saw no contradiction.

It was ironic that later on, in the underground, when we planned our strategy we very often spoke in French. The backbone of the resistance movement, the leadership—non-Communist and Communist—were graduates of French schooling.

In the spring of 1945, when the Japanese put the French in jail, a people's government was formed everywhere. That was such a happy time. Everyone was swept up in a tidal wave of patriotism. The rich people, the students, organized defense and prepared to rule the country. At that time with the French in jail, creating a vacuum of power, the Japanese gave us independence under Emperor Bao Dai.

I went to Saigon because a number of my father's cousins were in the Committee for South Vietnam. They had been university students before they organized the resistance to fight against the French. The Committee for South Vietnam negotiated with the British general Douglas Gracey, who was assigned to disarm the Japanese south of the seventeenth parallel (later known as the DMZ).

My uncle, Le Van Thuan, was a doctor who worked with a woman doctor named Nguyen Ngoc Suong. They were not Communists. Dr. Suong spoke English, so she and my uncle were members of the delegation that went to see General Gracey. The delegation wanted the British to recognize us as the legal government and not help the French to retake Vietnam.

I still remember waiting in Dr. Suong's home. When she came back from the meeting with Gracey she was crying. She said, "The British say it's not possible. General Gracey said that we have to negotiate with the French for our independence. The British are going to help the French reestablish order. We have no choice but to take arms and fight."

At this time, the Japanese were still keeping order in Saigon. They kept the French in jail. But Gracey let them out and gave them guns. What kind of arms did we have?

In our arsenal we had bamboo spears, swords, and a few French pistols.

At that time I was too young to understand everything that was happening in the independence movement. But the Communists under Ho Chi Minh were very clever. When we fought against the French I didn't care what form of government came out of it. Socialism, democracy, it didn't matter to me provided that we had independence. Because I thought that once the French were gone, all of the evil would be gone.

At that time we believed that Ho Chi Minh had the support of the Allies, especially the United States. Because Ho Chi Minh had offered to help downed American pilots at the end of World War II. And Ho had a photograph of the American general Chennault, with the general's autograph addressed to him, which Ho reproduced to show everyone.

And even more important, Ho had several photographs of an American OSS [Office of Strategic Services] team providing weapons and training to Ho's guerillas in North Vietnam. We had been shown those photographs by Ho's Communist agents in the south.

Toward the end of World War II Ho had come back to Vietnam from China through cunning tactics, tying onto larger non-Communist resistance organizations. In the South we had heard that Ho had formed a government of national union in Hanoi and had called upon all of the other nationalist parties to join him. We all believed that he had the support of the U.S. because of the photos.

But years later, in 1966, I met Allison Thomas in Ann Arbor, Michigan. He told me that he was an OSS major who had parachuted into North Vietnam. And I recognized that I had seen him in the number of photographs taken of Ho's guerillas taking American training. Thomas and Ho and Vo Nguyen Giap were in many pictures together. Ho had sent these pictures south and his agents told us: "Do you want independence? We have to go with the victorious Allies. And Ho is the person who has the Allies' blessing."

Major Allison Thomas is a good friend of mine today. I once asked him, "What was the purpose of giving the weapons to Ho Chi Minh?" He said, "My mission was to train and arm a number of guerillas in order to help downed American pilots, and cut the railroad linking Vietnam to China. But it was not for the purpose of supporting Ho Chi Minh. We never did that."

During that time, Ho never admitted to Major Thomas that he was a Communist. But on Thomas's last day, Ho gave him a big farewell dinner. Thomas asked Ho if he were a Communist. And Ho said, "Yes."

Beginning in 1945 I worked with the Viet Minh in Thot Not, my mother's hometown, in Long Xuyen Province. I joined the non-Communist women's Advance Guard Youth organization and was elected secretary. Among my jobs was to organize resistance in the villages and to train in and later teach guerilla tactics. We also learned to give emergency help to the wounded.

The Communists were very clever. They used myself and my cousin, both from very wealthy families, to solicit money from other landowning families who knew our parents. And later they used us to burn the houses of wealthy landowners. The rationale was to prevent the French from using the brick structures for military outposts. But in reality, the Communists wanted to destroy the whole structure of the old society. I was only nineteen years old. If they wanted me to burn houses, I went and burned houses. It was called the scorched earth policy.

In the south, the majority of the resistance groups were non-Communists who had only one short-term goal—to prevent the French from coming back. But the Communists had a long-term goal—to impose communism after our recovery of independence. In my home area there was no Communist Party at that time. Only a few Communists who had been released from Puolo Condore prison, who provided us with political indoctrination.

I still remember being in Thot Not, a medium-sized town on the Mekong River. We were expecting a visit from someone from Hanoi. We had always heard that Ho Chi Minh had a big army, supplied by the United States. They showed us a photograph of only two hundred guns, but we thought it was great. And by listening to the radio we heard President Roosevelt's promise to help liberate the colonies. And we saw that Stalin was allied with Roosevelt. So we felt that there was nothing wrong as nationalists with allying ourselves with the Vietnamese Communists.

So we waited for the big army from the north to help us. Because the French were eating us up piece by piece. We had to continually retreat, but we continued guerilla tactics sabotaging roads and shooting at ships on the river. In the beginning of 1946 we received some visitors from Hanoi. We hoisted a red banner to please them because we knew that they were Communists.

But when they came they said, "Put that banner down immediately. If the Allies, the U.S., see it we might have to fight for many decades." We didn't understand because we thought that Ho was an ally of the U.S. And because Stalin was an ally of the U.S., too.

In 1947, I got married to a fighter in my group. And my son was born in the underground. As the war continued to go against us, we finally had to retreat into the Plain of Reeds, a mostly uninhabitable marshy area. Sometimes we didn't have rice or regular meals. And we always dressed in rags.

I stayed in the underground until 1952, a couple of years before Mr. Diem came home. I left because I saw too many frightening things. The Communists were grabbing all the power by killing off the nationalists.

The Communists had organized in the resistance with us. We fought together and regarded them as comrades in arms. But sometimes in the middle of the night they would tell us, "Hold the area." And they would leave to indicate to the French where our nationalist positions were. The Communists betrayed us all the time. Ho Chi Minh's people began to kill off all of the strong non-Communist leaders and Trotskyite Communists in the resistance. One of my uncles, Le Trong, and friends like Dr. Suong, after collaborating with the Communists were killed by them. Huynh Phu So, the leader of the Hoa Hao Buddhist sect, whom I knew personally, was also killed by Ho's people.

I survived because at first I was too young to be considered a potential rival. I never dared to question what the Communists did. I didn't know what communism was. The rhetoric looked good. But they killed off a lot of patriots more intelligent and mature than I.

Ho was able to seize power in the north, thanks to all

those photographs of General Chennault and the OSS. And by eliminating all the other nationalist parties. In the south, the non-Communist parties like the Dai Viets and sects like the Cao Dai and Hoa Hao Buddhists and all the independent-minded people serving for the independence of our country were more powerful. But Ho's cunning tactics eliminated many and he imposed himself. And then, what sealed the fate of Vietnam—the United States helped the French.

That made it difficult, if not impossible, for independent-minded people to rally to the American-backed regime in Saigon [in 1954], no matter how much we loved democracy. And no matter how much we disliked communism.

Most of the leaders of the Saigon regimes were former officers in the French armies. It was difficult for me to believe that by a stroke of the French pen granting Vietnam independence in Geneva in 1954, that these collaborating officers could become bona fide nationalist leaders of an independent Vietnam.

# THE NATIONALIST FORCES

## Ha Thuc Ky

*Guerilla Leader*
*Dai Viet Party*
*Central Vietnam*

*1945–1954*

I was only eighteen years old in 1939, when the Japanese arrived to take over the country. I had been a student of forestry and engineering in Hue. At the end of World War II, I resigned my job as a forestry official and entered a unit of the nationalist forces to fight the French. We were not called Viet Minh. We were simply nationalist forces [of the Dai Viet Party].

The majority of the troops under my command were inexperienced young students. We would fight along Route 9 and in Laos. At the time the French were very weak and had not received any resupplies from France. They retreated as soon as we would attack. So we had many victories. And we captured a number of weapons.

But when our soldiers were wounded, it was very hard to get medical treatment. We tried to treat wounds, but quite often infections would set in and our soldiers would die. We had three or four hundred young men in each of two battalions. Around ten percent of them were lost during the first year.

During one attack on a French encampment, we were trapped inside, caught in a cross fire. An older commander turned to me and asked if I was afraid of dying. I said, "Yes, I am afraid. Everybody is afraid of dying. But when you're in this position of leadership, you must put your fear down and your sense of responsibility must rise." And we embraced.

In 1946 I first heard that Ho Chi Minh's agents were killing off rival nationalists. On March 6, 1946, there was a signing of an agreement between Ho and the French, where Ho betrayed our people. He allowed the French soldiers to move back into Hue and other areas of Vietnam in exchange for their recognizing him. When we discovered Ho's Communists were killing non-Communists throughout the country, we realized that our leaders were in danger. I received orders from Truong Tu Anh, the Dai Viet Party leader, to work undercover in Hanoi, to report on both the French and the Communist activities.

It's very difficult to give the exact number of Dai Viet Party members at that time. We were organized in secret cells in northern and central Vietnam, and weren't able to coordinate with members in the South. A physician, Buu Hiep, was the titular commander of the Dai Viet forces in central Vietnam. But the person who did all of the organization work was Hiep's brother, Buu Viem.

The Communists captured Viem and sent him to prison in Vinh, in the North. Viem succeeded in making Dai Viet cell organizations within the prison. And after a while, he killed a guard and escaped. But shortly thereafter he was assassinated by the Communists. His brother, Buu Hiep, was also murdered by the Communists in Hue, 1950. At that point, I was ordered to replace him as head of the Central Region Committee.

Our party leader, Truong Tu Anh, had been captured by the Communists while I was in Hanoi. Around that same time, the Communists killed the great Hoa Hao resistance leader, Huynh Phu So, who had two million followers in the Delta. A real hatred developed between the Viet Minh Communists and the non-Communist nationalist parties: the Vietnam Quoc Dan Dang (VNQDD), the Vietnam Phu Quoc Hoi, the Dai Viet, the Cao Dai, the Hoa Hao, and others. Even though we were fighting the French, the Viet Minh were our principal enemies. They killed off so many of us, destroying the emergence of a strong non-Communist leadership. This drove some of the nationalists to work with the French to oppose Ho Chi Minh.

The non-Communist nationalist organizations didn't have any experience in dealing with the outside world, most of us had only lived in Vietnam. Whereas Ho Chi Minh's Communist Party was an internationalist group.

They weren't that strong in terms of numbers, but they had the Communist world behind them. And for that reason they were able to prevail.

People in the villages during those years did admire and respect Ho Chi Minh because they thought he stood for an independent Vietnam, throwing out the colonial yoke. They were seduced by Communist propaganda and wanted to throw out the French by whatever means available. But, in those areas where the Communists took charge, the people found out the truth. Unfortunately, because they were being controlled by terror, they were afraid to speak out. By 1954 we already knew the truth about the Land Reform movement that was going on in North Vietnam.

Dai Viet representatives had come south. Because during the Land Reform terror, members of their families had been killed by the Communists.

# LAND REFORM

--------

## Hoang Van Chi

*Resistance Operative*
*Viet Minh*
*North Vietnam*

*1945–1954*

At the end of World War II, when the French came back and tried to reoccupy the country, many Vietnamese intellectuals and technicians joined the resistance movement to fight—knowing or not knowing that Ho Chi Minh who led that movement was a Communist. I was among them.

I knew perfectly well that Ho Chi Minh and his aides were Communists. But, at that time we were not concerned about their communism. We felt sure that as long as there was a Kuomintang China between Vietnam and the Soviet Union, the Communists would not show their real color and impose a dictatorship.

Most intellectuals who joined the resistance movement were sons and grandsons of former revolutionaries who had fought against French colonial rule. My grandfather had been involved in a nationalist resistance movement. And my father and uncle joined the Scholars Movement (around 1907). For this, they were imprisoned by the French on Puolo Condore Island.

I had been involved in various movements since I was in elementary school. During the students' strike to protest the arrest of Phan Boi Chau (scholar and nationalist leader), I was only twelve years old. And it cost me. I was thrown out of school and declared ineligible to graduate. So my family moved from Thanh Hoa (100 miles south of Hanoi), changed the spelling of my name slightly, and sent me to school in Hanoi.

I was in high school during the Popular Front Movement, when the Socialists were in power in France. In Vietnam we enjoyed a relative amount of political freedom. We were permitted to publish newspapers—provided they were written in the French language. And so, we formed a group that included anticolonialists of all tendencies: independents, nationalists, socialists, Stalinist Communists and Trotskyites. We published a newspaper in French—*Le Travail*. One day, at one of our regular meetings, someone in the audience raised a question: When Vietnam eventually became independent, what country would best serve as a model for us to follow?

Many people suggested Japan. They said that the Japanese were quite close to us culturally and had progressed very fast after the Meiji restoration. We should do the same.

Truong Chinh [a leader of the Stalinist Communists] offered a different view. He said, "Now it is too late to go the Japanese way. At the time of the restoration Western powers were utterly divided and could not join their efforts in stopping the Japanese. They are now united into a single bloc. If we imitate the Japanese they will destroy us immediately. There is, however, one solution to our problem: We have to go Communist and seek support from the Soviet Union."

Truong Chinh's argument well illustrates the fact that in the beginning Ho Chi Minh and his followers looked at Communism as a convenient means to be used in the struggle for national independence. They did not realize that in the long run the means will necessarily become an end in itself.

Ho's political career can be divided into three successive phases: In the very beginning he was a patriot. Next he became a Communist. And, when he came back to Vietnam, he played the nationalist game for the benefit of the Third International [Soviet Comintern]. He was so skillful in playing that game that a lot of naive outside observers got confused.

At the outset of the war against the French, I was a medical student. Viet Minh forces came to my province and didn't have a military doctor. They asked me to take care of them. After that group of soldiers moved south, I went back to Hanoi and met with Pham Van Dong, then

Minister of Finance. He made me director of the mints and his cabinet director. I oversaw the producing of the money that had Ho Chi Minh's effigy.

When the war broke out in December 1946, I moved my factory to the guerilla zone in Thanh Hoa and Nghe An provinces. But left without energy, I had to build a small hydroelectric plant from scratch. For that deed I received a "Nation-wide Citation" from Ho.

We were confident because the French were not very strong after World War II. They were in the cities, we were in the countryside. In 1946, 1947, and 1948 we knew it would be a long resistance. We intended to stay out in the forest until we won.

Non-Communists in the Viet Minh, like myself, knew that Ho, Pham Van Dong, and Truong Chinh were Communists. But we believed that with Chiang Kai-Shek in China, Ho would not dare to implement Communism. Moscow was too far away. And we did not anticipate that Chiang Kai-Shek would fall so quickly. And we got caught. Everything changed when Mao won in 'forty-nine.

Before March 1951, the Communist Party was secret. So in the field, we did not know who was a member. I was believed to be a Party member because I had a high position. And when people like Pham Van Dong or Truong Chinh would travel south, they would visit my home. We were friends because I had built a hydroelectric plant. And electricity was scarce in Vietnam. But I have a radio, a refrigerator. My wife would make ice cream. So they want to stop at my house and hear the latest news and enjoy ice cream.

At that time I have a thousand workers and they respect me very much because they thought I was a Central Committee member. Powerful and important people wanted influence with me. Then in 1951, when Ho returned from a visit to Peking, the Communist Party again appeared in the open, called the Lao Dong [Workers] Party. When my workers go to Party meetings, they didn't see me there. They realized I was not in the Party and began to behave with less respect. There was a rule: non-Party members cannot be director of an institution. But they could not replace me because I was the only technician in paper-making at that time.

To get out of that difficult and embarrassing situation I suggest to a friend—a Party member—who was in charge of the Chemical Department of the Defense Ministry to ask for my assistance in the making of explosives and to build a hot furnace to produce iron. He told higher authorities: "We need a chemist. Bring Hoang Van Chi to me." I got the job, as an obscure member of the technical board. It was a position that non-Party members were permitted to hold at that time.

Previously, most of our supplies and ammunition came from the French by confiscating it or bribery. And sometimes we could buy it from French Socialists or Communists in the army. But after Mao came to power, everything changed. The Chinese began sending advisors, supplies, and counselors for every branch of government—finance, education . . . everything.

In 1951, when the Party became very active, a so-called Rectification Campaign was instituted to make villagers learn the new socialist thought and dictates of Ho. In 1953, the Communists issued a Trade Tax that was aimed at crushing all private enterprise.

The first step was the ideological preparation, self-criticism among Party members. The second step was announcing a trade tax, based on the system Mao had applied in China. A Trade Office was established to give the Party monopoly of all trade. In the village where I lived, there was a merchant from the city who opened a watch-repair shop. Like every other shop owner he had to put up a sign, "Welcome Trade Tax!" Since he has a little education, he knew to put an exclamation mark to express enthusiasm. But this was very bad luck for him. In the new Maoist Chinese vocabulary an exclamation mark is the sign of complaint. At a village meeting to denounce "reactionaries," the Communist cadre who acted as chairman told him, "You are very clever. You say 'Welcome' but you use a mark of complaint." He was beaten to death. A victim of Western grammar.

Next they began Land Reform in the villages. The elimination of landowners was meant to begin the process of Communist collectivity of all land and labor. You weren't a landlord because of the acreage you possessed or your way of life; anyone who wasn't Communist was targeted.

There were public trials and torture sessions that the Party forced the whole village to attend. It turned into very vicious, what we would call kangaroo courts.

Peasants were forced into playing out retaliation against neighbors. For instance, if a father has been classified a "landlord," the cadre call in the children. If the eldest is a girl with younger brothers and sisters, she is told, "If you do not denounce your father, you will be classified as a landlord, too. But if you publicly denounce your father and say that he raped you, you can stay home to take care of your brothers and sisters." To save the rest of her family, she was obliged to go along. It was like a staged drama, orchestrated by the Party. Peasants and landowners had to play roles like in the theater.

I witnessed some of these rallies in villages in the resistance zone. The rallies were held at night because during the day we feared the French airplanes. Hundreds of people would be marched into an area the size of a football field, usually hidden by a hill. Surrounded by a circle of bamboo torches, the flames and clouds of smoke resembled temple paintings of Buddhist hell. The tribune had two wooden stages, one for the accused and a presidium for seven judges, all poor peasants. Among them was a police chief, usually a woman.

The tribune was lit by bicycle-powered generators. The people pumping the bicycles were behind the tribune's rear screen. Also behind the screen were Land Reform cadre, who directed and coached the judges in a low voice. Very often they were accompanied by Chinese advisors dressed in Vietnamese clothing, who helped to structure this program according to Mao's model. Each tribunal would last two or three nights.

On the first night, the accused landlord would be led to one stage and the witnesses against him to the other. The village guards would shout orders to the landlord at about five-minute intervals to stand up, kneel down, raise both arms horizontally. On top of the tribunal stood three portraits: Ho Chi Minh in the middle flanked by the Soviet Malenkov and Mao. Placards were posted with slogans like: "Down with traitorous reactionary landlords." And, "Let us give the masses a free hand in their struggle."

At first the accused is only denounced with minor crimes

of exploitation. If the victim denies this, the next night he is accused of bigger crimes by neighbors or relatives—rape or murder. If he does not confess, on the third night he is accused of serving French intelligence. That is treason to the country, which means death.

I always tried to stand away from the people being accused because they would be tortured while the cadre asked them, "Who is your partner?" Because they could not endure the pain, the victims might point a finger at anyone. The cadre did not mind what happened as long as the villagers were frightened into subservience to the Party. The final goal was to destroy the landowning mentality. Because for centuries each Vietnamese poor peasant aspired to own some land and be comfortable. The Party wanted to destroy this in order to pave the way for government-controlled cooperatives.

Cadre were ordered by the Party: "Better to kill ten innocents than let one reactionary escape." Quotas were set in every village: at least one must be publicly executed. But if a village was quite big, they increased the number. Others are sent to jail. But the number of people who died by violent execution is much smaller than those who died because of isolation. When the family is branded "landlord" nobody in the town is allowed to communicate with them. The family must live inside the house with nothing to eat. As a consequence, many people died of starvation, children and old people first.

Eventually Party members themselves became victims. Because at the beginning it was the thing to do to join the Communist Party. This included landowners and intellectuals. But later they became targets of accusation as the Party purged nonhard-core elements. Or people who had any democratic leanings and considered Communism a means, not an end.

Unfortunately, residents in Hanoi and Haiphong did not know about the Land Reform that was going on in the countryside, because it was happening in the Communist-controlled zone where communication is closed off and travel restricted by the Viet Minh. People do not even know what is happening in the next village. And the cities were controlled by the French until the end of the war. Only the Catholics knew. Because they were told of the terror and bloodshed by other Catholics. And so they fled en masse to the South.

I could bear all kinds of privations and hardships, including a chronic malaria. But there was an evil that I could not live with. It's a system of terror well orchestrated by the all-powerful Party, that resorted to mob violence to eliminate all potential opponents.

After the Chinese began supplying arms and ammunition, our hot furnace was closed down. I then became a high school teacher of math and science. In that modest position nobody watched me and I was able to escape from the country.

I left North Vietnam in February 1955, seven months after the Geneva Accords were signed. I told my wife, "Everything is changing. Now Diem is in the South. Let's go and see if we can help in some way." And we escaped.

But when northern refugees tried to tell southerners what Communism is like, they didn't believe us. They said: "The Communists are human beings. They cannot be *that* inhuman. And they are Vietnamese. Those killed must have committed some crime."

I spent a few years in Saigon and couldn't find any intelligent anti-Communist movements. Everybody was shouting, "Long live President Ngo [Diem]." And the Americans' problem was not understanding the Oriental mind. They didn't realize that a Confucian element would be involved even with a Vietnamese Catholic . . . which was Diem's downfall. It was the Confucian element that led to family favoritism and running his regime like a feudal emperor. Diem was from a well-respected nationalist family, but he knew nothing about politics and democracy.

John Foster Dulles saw the strong opposition to Communism in Poland and Hungary and the success of Magsaysay in the Philippines. All being Catholic countries. He believed that a Catholic Vietnamese president favoring a Catholic regime would be able to succeed against Communism.

# THE GENEVA CONFERENCE
--------
## Stephen Young

*Village Development Advisor*
*U.S. AID*
*Mekong Delta*
*1968–1971*

When Dien Bien Phu fell in June 1954, I was nine years old. I remember coming down to the dining room of our house in Washington, D.C.—my Dad was away negotiating at the Geneva Conference. I picked up the newspaper and saw big headlines: DIEN BIEN PHU FALLS, END OF WAR. I was really bothered by that and asked my mother, "What does it mean: 'falls, end of war'?" She said, "The war in Vietnam is over."

I said, "A war has been going on as long as I've been alive, and nobody ever told me about it." It didn't seem right somehow.

My father, Kenneth Young, was the State Department's number-two negotiator in the Korean War peace talks at Panmunjom, Korea, from 1952 until the talks were wrapped up at the Geneva Conference in 1954. John Foster Dulles, the secretary of state, asked my father to remain in Geneva for the second half of the conference, on Indochina. He got to know South Vietnamese nationalists who looked upon the Geneva agreement to divide Vietnam as another sell-out of Vietnam by the French and Communists.

In effect, the nationalists resented the two Westernized extremes of the political spectrum—colonialism and Communism. Neither of which truly represented the Vietnamese people. And they remembered Ho Chi Minh's betrayal in 1945 and 1946, when the Communists and French polarized the Vietnamese political system by murdering the good nationalist leaders.

The concern of the Americans in 1954 was how to give

the Vietnamese an alternative to both the French and
Communists. Very much in the minds of the Americans
at the time was the failure of an alternative to emerge in
China, in contrast to the emergence of parliamentary de-
mocracies in both India and Japan.

In October 1954, Eisenhower sent a letter to Ngo Dinh
Diem that said we would support South Vietnam directly.
The significance of that decision was that we broke with
the French to support an independent nationalist Vietnam, strong enough to prevent Hanoi from invading.

# THE NEW REPUBLIC

--------

## Gen. Edward Lansdale

*Commanding Officer for Pacification*
*Military Assistance Advisory Group*
*South Vietnam*

*1954–1956*


In early 1954, after my tour in the Philippines, I was invited to a meeting of the State and Defense departments. The French were asking for American aircraft for the Dien Bien Phu battle. We decided not to give it. The feelings were pretty strong.

John Foster Dulles turned to me and said, "We want you to go out there, Ed." I said, "Where?" He said, "To Vietnam." I said, "To do what? I'm not going to help the French with a colony. I don't like the way they treat the Vietnamese. I'm not going to help them mistreat any more people." And Dulles said, "What I want you to do is go out there and help those Vietnamese like you did in the Philippines."

When I arrived in Saigon in June 1954, there was a caretaker Vietnamese government taking orders from the French. I remember Saigon looked like a beautiful garden. The streets were narrow and lined with trees. And we came along, of course, and took down the trees to widen the streets. But I remember flowering trees and flowering shrubs. I was quite struck by the beauty of the place. The streets were just mobbed with bicycles.

South Vietnam wasn't ready at all for independence. The government started off with its head, Emperor Bao Dai, living in France. Most of this government was run by the French, who were leaving. Bao Dai appointed Ngo Dinh Diem prime minister about a month after I got there. Diem had been Interior Minister in the 1930s for six months. Back then, he had tried to introduce reforms against French rule that Bao Dai wouldn't support, so Diem resigned.

To help Diem, I ran the early pacification campaigns. The army went into areas from which the Viet Minh or French had departed and tried to get a government presence established there. In large areas, when the French administrators left, nobody was there to take over. The French had never trained the Vietnamese to be administrators.

I'd come from the Philippines, where we trained local people to run their own affairs and set up schools and colleges. But in Vietnam there were only one hundred doctors in the whole damned country. And they only had about a dozen lawyers. It was a very poorly trained country to take over and run their own affairs.

The original pacification was making use of the armed forces and civilian teams that were formed. Some ex-Viet Minh had come into the government and they were helping out. We were training teams to go into the villages and start self-government. But it was all sort of foredoomed by what we had agreed to at Geneva and what the French hadn't done in readying the people to run their own country.

The Viet Minh had learned by trying to run the territories where their troops were. They learned civil administration along with their military operations. They had originally recruited many of the brightest people, including a lot of people who left them when they discovered what the Viet Minh were really like. But these people didn't want to go into a French-led colony, which was the only other choice for years.

When Diem started running "A Vietnam for Vietnamese" it was an exciting period. Gradually, these former Viet Minh started believing it and came over to help. They were full of ideas, love of country, and idealism. I worked with many of these people. Most Americans coming from Washington would talk about civil service and, "We've got to get these bureaus going." I'd say, "What people are you talking about? Come on down to these ministries and see what's there." And they were setting up a school to teach administrative people. I said, "Fine, you do that. But at Geneva they decided there's going to be a plebiscite to see who runs this country. We haven't got people on our side in the provinces yet. And if there's a vote, the Communists can get cadre in there fast. They're training them now to come down south and take over. We've got to get people trained to start getting the people organized to keep the Communists out by a vote."

And the Americans were acting like the plebiscite would be in another hundred years, instead of 1956. They'd say, "Why are you so excited?" And I said, "Because it's coming right away. You should have had the schools started yesterday. And you're saying you'll be training them for four years before they can go into the provinces. That's too goddamned late."

So I used the army to go into the provinces to set up government as quickly as I could. Then we brought in the civilian teams and really tried to start a Vietnamese government going. Meanwhile the Viet Minh were telling people, "The new army eat babies for breakfast, they rape women," and all sorts of stories.

# PACIFICATION
--------

## Rufus Phillips

*Military Advisor*
*Military Assistance Advisory Group*
*South Vietnam*

*1954–1956*


In 1954 I was an Army lieutenant assigned to an air/sea rescue unit in Korea. I wasn't doing much of anything when Ed Lansdale's Saigon military mission was looking for people who spoke French, and there weren't very many. So I got chosen.

I arrived in Saigon on August 8, four days before the Geneva Accords went into effect. August 10 was my twenty-fourth birthday.

Diem had just been appointed by Bao Dai as the premier. He arrived and had very little support. Bao Dai had sold the police to the Binh Xuyen gangsters. French soldiers were coming down from the north and were really bitter. French paratroopers would come into the nightclubs, sit on the floor, take their shoes off, and bang them on the floor.

People were drunk all over the place. And there were two monstrous gambling places that went literally all night—with no table space. It was a wide-open city. And everybody anticipated that it was just a matter of time before the rest of South Vietnam went down the tubes.

Ngo Dinh Diem was a very strong nationalist. He was the last well-known non-Communist Vietnamese who had an independent reputation. Because he had always refused to cooperate with the French. When Diem arrived in Saigon, the first thing he encountered was that the French governor-generals didn't want to let go of the power. Diem raised hell about that, and the governor-generals had to move out. But the French were still pretty much in control of the country. And then nearly one million refugees started coming down from the North. And that was a hell of a problem.

Today there are some people who say that the only reason that the people from the North fled to South Vietnam was because Lansdale was doing things to spread rumors. That's not true. Jesus, they came because the priests were very afraid of the Viet Minh. They'd seen what the hell the Communists were doing.

Diem was trying to put together a government and deal with the refugee problem. And almost immediately he had a semirevolt on his hands by the head of the army, General Hinh. Hinh was a very charming guy who also was holding a general's rank in the French army and had dual citizenship. He was being egged on by the French to undermine Diem.

The French were famous for intrigue. In 1945–46, the French and Ho's Communists worked together to eliminate the non-Communist nationalist Vietnamese organizations. In this deal, the French turned over their files on the VNQDD and Dai Viets to Ho Chi Minh. This perpetrated a massacre of nationalist leaders all over Vietnam. In one particular case, I met a VNQDD guy who had escaped. He was still fairly young at the time. He told me that nationalists were simply hit on the head, sewn up in sacks, and dumped into the rivers—literally hundreds and hundreds.

Obviously, the French never wanted the story to receive much publicity. But I remember talking to some French officers about it in 1955. They were complaining about the Americans coming in and the Vietnamese turning against them. I said, "Well, what about this collaboration you had with Ho's people?" And God, they were so upset. They had to admit it was true.

To understand the intensity of feeling and fear the non-Communist Vietnamese had, you have to go back to those experiences. In the 1954–55 period, when the Vietnamese really opened up and said what was bothering them, we knew that if the U.S. simply went home, that was not going to be a solution. The reason we were there to begin with was to try to help the non-Communist Vietnamese to have a country of their own. And it's funny that the myth of Ho Chi Minh is still a very successful image of a benign figure. But that's not the way he is known to one hell of a lot of Vietnamese who had to deal with him.

Even in North Vietnam people did not take easily to Ho's dictates. There was an uprising in Nghe An, Ho's home province, in 1956. It didn't receive much publicity, because of the Hungarian revolt against the Russians at that time. But it was very significant.

As the French were trying to undermine Diem, he had all these other problems, including what to do about the areas that the Viet Minh were evacuating. The Communists left behind a lot of their political cadre. And they did two things which built a path for them to come back. One, they encouraged each soldier to marry a local girl and try to get her pregnant before evacuating. This meant that she would have a child by him, creating an allegiance to North Vietnam. Second, they conscripted a lot of ten- and twelve-year-olds from families that had no previous strong contact with the Viet Minh. And they took these children up north.

The South was a mixed bag. The Viet Minh controlled the Ca Mau peninsula and the Ben Tre area in Cochinchina [Mekong Delta]. And they had coastal areas north of Saigon from Quang Ngai down to Nha Trang. They had controlled these areas for almost nine years. So there had to be a way of putting a new government on its feet in those areas. And that's what I got involved in.

We had a joint military mission with the French called TRIM to train and instruct the Vietnamese. It had an American program officer and a French intelligence officer. But most of us weren't working on intelligence at all. We were either doing things for the refugees or involved in this pacification—taking the name from the French—to put government on its feet.

I worked with the Vietnamese army on this. I went with them into Ca Mau as a liaison. The Vietnamese troops were not prepared for the operation. They had not been well trained in civic affairs and didn't have a clear concept of what we were supposed to do. We tried some civic action, being helpful to people by trying to restore roads. We brought in medical assistance, Operation Brotherhood, mainly Filipino doctors sponsored by the International Jaycees. And they were effective. But where the operation broke down was that the military didn't have a clear idea of how to win acceptance by the local population.

In one incident, we went down to the tip of Ca Mau in a boat. A lot of charcoal is produced in the mangrove there. It's also the worst mosquito area I've ever been in. You can see thick swarms of them like clouds coming out of the swamp as sunlight starts to fade.

We arrived in a little town at dusk. They took us to this sort of restaurant and gave us some hot tea. They put smoke pots under our table to ward off mosquitoes. So you're either fighting mosquitoes or choking to death. A large crowd gathered around us. And I hear this murmur growing louder and louder. So I said to this Vietnamese colonel, "I think they think I'm a Frenchman. You could get up and tell them something. Because I've got a feeling that I'm going to be lynched."

So he got up and introduced me as an American. And the whole crowd relaxed. The reason was that this had been one of the Viet Minh's supply bases that the French had bombed repeatedly. Coming out of this experience, I wrote a series of "lessons learned" that were applied quite successfully in Quang Ngai and Binh Dinh.

There was a wonderful guy named Colonel Le Van Kim. He was a very bright and articulate Vietnamese army officer, in command of this operation. We set up a training program for the troops. One of the factors they had to overcome was their lack of self-confidence. They'd never been allowed to operate independently under the French. After Geneva, all of a sudden they were on their own. And they had tremendous problems.

As the Viet Minh would evacuate part of a zone, the ARVN [South Vietnamese Army] would come in. There was supposed to be a French buffer. But the French were negative on the whole thing, and they weren't being cooperative with anybody.

It took almost a month and a half to reoccupy the coastal area. And despite the fact that we had two Vietnamese divisions, there was not one single incident between a soldier and civilian. And the morale was very good.

I'd pass myself off as a reporter so that nobody would

feel that I was intruding. I saw troops start being helpful to people, but the people were really hanging back. The Viet Minh propaganda was that we were going to rape and pillage. And their experience with French and Vietnamese troops before that hadn't been very salutary. Because the Vietnamese troops had been trained to shoot anything that moved.

But as the operation went on, the word got around that the soldiers were not doing what people expected. In fact, they were being quite helpful. So the further into the countryside we went, the warmer our reception. People were coming to meet us with water and food for the troops. We'd march into a war-torn town and help rebuild the marketplace, rebuilding clinics and schools. And the troops couldn't believe it—but girls started coming up and scattering flowers along the road.

The troops liked the adulation and began volunteering very sincerely to continue this work. Originally officers had to force them to do this. But they liked the garlands of roses around their necks. The "I'm a hero" type feeling is a self-perpetuating kind of thing.

News was getting around that Diem was standing up to the French and the Binh Xuyen gangsters. He was gaining very strong nationalist sentiment among the population of being the Vietnamese who really threw the French out. It wasn't Ho Chi Minh, it was Diem.

Diem sent a message to Colonel Kim that he wanted to come up to Binh Dinh right away. Kim was very nervous. We didn't know what the hell would happen. But Diem insisted, and came about ten days later. I've got a photograph of him riding around in a jeep. And he got a tremendous welcome.

The people put Diem on their shoulders, taking him around and cheering. I have pictures of Diem up on people's shoulders, hanging on to their heads, with a look on his face, "You're going to drop me." But women, old men, young boys, and young girls were cheering with big smiles.

The Vietnamese wanted to have a country where the leader is one of them and the troops are looking out for them. But there were a lot of Viet Minh cadre still out there.

# THE SEEDS OF WAR

## Nguyen Tuong Lai

*Guerilla Leader*
*Viet Cong*
*South Vietnam*

*1954–1968*

I was born in Bac Lieu, in southern Vietnam. In 1954, at the age of fourteen, I joined Regiment 1094 of the Vietnam People's Army [Viet Minh]. After the signing of the Geneva Accords my regiment went to North Vietnam, where I was trained in the Political Action Group. Then in 1955 I was assigned back to South Vietnam to organize activities to make pressure on Bao Dai's government.

In 1955 Bao Dai was deposed by Mr. Ngo Dinh Diem with the help of the U.S. I was the leader of a sapper [saboteur] team running commando missions in the Soc Trang area when in 1957 we were instructed by the Communist Party's Central Committee to now begin the war. At that time we were prepared to struggle against American interventionism.

# THE UNDERGROUND
# SCHOOL
--------
### Truong Mealy

*Viet Minh and Viet Cong Agent
Mekong Delta and Saigon*

*1952–1960*

As part of the Geneva agreement, all of the Communist
cadre in the Can Tho–Nha Be area were supposed to go
down to Ca Mau to take a boat to North Vietnam. As
they left, they ordered small children between seven and
fifteen years old to go with them. I escaped that. But
many cadre stayed behind to train local children and organize subversive activities.

I was ten years old when a Viet Minh convinced me to
go to a secret school. My father had been dead since I
was eight years old. And these people recruited me without the knowledge of my mother. I just followed their
instructions. They had me distribute handwritten leaflets
around the marketplace saying things about higher salar-
ies and justice. And they asked me to introduce them to
three of my friends: "One becomes three; three becomes
nine, and this way we will have many people."

The cadre promised I could go to school. At night they
took me into a cemetery, behind a gravemound where two
people can sit unnoticed. For example, after South Vietnam achieved independence, my teacher told me, "Do
you know why Ngo Dinh Diem came to Vietnam? He was
sent by the U.S. Now his whole family has power and all
the poor people must work to feed them. Who should run
Vietnam—Diem or Ho Chi Minh?"

They never called themselves Communists during this
time. But they said, "The Vietnamese people want to have
a free government. Nothing is better than independence
and liberty. Our best friend is the Soviet Union. It took

58

the United States a hundred years to have progress but in only forty years the Soviet Union has become prosperous. Why? Because the Americans are capitalists, a few people take power. But in the Soviet Union the power is in the hands of all the people."

I said, "That's wonderful. Really wonderful." And I tried to march along with them. The first step is to recruit my friends. We studied together to get good marks on the Communist teacher's examinations. I belonged to the Cambodian minority, so the cadre told me: "Ngo Dinh Diem will not let you have equality with the Vietnamese. So you must fight against him." Some of my friends went along just because of their hatred for rich people. The cadre said, "You work ten or twelve hours a day, while people in the city only work two hours. But their gain is much bigger than yours."

In the beginning the cadre just drank coffee and talked with me. I only wanted to make a friend. I didn't know anything about politics. But after we became friends he trained me in politics and planted a weapon inside me. The farther and farther we got into the discussions, I discovered he's not really good to me. But it's too late . . . you are afraid to refuse his wishes.

If a child tried to break away they used blackmail tactics. The cadre would say, "If you leave us, somebody will tell the government that you worked as a Communist." We were trapped.

I completed all of the underground training. The last grade was honor in front of a photo of Ho Chi Minh. It was only my teacher and me. Kind of a religious ceremony where Uncle Ho is worshipped as some kind of god. We stood in front of the picture meditating with our eyes glued. Praying: Thanks to Uncle Ho we have independence in Vietnam, minorities have freedom, and so on.

After I was sworn in, the cadre taught me how to cheat my mother so I could go on missions with them. I had to prepare a week or two beforehand. I'd tell my mother, "I am working so hard now. I would like to go on a holiday with my friend. Will you agree?" For two or three days I'd repeat the question. By the fifth time, my mother would say, "If you want to go with your friend, that's okay."

I told nobody where I was going. On some of these missions I had to run away from the Diem government soldiers on patrol. They walked over my head as we hid beneath the ground in tunnels. The cadre taught me to be courageous: "You should not be afraid. Because in this world either you are alive or dead. And if you show yourself to be a coward, you will be ashamed for your whole life. It is better to be courageous and dead." To a ten- to twelve-year-old child this is very impressionable. It stays with you for the rest of your life.

This helps explain the difference at times between the Viet Cong and the South Vietnamese soldiers, who were drafted at eighteen or twenty years old. It's a great difference when you train an eight- to ten-year-old soldier not to be afraid and to have a religious attitude toward Ho Chi Minh.

In the underground school I read a whole book about courageous children. In one story, a Vietnamese boy put his head into the barrel of a cannon to block it, so other soldiers could capture it. The child died. But his life is better than the ones who lived, because they are ashamed for not being courageous.

From the very beginning we were taught the art of deception. Telling lies is a part of winning the victory. You do anything to overthrow the government and defeat the enemy. We say: The victory will justify everything.

Sometimes they only train a child for one or two months before they send him somewhere with a hand grenade—inside the city or a marketplace. And he wouldn't know for whom, because we were only told the first names of our teachers. So if you are caught, the police cannot trace you back to anybody.

My teacher would instruct me, "When you get to the city, get in touch with a person named Tiger. Take this cut half of paper money, and Tiger will have the other half." I'd go to that city, walk into a restaurant, and order coffee. My contact doesn't know me, but since I am new in the town he will notice me. He comes to my table to speak with me and pulls out his half of the bill. We join the two halves together and make friends. I operated this way in Soc Trang, Can Tho, all the way to Saigon. The cadre would tell me what district to go to in Saigon, what restaurant or coffee shop, what kind of bicycle to use for my identity. But I never knew who exactly I worked for.

Children were trained by the Communists to throw grenades, not only for the terror factor, but so the government or American soldiers would have to shoot them. Then the Americans feel very ashamed. And they blame themselves and call their soldiers "war criminals."

What happens to the psychology of any soldier, especially those who are not professionals, when a child throws a grenade and kills your friends once, twice . . . you start suspecting all kids. It creates a very paranoid mentality for the visiting soldiers. They don't know which children are friendly. They start disliking and hating everybody. You believe that you can't make friends with people in the villages because you think that they are all trying to kill you.

This is where the Communists are so smart and very successful. Their most powerful weapon is psychological warfare.

# THE BAREFOOT DANCER
--------
## Gen. Edward Lansdale

*Commanding Officer for Pacification*
*Military Assistance Advisory Group*
*South Vietnam*

*1954–1956*

*The Cao Dai are a religious/political sect with around 1.5 million members in southern Vietnam.*

Trinh Minh The [pronounced Tay] was a Cao Dai guerilla leader who fought both the French and the Communists. President Diem asked me to see him and talk him into joining the national army. I received a safe pass from a Cao Dai minister in Diem's government. So I drove up to Tay Ninh Province, to the jungle area around Nui Ba Den Mountain.

Trinh Minh The had a reputation for his unusual way of fighting. Going up against an enemy, he'd go in and kill the leader. Fighting against the French, he knocked off a general. And the French took an awful dim view of that. But Trinh was really loved by the people in the countryside where these guerillas fought. The men, women, and children out there were very protective of him.

I was watching a group of children walk barefoot on a paddy dike when a group of Cao Dai guerillas emerged from the jungle. One of them looked to be a youth of high-school age, about five feet tall and ninety pounds. He was wearing a faded khaki shirt and trousers, tennis shoes, and not carrying any kind of weapon. He had a big smile on his face as he introduced himself. This was Trinh Minh The, the notorious guerilla leader. He suggested that we get off the road quickly because French forces were nearby.

We hid my car in the jungle and took off on foot up the mountain. I had to climb over all these goddamned rocks to get up to his camp. His officers were all dressed up and they begged me to review their troops. I didn't wear a uniform, I was wearing civilian clothes. They lined up into what looked like big squads, not even platoon size. And the officers only had one set of epaulets among them. So as I walked by each group, they'd run and pin the epaulets [insignias of rank] on the captain or major in the next group. I got to laughing so hard. I said, "Don't do that. Look, I'm not in uniform." But they said, "Oh, no, no, you're an American colonel. You've got to review our troops."

I talked Trinh into coming to Saigon. And he was made a general in the army. We became very close friends. I couldn't speak his language at all, and he couldn't speak mine. We had to use interpreters. But he and I looked at each other and understood an awful lot. When I could tell he wanted to do something, I would put my arm around his shoulder and give him a little squeeze. And we'd communicate without words.

He came over to my house one evening when I had a lot of Filipinos from Operation Brotherhood there. We got to folk dancing with bamboo poles. And Trinh was watching these people of different races so close to each other. I could see this look of longing come over his face. So I said, "Hey, we've got a Vietnamese friend here who's got to learn to dance." I grabbed him, made him take off his shoes, and made him dance barefoot as we were doing. He started laughing and he turned around and gave me a great big hug.

On one occasion in 1954, before Trinh joined the national army, the French came to see me in Saigon. They said, "We've got intelligence that Trinh is coming to see you. We've got the whole neighborhood surrounded. And we're going to kill him."

So they waited. And here came Trinh, driving right up to my house. He was disguised as a pedicab driver. He had a nobody all dressed up in a white suit sitting in the back of the cab. And out stepped Trinh, the poor barefoot driver.

As he came up to my house, I told the "driver" to go to the kitchen. I had some food for him there. The French hit men were all around us. I said, "My God, Trinh, these guys are going to kill you. They've been waiting for you here." And he said, "They're stupid. They couldn't hit anything."

Many times the French would be hunting for him. And Trinh would come by on his bicycle. And they'd think he was a little kid. Because he didn't fit the mental picture they had of him as the fierce guerilla leader. And he would stand there and talk with them. They'd ask if he'd seen Trinh Minh The. And he'd say, "Yeah, I've heard of him. He's out in that area over there."

Trinh was killed in Saigon in 1955 fighting against the Binh Xuyen gangsters. This was the critical battle that led to the founding of the Republic of Vietnam under Diem. The government named a street in Saigon after Trinh. And a bridge, where he was killed . . . on the bridge.

There was a big funeral ceremony for him on Nui Ba Den Mountain. His men went up the mountain and buried him. I had Trinh's young son in my arms. I was crying and sweating all the way up. It was misty as I took Trinh's son with me to the grave. The troops insisted I go. The child and I stood at the grave alone.

On the way back to the ceremony site, I heard this chanting. And I thought, "Now what's their story?" I asked the political advisor what it was. He said, "The men are pledging allegiance to you because you are the brother of their leader."

I said, "I'm a foreigner. They can't do that. They should pledge allegiance to their country and to its government. And as long as this government is true to them, they should be true to it."

When I returned to Vietnam in 1965, Trinh's son was grown up, just finishing high school. He married the daughter of another general. And his mother said, "My husband used to tell all of us in the family that you were his brother. But all of the men in the family have been killed. You're the only one left alive. So would you please act as the groom's father in the wedding?" I said, "I'd be honored to do it."

The son went into the army and became a helicopter pilot. He was shot down and captured. I've never received any word of him. His mother disappeared and I can't even get in touch with her. But he's got a young son and daughter, and a sister, now living in Canada. I'm trying to look out for them up there.

# INVITATION TO A SIDESHOW

## Penn Nouth

*Prime Minister and Presidential Advisor*
*Kingdom of Cambodia*

*1953–1970*

At the time of Cambodian independence in 1953, I was prime minister. We attained our independence by a separate agreement with France, many months before the Geneva Conference was resolved. The Geneva Accords of 1954 not only confirmed Cambodia's independence, but had the merit of getting the evacuation of Vietnamese Communist forces illegally residing in Cambodia.

The Vietnamese Communist Party—Viet Minh—were supporting a handful of Khmer Communists to make subversive activities. This subversion was not only in Cambodia, but in Laos and Cochin-china. It started in 1930 when Ho Chi Minh formed the Communist Party of Indochina. But through 1945–54 there were only a handful of these Khmer Viet Minh.

The objective of the Indochina Communist Party was to make propaganda always to the theme of liberation from French domination. In Cambodia, due to our history of Vietnam invading and absorbing our country, this was not successful. But in 1954, when the Vietnamese withdrew their troops they took with them the Khmer Communists. They also took by force a large number of Cambodian peasants. These people were brought to Hanoi for political and ideological training. That is the origin of the Khmer Communist Party.

At Geneva, even though I had negotiated our independence from the French months earlier, the Vietnamese Communists pushed to have Cambodia partitioned into two zones. They wanted a Communist Cambodia under

Vietnamese control, similar to the Heng Samrin regime
in Cambodia today. But the leader who saved us was Chou
En-lai. Chou said that China already had so many Communists that they didn't need Cambodia. Rather, Cambodia would serve as a buffer between China and the
Western world.

After Cambodia gained independence I made a broad-
cast to the North Vietnamese to withdraw their troops
from my country. Since Cambodia was free, their presence was not justified. Though we had no hostility toward
them. Unfortunately, the text of my speech did not please
the U.S. State Department under John Foster Dulles. They
said our position of neutrality vis-à-vis the Vietnamese
Communists was immoral. But at that time I was naive
enough to believe we could coexist with our Communist
neighbors.

In 1954 the U.S. created SEATO [Southeast Asia Treaty
Organization]. I received a visit by a U.S. congressional
delegation led by my friend, Mike Mansfield. They came
to talk about SEATO as a league against Communism. I
said, "We cannot join SEATO because the Geneva Accords imposed that we be neutral. However, independent
Cambodia would very much appreciate the friendship of
the U.S."

The U.S. had just engaged China in the Korean War
and feared that China, who had an aggressive policy at
that time, would spread Communism, in Indochina first
and then the rest of Asia. I had a lot of American officials
in Phnom Penh ask me, "Aren't you afraid of an invasion
by China?"

Our diplomatic relations with China began in 1955 at
the time of the Asian–African Conference at Ban Doeng,
Indonesia. Chou En-lai, Nehru, Nasser, and Sihanouk all
participated. This conference later led to the formation
of the non-aligned movement. We Cambodians told the
Americans, "We have known French control for ninety
years. And we don't want any Communist country—Soviet, Chinese, or Vietnamese—to colonize us. Even if
they declare themselves our friends."

In 1956 there was no referendum for the reunification
of Vietnam. A new war developed between South Vietnam and Hanoi. This was also a pretext for Hanoi to

spread their troops throughout Indochina. In Laos there already existed a zone controlled by the Communists. Hanoi sent many regiments to South Vietnam through Laos. But the infiltration and staging in Cambodia was not significant until 1963–64 when Prince Sihanouk signed a pact with Hanoi allowing them on our eastern border and later, the use of our southern port of Sihanoukville [Kompong Som] as their supply base.

We thought the presence of Vietnamese Communists would only be on the border of South Vietnam. But against our knowledge, the North Vietnamese brought some Khmer Communist elements trained in Hanoi back into Cambodia to create a movement.

The South Vietnamese forces of Diem invaded Cambodian territory under the claim of hot pursuit of the Viet Cong. And the U.S. supported Diem when we complained. South Vietnamese troops incurred into Ratanikiri and displaced the border markers. Cambodian troops intervened and pushed them back. Afterwards the U.S. Embassy in Phnom Penh had strong words:

"We gave you the arms to fight against the North Vietnamese, not against the South Vietnamese, who are our allies, or against the Thais." We replied, "We used these weapons to defend our frontier and territorial integrity."

We clashed with the Thais less than with the South Vietnamese. But Thailand had claimed Cambodian territory at Preah Vihear. And the U.S. supported all of the rival neighboring regimes. So Sihanouk and other Cambodians began to discuss the question, "Can we rely on American equity, if we cannot use these arms against our enemies?" Because of these events, we denounced the Accords of Friendship with the U.S. in 1963.

Even though Sihanouk was suffering the North Vietnamese and Viet Cong occupation of some of our provinces, in 1963 we signed an agreement with Pham Van Dong in Hanoi. The North Vietnamese and NLF agreed in writing to accept our borders. Years later we realized it was false promises. But since China said she was morally committed, and backed the Vietnamese Communists, we felt this was in our best interest.

We made trade agreements with both China and the Soviet Union to keep a balance between those two powers to defend our interests. By these agreements, we allowed supplies to be delivered to our port and be coordinated through the Chinese and North Vietnamese embassies to be shipped to North Vietnamese troops staging on our border with South Vietnam.

Simultaneously began the rise of the Communist movement in Cambodia. At the outset there were no more than two to three hundred Communists. But supported by North Vietnam, China, and the Soviets, they instigated feelings of hostility among peasants in remote regions.

# THE SCRABBLE GAME
--------
## Gen. Edward Lansdale

*Commanding Officer for Pacification*
*Military Assistance Advisory Group*
*South Vietnam*

*1954–1956*

President Diem was a complex person. He was a great patriot, knew a lot about his people, and had tremendous feeling for them. But things started going downhill with Diem for a combination of reasons.

Diem had a number of faults. Some were endemic to Vietnam because of the way politics developed under a hundred years of French occupation. Every Vietnamese had to be conspiratorial to survive. Not trusting anybody was second nature. But to operate an open political system you must be able to tell people what you think and try to get their support. Unfortunately, Diem wasn't able to get himself out of that conspiratorial atmosphere. He was prone to people whom he trusted, who would play on his paranoia. Particularly his brother Nhu, who became more and more influential.

Diem's father, on his deathbed, asked Diem to look after his younger brother Nhu. So Diem always had Nhu close to him. And secretly, Nhu thought, "I'm a hundred times smarter than you." And he was very cocky. This used to worry me.

I remember once we were up at Dalat. Nhu was playing Scrabble in French, and asked me to play with him. I said, "Yeah, I will." And his wife, Madame Nhu, said, "Don't beat him. He can't stand being beat. He thinks he's the smartest guy in the world."

So I went and beat him. And, oh God, he hollered. "Cheating! You cheated!" Nobody could win fairly against him. His ego was too big.

Nhu put intelligence systems together to help his brother. Initially I thought it was good, because he was very good at catching Communist intentions, particularly watching Hanoi. Diem asked me to work on his intelligence systems, which I did. But Nhu wouldn't let me into what he was doing. He was feeding political intelligence to his brother daily.

Diem would tell me about various individuals, what they'd done the night before, and gossip about them. Like when troops were ambushed and killed, he would know where they were drinking, what they had said beforehand. The names of the officers, intimate details of their families. His brother Nhu, I discovered, was giving him this information.

But I told Diem, "I want you to go out into the country and learn these things for yourself. Because some of this information strikes my ear as wrong." So he sent some of his trusted people out to check, and discovered that I was right. His brother had given him colored information.

When I left Vietnam, there was nobody to stand up the way I did to try and guide Diem. I left at the end of 'fifty-six. Diem had elections after that, and they were cheating in it. I was hearing from Vietnamese that those who lost the elections were mad at Diem.

# THE THIRD FORCE

## Ha Thuc Ky

*Opposition Leader*
*Dai Viet Party*
*Central Vietnam and Saigon*
*1954–1963*

After our struggle against both the French and the Communists we in the Dai Viet nationalist party were happy to see the Americans come. But we were disappointed that they picked Mr. Ngo Dinh Diem to be the new president.

It wasn't so much Diem, it was his brother Nhu. During the organization period, after the French conceded and before Diem took office, Nhu had been chief of a solidarity party in the Hue area. This was an attempt to bring together the various nationalist groups in the Hue area. I was a deputy in that Dai Doan Ket Party and we Dai Viets associated with Nhu at that point.

But as soon as Diem took office and Nhu went to join him, there were arrests. They broke up by every means possible the various nationalist organizations like the Dai Viets and the Dai Doan Ket. Diem and his brother didn't want to share power with anybody. And for that reason, we opposed them. All the people who opposed the Communists, all the various factions that had fought for the liberation of Vietnam in the South, should have been brought together. They should have had a major advisory role in the Diem government. Instead, we became disaffected.

The Dai Viets were among the most threatening in the minds of Diem and Nhu. Members were arrested and not allowed to associate with people imprisoned from other political parties.

In 1954, I stayed in Quang Tri Province and created the

71

Dai Viet broadcasting station to fight both Hanoi and Ngo Dinh Diem. Nhu was going to imprison us one way or another. So we were basically attempting self-defense. Although we knew it was a lost cause. The Americans were supporting Diem. So, of course, he was going to prevail against us. But we didn't hate the Americans, because we knew that the Americans had to support Diem. And we had experienced the barbarity of Ho Chi Minh's people.

Our resistance base finally broke after one year of constant attacks by Diem's army and Hanoi's forces. I escaped to Saigon, where I reestablished the broadcasting station and continued to fight against Diem. My wife and I lived underground with our six children.

After a year in one house, I realized that the police were using a method that would eventually get me. So I got rid of the radio equipment and rented the house to an American. I hid caches of weapons and supplies in the basement. When the intelligence service found this house, the American and his wife were surprised to see men come in and dig up weapons from down below. It was quite a shock for them.

I was captured in October 1958. I was put in a prison in Saigon within the army camp named Le Loi. It was an old French prison with great thick walls. For the next five years there was no place to go.

At the time of the overthrow of the Diem regime, I had an infection and my face was badly swollen. So I was moved to a jail in Saigon where there were mostly Communist prisoners. And during the three or four days following the Diem assassination, my own life was in jeopardy. I was told by a nun who gave the prisoners food and water that if the Communists knew I was a nationalist they would kill me. So I told them I was a Communist in deep cover. Fortunately, General Khiem, one of the coup leaders, sent someone out to look for me. And he pulled me out in time.

When the military took over following the coup, it was the opposite of democracy. This was a bunch of generals with no experience in administration. They came to power and told the people what they wanted them to do. Unfortunately, even today there are people who think that during the early phase of a country's existence—especially after coming out of colonialism and facing an enemy using the tactics of a war of national liberation—it may be necessary to use more rigorous, less democratic means to accomplish your ends.

But a government's strength is not defined by large quantities of weapons, but by capturing the hearts and minds of the people. That's the way to strengthen your country. And you do that by having a regime that people identify as fair and just. Maybe not fully democratic, but it must have other qualities that people can trust.

In those early years of the republic, the only people who were allowed to fight or contribute in any way in the war effort against the Communists were soldiers loyal to the generals. The government should have capitalized on all the nationalist parties. We were all surely interested in fighting the Communists. But the generals said the parties were disorganized and factionalized. However, the real reason was they did not want to lose any of their authority.

The people, of course, were separated and factionalized. And the Americans were dealing only with the generals, whose units did fight on occasion. But the only way to defeat a clever enemy like the Communists is to get as much participation from as many nationalist groups as possible. And try to bring them together.

# THE HO CHI MINH TRAIL

## Nguyen Tuong Lai

*Guerilla Leader*
*Viet Cong*
*South Vietnam*

*1954—1968*

Since 1957, I was a lieutenant in the revolutionary army.
My sapper team was based in Soc Trang, Ba Xuyen Province. By the time I was nineteen years old I was an experienced combat veteran against Ngo Dinh Diem's army.
I was allowed to become a full member of the Communist
Party in 1959. That year, the Party's Central Committee
in Hanoi issued Document 14, to make a concerted uprising against Ngo Dinh Diem in 1960. In May 1959, Group
559 was formed in North Vietnam to transport people,
weapons, and supplies to the South. To accomplish this
task a strategic route was created, bearing the name of
Ho Chi Minh.

# THE NATIONAL LIBERATION FRONT

## Truong Nhu Tang

*Founding Member*
*National Liberation Front*
*South Vietnam*

*1960–1976*

I returned to Vietnam from university studies in France in 1955. I saw that the nonrealization of the Geneva Accords would lead to war between the North and South. But I stayed away from political acts and worked in a private bank in Saigon.

Watching the political evolution of my country, I saw that the Diem government made many fundamental errors: First, it was a government of one family. Second, Diem suppressed many patriots who participated in the war against the French. Third, he put the Christian religion above the interest of the nation. I am personally not a Buddhist, but eighty percent of the Vietnamese population are Confucian or Buddhist.

From 1958 some resistance was formed, which led to the formation of the National Liberation Front in December 1960 in Tay Ninh Province, near the Cambodian border. I had been contacted by former resistance members and others who were unhappy with the Diem regime. I belonged to a well-known family in the South. I had relations in every stratum of society. I had been the comptroller of a large bank, and later became Director General of the Sugar Company of Vietnam and secretary-general of the Self-Determination Movement.

The mobilization committee for the National Liberation Front was formed by intellectuals: the architect Huynh Tan Phat; the doctor Phung Van Cung; the lawyer Trinh Dinh Thao; myself; and others. We were all mostly educated in France. Our idea of independence came from what we saw in free countries in the West. Whereas Ho Chi Minh and the Communists in the liberation front were formed by the Soviet Comintern under Lenin and Stalin.

I was not Communist. I joined the resistance movement believing that Ho Chi Minh, Pham Van Dong, and the Vietnamese Communist Party were patriotic and would place the national interest above personal and ideological desires. I believed that we would consolidate our divided nation and begin the task of reconstruction. I believed the people of Vietnam would find peace, well-being, and freedom once the war ended. Because of love for my country, I gave up my family, everything, for this dream.

I would not listen when my father warned me, "In return for your service, the Communists will not even give you a part of what we have now. Worse, they will betray you and persecute you all of your life."

But I was adamant, because the North Vietnamese insisted that they never wanted to impose Communism on the South. We were, in fact, dependent on the North Vietnamese for weapons, communications, and especially for our propaganda network. And our movement was reinforced by troops coming from North Vietnam.

Beginning in 1959, the northerners came down through Laos and Cambodia on the Ho Chi Minh Trail. Many of these soldiers remained posted along the trail to protect the flow of arms and munitions coming from the North.

# THE CHINESE PRIEST

--------

## Gen. Edward Lansdale

*Assistant Secretary of Defense*
*Observation Visit*
*South Vietnam*

*1961*

I was stationed at the Pentagon in December 1960. I was an air force general and an assistant secretary of defense. I had been in on the early planning for what became the Bay of Pigs fiasco. I thought it was going to be a failure and said so. They asked me not to hang around in policy meetings because I kept saying, "No, don't do it. It's going to be a big flop."

So I requested, "Please send me out of the country. I want to see what's happening in Vietnam." And both the secretary of defense and secretary of state told me, "We didn't know that our staffs hated your guts so much." That was because I had my own views on our effort in Vietnam.

I wanted the Americans to train Vietnamese to run their own affairs. To take our hands off helping too directly, running things ourselves. But I'm not sure American nature is fitted for that. We're a can-do, take-charge people. We kept sending in people with the best spirit in the world, wanting to help the Vietnamese. Even when they pronounced the names wrong and everything. Idealistic, running food programs or whatever.

When I'd get down to the provinces from Saigon, there'd be truckloads of rice coming in. The American rep would wait for the province chief or district chief to start distributing. And if he wouldn't act promptly the Americans—for the best reasons in the world—would grab the rice and do the distributing themselves. This took initiative away from the Vietnamese.

Some of the very finest Americans, who were heroes

to the Vietnamese, like John Paul Vann who was a tremendous individual, were very much that way. I'd say, "Let the Vietnamese do it and learn. If they make a mistake, talk it over with them very quietly. And the next time it won't go wrong."

When I visited Vietnam in 1961, I was very independent with Diem, as I was with the ambassador and generals commanding out there. I was going for the truth, or what I felt would bring the truth. I told Diem, "I'd like to borrow a helicopter." He said, "Where are you going?" I said, "I'll tell the pilot." Because I was going places where I knew they'd say "No."

I got Diem's secretary of defense to go with me. We went way down to the foot of Ca Mau, right in the middle of Viet Cong territory. Some ethnic Chinese refugees from North Vietnam had resettled down there. And I'd heard some fine things about what a Chinese priest was doing and the defense the villagers were making against the VC [Viet Cong].

The U Minh Forest was a malaria-ridden mangrove jungle—a lousy place infested with mosquitoes and great big snakes. The world's worst place to have a hideout. Unbelievably, the Viet Cong used the U Minh as a major base. And the Chinese priest moved in below that, in the unsettled portion of Ca Mau.

Our helicopter landed in mud, just as some wounded soldiers were coming out of a canal after a big VC ambush. There were walking, swimming wounded coming up. I put them in the helicopter and flew them to a province hospital. After that I stayed in the village of the Chinese priest and learned his methods. He was fighting the war correctly.

Everybody in the village was spiritually on his side. They were all Catholics. So there wasn't a single Communist who could ever come in and start talking bad, because the villagers would take out their knives right away. They had escaped the terror in North Vietnam. They knew who was the enemy.

All the villagers acted as a defense force. The women weren't soldiers, but they'd support the combat soldiers. The village bakers ran the mortars. And they'd cook French rolls that the troops would stick in their pockets— those were their rations.

The first night, I was there, the priest said, "Are you a Catholic?" I said, "No, I'm not." He said, "Come along anyway, I have a midnight mass tonight. I want you to see what happens." They rang a bell and turned on big floodlights up on some of the roofs to call the people to church. It was a tiny little village. And there were swamps with very watery terrain around them.

As the priest started the mass, some people would come up and whisper to him, then go away. They were reporting—they had scouts all over the countryside watching the enemy coming. The VC were attracted by the lights and the bell ringing. And they were preparing to attack.

The scouts had little radios on their belts that could use Morse code. And the priest was getting the coordinates of where the VC were massing. At one point, he turned and nodded. A whole bunch of men excused themselves and bowed out of church. They got their mortars, checked the coordinates on their map, and started firing rounds. Caught the VC right out in the open in the swamps. It was pitch-dark, but these guys knew exactly where to fire.

The VC were really scared of that priest. He captured around three times as many VC as he had villagers. And he had them trying to dry out land around the village so they could build houses and farms.

When I got back to Washington, John Kennedy had just been inaugurated as president. And my boss, the deputy secretary of defense, gave my reports to the Kennedy people. I got a phone call in my Pentagon office, and there was this Massachusetts accent. It sounded like Kennedy, whom I didn't know at all. He told me that he'd read the report about the Catholic priest in Ca Mau and he wanted to run it in the *Saturday Evening Post*. I was listening very hard to the voice, trying to figure out, "Is this my apprentice trying to pull my leg?"

I said, "Any money from the article I want to go for medical supplies for this village." And we got quite a bit for them.

Kennedy's attitude when he first came in was one of great compassion for the Vietnamese people—what their aims were and their hope. I was very concerned. I felt we were doing some things wrong, and we had to change our ways. I was worried when I saw artillery being used against villages.

I was coming out of My Tho, along the highway, when I saw it. And I knew that a Vietnamese general was doing it. I went up and called him dirty names. Afterwards, I saw one of Diem's brothers who was living nearby. He told me that all the people had been telling him what I said to this general. He said, "Is he really a son of a bitch?" I said, "He sure is, for using artillery."

The general had told me, "The VC are over there, that's why I'm doing it." He was scared to death to go anywhere near there. Americans had taught them how to save infantry lives by using artillery.

And years later I was witness to another incident: Cholon District in Saigon was a real working-class district. We went in there and started uplifting the people. God . . . they lived in mud. We showed them how to lay bricks to come up off the mud and build huts on the dryer ground. And they started some cottage industries—egg hatcheries, tileworks, and so on.

We got people to help themselves. Many of their sons were VC. And when the VC would come up to us and tell us to stop what we were doing, these people would yell to their sons, "Come back to us. You're on the wrong side." And these sons started crossing over when we had the Chieu Hoi amnesty program.

It all ended in 'sixty-eight in the Tet offensive. Because the U.S. Army went in and leveled the place. A friend of mine was commanding a brigade that was defending Saigon. And the VC got into only one house in the whole damned district. The people were coming out and trying to tell the American troops, "We'll show you where the enemy is. They're in one house."

But this commander said, "I don't want my infantry going in there with hand-held weapons. I've got artillery. These are only a bunch of shacks in there, anyhow." So he opened up with artillery and leveled the district.

My people got there about ten minutes too late. The people told them, "Never come back here again. You were our friends up to this time. No more. We don't trust the Americans anymore."

# THE FOREST OF PENCILS

--------

## Anne Miller

*Writer*
*U.S. Information Service*
*Indochina*
*1954–1960*

The whole character of American aid changed after the Korean War. Up until that time it had been very specific technical assistance, patterned on the Marshall Plan. And on President Truman's idea of technical aid and sending in teachers.

In Vietnam, good settlements were established. Wolf Ladejinski had arrived for USOM [U.S. Operations Mission] to do a land reform program. He had started the economic development of Taiwan by doing exactly the same thing. And he had done one in Japan that set them on the proper road. It was a great asset to have him.

Well, Joe McCarthy was after him. And McCarthyites who were crusading after 1954 got Wolf fired. But President Diem took him on as his personal advisor, because everything Wolf was saying made sense. Agricultural banks were set up by USOM where people could get loans. They got free small tools from USOM. And they received water buffalo sent in from Thailand. The Communists had a terrible time with that. They spread rumors: the water buffalo wouldn't understand Vietnamese, and their legs were so short they would drown in the paddies.

We started building schools in 'fifty-four, under Sam Adams, a Negro, who had started a massive education program in North Vietnam. He later received the Springerly Award for the work he did in Indochina, setting up what he called "community schools."

French colonialism had destroyed the traditional education system, which was a series of examinations on literary subjects, called the "Forest of Pencils." These exams went on for days. Students were put into cells and guarded, so they couldn't cheat.

We set up a number of community schools. Each village gave eight hectares of land on both sides of a road, and the school was built there. The teacher was given a house on the same land. These were open-air buildings. I went to the opening of the first community school, near Hue in a little town called Bung.

The parents and children were taught to experiment with new kinds of seeds and new methods of farming, poultry and pig-raising to improve self-sufficiency in the villages. A school like this became the center of activity for the village. Because they also received first aid at the school, simple medical care that could be taught to a teacher. And they formed youth groups, patterned after the Boy Scouts, to perform good deeds around the community.

At first the U.S. aid mission didn't have many people. And we had a precept: Do everything you can in a given situation before you try to spend money. Everybody was geared to this. But it eventually became a scene like *The Mouse that Roared*, when the little country said, "I'd like to borrow a million dollars." And the big country said, "I don't think I can get that for you. I can get you a billion, but I can't get you a million."

It's just like when the U.S. Army went in. They sent in 5,000 troops and what happened? It got to be 500,000. We did the same thing in our AID and our USIS. These little empires. People had their own Vietnamese and their own little project, which had no consideration of the whole picture.

In the early days, every aim was stated, worked over. Our contact was directly with the people we wanted to help. We were trying to find outlets for their resources. Build roads so that they could get to markets. And that's totally different from gathering your little group of intellectuals around you and saying, "Now what do we wish to do?" God, it was sad. As our involvement expanded, many Vietnamese weren't happy about it. They were cross-grained people, like West Virginians. They didn't care for all that aid. They would rather do it themselves.

I remember in 1955, USIS explained to the Vietnamese information ministry how we would set up an information center for them. And they became very silent. Soon the Vietnamese had an opening on Rue Catinat of their own beautiful Information Center, with an art show and published works. USIS hadn't even gotten to advise them . . . You never saw such angry people in your life. This was a hint of things to come: instead of being impressed that the Vietnamese had organized and put this beautiful place together, the USIS people were furious.

Eisenhower and Foster Dulles—both of whom I don't give much to because I'm a Democrat—were aware of the dangers in that country and to ourselves. And they damned well did everything to try to stop it. But from the time Eisenhower left office, nobody had this vision. All these numerous little projects were only candles on a birthday cake. And the birthday cake was that we encourage South Vietnamese self-reliance and keep them out of the Communist orbit.

But it just became a sprawl—an uncoordinated, undesignated bunch of money, bunch of people, bunch of materials. And I could see what this would do to President Diem. There was nobody to talk with him about the future.

Eisenhower, being a military man, opposed the Korean War and was adamant that we never be involved militarily in Vietnam. At the outset, we had a minimum of military men there. And all of them were working on village projects, not only military training. Because the most important effort was to try to teach the Vietnamese army not only how to defend itself, but how to be accepted by a village.

I could not believe it when Kennedy announced that he was going to send in regular troops. That was the beginning of the end.

# THE CYCLOPS

**Rufus Phillips**

*Assistant Director of Rural Affairs*
*U.S. AID*
*Vietnam*

*September 1962—November 1963*

By the end of the Diem period, there was a lack of confidence in the Americans. We got into some very funny kinds of syndromes. The AID mission became convinced that the solution to the Vietnam problem was the industrialization of Vietnam and development in the cities. But Diem knew the problem was in the countryside. And he kept telling the Americans this.

Diem asked the U.S. to provide community development volunteers. And some of us old hands tried to persuade AID to do that. But AID wasn't interested.

The U.S. position became that we had to create a regular army. And we let Michigan State University train the Civil Guard. The problem was that the Civil Guard were left without any strong backing. The province chiefs started using them to cut grass. Nobody in the Michigan State group was forceful enough to take control.

When I got back to Saigon in 'sixty-two, the Vietnamese were already implementing the strategic hamlet program. But I found that there wasn't a single guy in our embassy or anywhere else who had a copy of what the hell this program was all about. That was characteristic of the American involvement . . . the bigger it got, the blinder it got. So the Vietnamese were off operating on their own. And they adopted some bad programs.

Nhu became a victim of his own paranoia. And this got Diem into very deep political trouble. He became isolated from almost all other Vietnamese nationalists, except those who passed Nhu's scrutiny.

Ambassador Nolting was a nice guy and tried to be helpful. But, my God, it takes a very unusual person with a very unconventional background to size up the kind of political situations that you have in places like Vietnam. You've got to have sources of information and people talking with you very frankly, who are coming from all different directions, in order to sort out what the hell's really going on.

Nolting didn't have that kind of feel for Vietnam. He came to Vietnam brand-new. He was a very decent guy and trying to do what was right. But in some ways he was blindly supportive of Diem. And then Nolting left and Ambassador Lodge came. I think Lodge had written off Diem before he ever got there. So we had this radical swing the other way, without thinking about, "If you write this guy off, who's going to replace him?"

The Diem coup was a horrible mistake, with a war going on. There were some things going wrong with Diem that we could have changed by persuasion. Instead, we chose a forceful way of change. And among other things, when Diem was overthrown the Constitution, the constitutional government, and the people running the government infrastructure throughout the country were all eliminated. We had carefully, painfully for nearly ten years tried to build up this very fragile new nation. Then we destroyed any kind of stability.

And every new time a general would run a coup during this "revolving door" period, all the previous guys were kicked out. We were getting people in power who just didn't know the score at all. And the bigger our involvement became out there to compensate for the chaos, the more we displaced the Vietnamese leadership.

We decided that we were going to win the war and then give the country back to the Vietnamese. That was the coup de grace to Vietnamese nationalism. How the hell could the Vietnamese stand on their own feet? And this became the basic issue that the Communists played on.

If Vietnam hadn't been such a tragedy, it would have been one of the world's greatest farces. The American view of the world is run on the basis of objective facts. Whereas, the Vietnamese are impressionistic and full of intuition. They deal almost entirely on what they think

people said or what they think happened. And like most
Asians, they don't readily express what's on their minds.
You've got to pick up a lot from them by intuition.

The Americans would expostulate some point of view.
The Vietnamese would smile and nod. And the Americans
would think that they were agreeing. But in reality, either
the Vietnamese didn't agree with you at all or didn't
understand what you had said, but they were too polite
to tell you. The American tendency was to overwhelm
the Vietnamese. And the Vietnamese know how to play
to people. So they would do the thing to make the Americans happy and get them off their backs.

In 1964, General Nguyen Khanh took over from the
generals who pulled the Diem coup. Ambassador Lodge's
attitude was benignly strange: "Well, it's just like in the
U.S. A guy gets defeated in politics and who the hell
remembers him. These generals came in, they didn't do
any good. So Khanh kicked them out. Forget them. Let's
go on to the next one."

And so Lodge kind of encouraged Khanh. Then Robert
McNamara came out and paraded around the country,
raising Khanh's hand in the air like a prizefighter. Something guaranteed to hang the American puppet label on
the guy.

Maxwell Taylor replaced Lodge as ambassador. And
the Americans were pressing Khanh to institutionalize his
regime: "You've got to have a constitution." So one day
a close friend of mine was wandering around the Vietnamese General Staff office and came across this Vietnamese major whose desk was piled high with books. He
asked, "What are you doing?" The major said, "I'm helping to write a constitution." He asked, "Have you ever
done this?" The major said, "No. But I got this assignment
from General Khanh." In front of him he's got the American Constitution, the French Constitution, and all the
previous Vietnamese constitutions.

Khanh looked at the constitution draft and said, "It
looks okay to me. But the Americans know a lot more
about this than we do. I'll send it down to the embassy."
Well, the embassy reviewed it, but not as a political concept. They reviewed it like, "You forgot to cross this T
and dot that I." And sent it back to Khanh.

So General Khanh thinks the Americans have approved it. He calls a big meeting for all of the general officers. It was an all-day affair. Lots of arguments: "No, you can't proclaim this." But Khanh said, "The Americans want me to do this. Obviously they know what they're doing." And he carried the day.

The next day Khanh proclaimed the Constitution by fiat. As a result, the Buddhists went into the street, the students went into the streets. And Khanh called up a CIA guy to ask Taylor to come out with a statement of support. Khanh said, "Look, I've done what the Americans wanted me to do. Now all I've got is trouble."

And Taylor responded, "We didn't approve that Constitution." Khanh said, "What the hell do you mean, you didn't approve it? By God, I sent it to you, and you sent it back to me with comments on it. What does that mean?" So they had a total falling-out. And of course, Khanh went down the tubes. He was replaced by an air force general, Nguyen Cao Ky.

In 1965, I made a return visit to Vietnam. I went to see a friend named Chau, a very decent guy down in Ben Tre Province. We got to talking about what was going on. He said, "I just can't make any sense out of what the hell the Americans are doing. Do they have some plan?" I looked at him, I got tears in my eyes, and said, "Chau, I wish I could tell you that the Americans have a plan. But I have to be honest with you. They don't have a plan. We really don't know what the hell we're doing."

# POW

## Dan Pitzer

*Prisoner of War*
*U Minh Forest*

*October 1963–November 1967*

The second Special Forces detachment from Fort Bragg was the second group of A Teams to Vietnam. We hit country in July 1963. I was assigned to a twelve-man A Team site in An Xuyen Province, way down in the Delta about as far south as you can go. Our commitment was to train locals to defend themselves. In six months we were to have five hundred people trained.

We were in the little village of Tan Phu, an old French fortress built on an intersection of canals. In fact, there still were some old rifles in a cement bunker from the days when the Viet Minh had come in and wiped the French out. Ironically, the Vietnamese Special Forces major in charge of the camp, Major Phong, had previously been Viet Minh. So he called in all of his old Viet Minh company commanders. They had a big conference. He gave them money and sent them out.

Two or three weeks later we'd get a phone call, "Some guy is in the area. He's got a hundred men, and needs transportation to your place." All these old Viet Minh troops came in and we'd train them. Most of our trained combatants were ethnic Cambodians. The entire Mekong Delta had once been Cambodia before the Vietnamese conquered it. And our guys admitted that when they went out on patrols they'd cache ammo and weapons. Because at the right time they were going to claim the land back.

They weren't fighting for the damned Vietnamese, even though they lived in Vietnam and they all spoke Vietnamese. And they didn't like our counterparts, the Vietnamese Special Forces. They liked the Americans.

The feelings between our guys and the VC were pretty

88

intense. The VC headquarters was someplace in Cambodia. Two of our soldiers had been captured by the VC and pretty badly mutilated. We found two-foot-long steel rods rammed up their anus and their penis.

The more populated areas were under government control, Diem's picture was up all over the place. Flags were flying everywhere. The Viet Cong controlled the rural areas. They didn't have an abundance of ammunition or men. But they would sneak into a village at night, pull out some of the prominent people, and mutilate them for the rest of the villagers to see. The village was compliant after that. The VC would blame the Americans, saying, "We're doing this to you because the Americans are bombing."

We had a pretty heavy workload with pacification. We would go into a village with a medical team, right in the middle of VC-controlled areas. Even if they didn't like you, two or three hundred people would flock to the village. We made a medical run up and down the canals every day. The people were very appreciative of getting medicine. The Special Forces pacification program was working out well.

But if we spread out too thin and our soldiers moved out of the village we pacified, the Viet Cong came right back in again. It was the old problem: We controlled the daytime, but the night belonged to Uncle Charlie.

The guy who might have been your cook during the day, or the guy across the street cutting hair . . . that night he'd put his black pajamas on and bring his AK-47 out from under his mattress. He went out to your camp and was shooting at you.

After one skirmish, we captured the village chief's son. Even in our camp, some of our troops said, "I'm fighting for the Saigon government. But my brother's fighting for the liberation army." And in the deep South the people felt no connection to any government in Saigon. In those rural areas, Viet Cong propaganda was stronger than Saigon's because it was present all the time. The Saigon people would come in occasionally with their movies and broadcasting units, run a quick medical unit through, and leave.

We went in under gentle persuasion, trying to take care

of everything: medicine, civil affairs, building boat docks, bridges. But as soon as we moved on, here comes the Viet Cong. And they burn those villages, blow the dock up, destroy everything that the Americans and Saigon government built. If there was some way that we could have stayed there to protect the villages, the Saigon government could have had more support.

On October 29, 1963, we received information that there was a Viet Cong hard-core outfit—"regulars"—out in an area called Le Coeur, a canal section. We took two companies of CIDG [Civilian Irregular Defense Groups] and went out early in the morning to put one of these hammer-and-anvil operations [a sweep force pushing enemy into stationary forces] on the VC.

We found nothing there. But I had that eerie feeling that something was wrong. I was walking along a canal and found a brand-new rifle cartridge. That should have told us something. Nick Rowe and I decided, "Hell, there's nothing here. We'll just go up another two or three canals and leisurely take our time. Pick some pineapples and then go back to our campsite."

We ran into one whole battalion of regular VC forces. Then the local VC got into it. And they really socked it to us. The way I was captured—everyone likes to tell John Wayne stories: "It took twenty people to wrestle me to the ground." But it wasn't like that.

During the intense fires, as we ran low of ammunition, we crawled into some reeds off the main canal. We were blocked in. The Cong were coming in behind us.

I had a map case, which I buried to hide. I had my .45 pistol. My plan was to swim under the canal, about twenty or thirty meters, to boats turned upside down on the other side. I thought, "If I can get to the other side of the canal and hide under the boats until dark, I'm home free."

Rocky Versace was yelling, "I'm hit. I'm hit, Dan." I was the team medic at the time. So I went over to see what I could do for Rocky. Either a grenade or mortar round hit nearby, splashing mud up my eyes. I had to stop and wash the dirt out of my eyes. The next thing I knew, a weapon was being shoved into my back. I heard in Vietnamese, *"Dung lai!"* ["Don't move!"]

The Viet Cong captured Rocky, Nick, and me. They

moved us at night by sampan [small boat] on the canals. As we moved past villages, you could tell what kind of village each one was by the radio stations they would be playing. If they played a mixture of all stations, the VC guard would say, "No good. These people are bad." In the Viet Cong areas, they only listened to one station, Radio Giai Phong—Liberation Radio. That's all they were allowed.

We were taken into the U Minh Forest, an area the Saigon military never ventured into. Up to that time, very few people had been captured. Of four Special Forces guys previously captured, two of them were killed and the other two held for twenty-five days and then released. So in the back of my mind I thought, "These people are only going to question me, find out what we are doing, and kick us out." But I was a prisoner for four years in the U Minh Forest.

They kept me in a bamboo cage all those years, four feet wide, six feet long, just big enough to sit up in. I never gave up hope unless I was extremely ill or mad within myself . . . A lot of times I didn't understand it. I'd see a helicopter fly over—it would be so close that I could read the name tag, and wonder why that guy couldn't come down and get me. I'd dream about it, have nightmares about it. But I had to accept the fact that this was the way it was going to be.

When I think about all the guys that died in captivity and the guys that lived, it was a difference of just two words: "if" and "when." A guy saying, "If I go home" or "If I'm released"—he's buried. But those who said, "When I go home" or "When I escape" or "When the war is over"—we survived.

For our first year in captivity, we were held in isolation, not allowed to communicate with each other. There was a constant barrage of indoctrination: "Sign a statement that you support what we're doing and we'll let you go."

During my four years, there was a total of eight prisoners. Not all at one time. There were three of us captured to begin with. And at no time did we have more than five held in this one camp. Out of the eight total, Tadeos, Walker, and Joe Park died of starvation. And Rocky Versace was executed. That left Nick Rowe—who escaped later—myself, Jackson, and Johnson. Four out of eight made it out alive.

It's amazing the defenses both your mind and body will come up with. I had a piece of shrapnel in my right shoulder that became infected. The infection kept getting worse and worse. Finally the lymph node under my left arm swelled to about the size of a lemon, stopping the infection from going through the rest of my body. And one night it just burst. All this blood, pus, and fluid went all over everything. If I had had penicillin this would not have happened. In the tropics, one little mosquito bite scratched could become infected. And we had ringworm that would start in the warmest parts of our body and eat all the way down to the tips of our fingers. I came back with practically no fingernails.

The levers the VC used on us were food deprivation, sleep deprivation, and illness. Physical torture was to heighten the psychological pressure, intimidate. This would create a pain reflex, so whenever they would threaten you, your mind would create the previous physical trauma. They used the term "correctional period" instead of torture. They used these twisted semantics because "torture" is against their "humane and lenient policy." They would say, "We are not torturing you. You are being corrected because you erred and have done this to yourself."

They also threatened, "If you don't repent your crimes..." The first thing that hit me and stuck with me the whole time in captivity was what the first interrogator who spoke English said: "You can stay here forever. This war can end tomorrow, but you can be here for the rest of your life."

Nick and I made an agreement that no matter what the VC did to us, even if we had to die, we were not going to disclose any information. We worked on a cover story to divert the interrogators. We did not let on that we knew how to speak French and Vietnamese. But Rocky Versace tipped his card. And they went after him with a vengeance.

Rocky was strong in some ways and naive in others. He believed in the Geneva Convention [rules for treatment of prisoners of war]. He believed in the Code of Conduct [U.S. military code of honor]. He never believed that the Vietnamese would ignore the Geneva Convention. But Nick and I could tell right away that it was no protection. So our intention was to dummy up and take the punches as they came.

The VC realized Rocky was a captain, Nick a lieutenant, and I a sergeant, so they singled him out as ranking man. Rocky stood toe to toe with them. He told them to go to hell in Vietnamese, French, and English. He got a lot of pressure and torture, but he held his path. As a West Point grad, it was Duty, Honor, Country. There was no other way. He was brutally murdered because of it.

Up until the time I was released in 1967, the main interrogator, Mafia, asked me what made Rocky work. The VC could understand somebody dying for a political cause or a political god, but they couldn't understand Rocky dying for something they didn't understand. That in itself was a triumph for Rocky. He flat beat them on their own ground.

They picked on the blacks a little bit more than on Nick or me. The VC were very smart at that. The liberation front had enough moxie to get into a guy's mind. They would taunt us—"Who is sleeping with your wife tonight?" Especially with those prisoners who expressed response to insults about their families. A guy named Johnson was pushed very much. He was black and his wife German. The Cong honed in on the racial problem in the U.S. They had some black prisoners in other camps write propaganda pamphlets directed to black GIs. They'd translate these into Vietnamese so that the villagers could read them, too.

Our main punishment was the night. I've seen mosquitoes so thick on my ankles that I thought I had black socks on. A guard would say, "Under the lenient policy of the National Liberation Front we're going to wash your mosquito net . . . and we want your pajamas, too." So overnight they would leave us naked and in leg irons. And if you think that wasn't torture . . .

I did get strung up once. I had the great pleasure of decking a guard, whose name was Shithead. I didn't know that Nick Rowe had decked him the week before. When I hit this guy I felt that I broke his jaw. The guards came in and strung me up in the rafters outside my cage. They stripped me naked and tied ropes around my wrists and ankles. They let me hang all night. The next morning, my eyes were swollen shut from mosquito bites. They stayed shut for a whole week.

The camp cadre kept getting messages from the head-quarters of the Viet Cong about what to do with us. There were some attempts to get a release lined up. They'd give us a clean, brand-new set of pajamas. All we wore was black pajamas and we were barefoot. Then these digni-taries would come in, the higher-ups of the Viet Cong. There'd be a lot of indoctrination, "education" as they called it. We sat there and they'd have bullshit sessions for propaganda purposes. They'd say how they were fight-ing for no pay. That so many weeks of the year, during harvest time, they went out to local farms and helped harvest the rice. They would take the amount that they expected to eat for the rest of the year. And they had this stuff cached all over the Delta—rice, ammo, everything.

The Mat Tran—the National Liberation Front—was their own government. They'd say, "Hanoi is our big brother. They are supporting us, sending us weapons. When this war is over, the two countries are going to be united. But we'll have our own government. The Liber-ation Front will be the government down here." They were in for a big shock after 1975.

The Viet Cong did sacrifice. Their main drive, main theory, was, "We're freedom fighters. Don't call me by my name. Address me as Mr. Giai Phong [Mr. Freedom]." They thrived on that. Young kids, anywhere from eighteen years old to their early twenties. With one or two older cadre to guide them. They thrived on being combatants.

The VC ran a tight ship among their own people. We had one little guard we named Abortion. He was picked on by the other guards, no one wanted him as a friend. But he was in a typical cell group of three or four men. They all worked together, critiqued each other, and squealed on each other. And they'd all sing the liberation songs together.

One day Abortion was told to go out and get medicine for the American prisoners in his little sampan. And he says, "I'm not going onto the main canals or river, I'll be shot by American aircraft." And they said, "Well, Major

So-and-So says you will go." He said, "I'm not going. I'm tired of this business. I'm going home. 'Bye." He packed up his little shit and left.

The others had a long talk. They came out of the conference all full of piss and vinegar. And they went out in two or three sampans. The next morning they came back. I heard them over in the kitchen talking. "Did you meet him? What did you do?" *"Ban chet."* They killed him.

Being a prisoner, I could see both sides of the war. Prior to being captured, in a village everything outside was "Viet Cong are animals out there, they're going to kill you." And when I was a prisoner in a Viet Cong–controlled village, the hatred was there: "Don't venture out. The Saigon soldiers will get you."

The villagers in reality were afraid of both sides. Scared to death. And the Viet Cong were terrified at the sound of an aircraft. They hid everything. I mean, you didn't have a jockstrap hanging out on a clothesline. We nicknamed a guard named Muy, "May Bay Muy." *May bay* means "aircraft." That son of a bitch could hear a plane take off two hundred miles away. He'd scream *"May bay! May bay!"* And ten minutes later, an aircraft would appear overhead.

At one point, B-52 strikes were so close it was like standing on a beach and leaning into the wind. I could pin my black pajamas to the concussion from the bombing.

At one point there came a lot of women who wanted to learn English. The Viet Cong told people, "If you learn English, you don't have to be a combatant. You can be an interpreter, you don't have to go out and get shot at." They'd make me read a whole sentence to them in English. They thought they could memorize it. But they didn't know what the hell I was talking about. We'd point to our nose, "This is your ass." Until the interpreter came around and chewed me out for it.

A POW camp is nothing more than a punishment-and-reward system. A human being can be conditioned to respond when reduced to the state of an animal struggling for physical survival. As for plans to escape, you don't know what's out there in the jungle surrounding your bamboo cage. We were more prisoners of the terrain than we were of the people standing there with guns.

We were in jungle-swamp areas where we were up to our waists in muck . . . leeches. Snakes.

I'm five feet eight and I weighed maybe ninety-five or a hundred pounds. I had amoebic dysentery—I was going to the toilet ten, twenty times a day. I had malaria. So the guards knew we were not going anywhere. You learn to live day to day. When I got up in the morning, "If I can just make it until noon . . . Okay, now I've made it to noon. Now if I can just make it till the evening meal and then go to bed. Then it's all over with." Sleep was an escape.

When I was extremely ill, I got into a very dangerous thing—astral projection. I could separate my mind from my body. Go any place I wanted with physical sensation. I could set my mind up on top of the cage I was being held in with leg irons. I'd look down at my body and say, "That physical wreck of skin and bones, eaten up with ringworm, doesn't belong to me." But then my mind would say, "But that is my main mode of transportation, so I have to get back to that filth." At that point I really had one foot in the grave.

The most recently arrived prisoner would be put in isolation. But every American used one latrine that we had dug. We almost always established communication there. For instance like when Johnson took over as president after Kennedy was assassinated. The first question we asked the new prisoner was, "Who won the Army-Navy game?" Then the second question was, "Is it true that Kennedy was assassinated?" Because we just thought it was Communist propaganda to discourage us. We really couldn't believe it.

# THE SHORT TOUR

--------

## Chuck Allen

*Commanding Officer*
*U.S. Army Special Forces Detachment*
*An Sanh and Khe Sanh*

*October 1962–April 1963*

In October 1962, I was assigned for temporary duty in Vietnam to do surveillance missions on the Laos border. We moved initially into Camp An Sanh, outside the town of Khe Sanh. Then we moved the camp over to the airstrip on a plateau that later became the Khe Sanh camp. We had responsibility for the western half of the DMZ and the Laos border, from the DMZ down to thirty miles below Khe Sanh.

The North Vietnamese were infiltrating South Vietnam. Portions of the Ho Chi Minh Trail ran into our area. Our patrols and operations did establish that NVA were up there. We ambushed a patrol and killed two or three of them, capturing their weapons. We also received incoming rocket fire and 120-mm mortars that were not in the Viet Cong arsenal at that time.

Most of the people in A Team detachments in Vietnam during that period had a tremendous sense of pride and accomplishment in what they were doing. But in some of the camps, particularly working with the LLDB—Lousy Little Dirty Bastards—the Vietnamese Special Forces, there was a tremendous sense of frustration. Because it could be hard to get your counterparts out on an operation. They didn't want to leave the camp. Sometimes we had to bribe them with extra food or clothing. That was very frustrating.

Sometimes they'd have an accidental weapon discharge while on a patrol in the woods. That was nothing more than a signal to let the VC know we were coming. Because they didn't want to get into a firefight. Or at night we'd catch them cooking rice with an eight-foot bonfire smoking up the whole valley, letting everybody know where we were.

We knew damn well that they wanted to give their positions away to try to avoid a firefight. Which on several occasions did get us ambushed on the Laotian border. They'd get out into the open and walk along the riverbank. And, goddamn, we'd get ambushed from Laos. The North Vietnamese would shoot across the river and hit us.

Being an advisor was a very difficult position. Because you want to get them to do it right. It takes a while to learn that the American way isn't always the right way, when you're dealing with foreign armies. In Vietnam, the poor bastards had been at war for fifteen years. And here we come, full of piss and vinegar, wanting to win the war in six months, build a new camp, and run operations. The Vietnamese had a whole lot better appreciation of what it means to have someone in your family killed or wounded, because most of them had lost someone. So they took a more realistic approach to the war than we did.

We learned very quickly not to push them too fast or too hard, probably within the first thirty days we were in country. It takes that kind of realization when you're working with indigenous people. You have to learn their outlook and what the situation is to them, not to you. That's the secret to working with foreigners, indigenous ...whatever the hell you want to call them.

The Montagnards' motivation was completely different. We hardly ever had problems with the mountain people. All the Montagnards I worked with were pure, good-hearted, hard-working people. They were very appreciative of what we were trying to do, particularly the civic action program, where we helped with their farming. We put wells in their villages. We ran a terrific sick-call MED-CAP program throughout all the villages. And we provided employment for them, filling sandbags at the camp, cutting grass, making punji [sharp bamboo] stakes for defense. And most of the Special Forces people respected them as individuals. We didn't treat them like *moi*, which means "dog," like the Vietnamese traditionally did.

Most of the Montagnards were recruited into what we

called CIDG programs, Civilian Irregular Defense Groups, or the RF/PF, Regional and Popular Forces [similar to the National Guard]. They were not uniformed soldiers like the Vietnamese were. And they were on for monthly wage. If they wanted to go home to farm their fields or take care of their family, they were free to go and come. With certain reservations, of course.

A typical Montagnard village in the western Quang Tri Province area was made up of between twenty and fifty long straw huts built on six- to eight-foot-tall pole platforms. Their chickens and pigs ran loose underneath the buildings. Families cooked inside their longhouses. The villages were usually on the side of a hill, fairly close to a decent water supply.

As soldiers, the Montagnards were good under fire, easy to work with, good people . . . they didn't get discouraged. Some of the biggest problems we had was keeping them in uniforms. Boots hurt their feet. And we didn't realize that at first. We had to learn by experience. Some factors were not in our premission training. Sure, we had special training on the area and the background of the tribes. But nowhere in the training did it say, "Hey, you don't put Montagnards in the wrong kind of boots or they get blisters on the tops of their feet."

The VC, of course, were politically motivated. There was a hell of a psy-war going on in Quang Tri Province. The VC had the capability to print leaflets. And the NVA had political cadre that would come into the villages. In many cases, the villages were not armed. So they lived under the threat of having their families wiped out. Assassinations were being conducted by the VC infrastructure. Political cadre would come in and tie the tribal chief or members of his family to a tree and hose them down. Leave them dead and bleeding as an example for the rest of the village. There was a tribal council in a village just outside of Khe Sanh who were lined up on a riverbank and grenaded and shot. About ten of them were killed.

NVA activity was north of us, toward the DMZ, and west, across the Laotian border. They'd make incursions to hold political rallies. We never did find out if that mass assassination was by the NVA or VC.

When I left that first tour at Khe Sanh, I was real sad

to go home. Because we had not completely finished building the camp. Also, after six months, we had only just reached the point of establishing the right kind of rapport with our counterparts and the local people. We were really getting effective.

I don't think that anyone who was working with the Vietnamese and the CIDG had any feelings that the war was going to end right away. There were no big battles. We knew that it was going to string on and on. There were always rumors of American ground troops coming in. But people in the Special Forces camps felt that they were winning their war in their own little area.

But we saw that the U.S. support base was growing like a goddamned mushroom. Everytime we'd take a trip back to Nha Trang, Danang, or Cam Ranh Bay we could see this tremendous buildup coming. More and more permanent-type installations were being built. The hospitals weren't operating in tents anymore, they were in Quonset huts. I figured, "Something is going to happen. We're going to be here a long time."

# SECTION III

# WAR WITHOUT GLORY

# KENNEDY'S SOLDIERS

## Frank McCarthy

*Rifleman*
*1st Infantry Division*
*Iron Triangle*

*October 1965–March 1967*

I was in the first wave of army infantry who went to Vietnam in the 1st Infantry Division in October 1965. After a year of counterinsurgency, counterguerilla training at Fort Riley, Kansas, we believed we were ready.

We were trained to do a mop-up operation in a country the size of Washington State in about a year, then come home. This was another confrontation with the Communists around the world, as were the Berlin crisis and the Cuban missile crisis. We truly believed that we could do the job.

I was born in Camden, New Jersey. I lived in Philadelphia in my youth. I was from an Italian-Irish family: myself, a brother, and three sisters. Pretty tough kid, pretty rebellious. I didn't like school much. I felt even as a child that my career was going to be in the military. Because my Uncle Frank, who was my role model as a child, was a career soldier. My mother divorced when I was young. So I was gung ho all my life.

The Kennedy assassination was traumatic for everybody in the military. Because as far as we were concerned, we were the defenders of freedom and liberty throughout the world. We were Kennedy's soldiers and we were proud of it. It was an honor and a privilege to be a soldier under JFK. I remember when he died, going into the mess hall and looking at it on television . . . seeing hardened World War II and Korean War combat veterans sitting there with tears rolling from their eyes when they heard the president was dead.

Most of the NCO's [noncommissioned officers] were either World War II or Korean War veterans. My platoon sergeant had been in both. He had eight Purple Hearts, four Bronze Stars. He was a real combat soldier. And our battalion commander was the recipient of the Congressional Medal of Honor in Korea. He went to West Point after the war. And we all loved him. We had a tremendous amount of esprit de corps. For a year we learned everything about the 1st Division and all its traditions and great battles, being the first in combat. The D-Day Normandy invasion, Italy, Africa . . . they were everywhere and just great. We were going to carry on that tradition.

We went on a monstrous train from Fort Riley to Oakland, California. We got on three ships and sailed to Vietnam. We landed at Vung Tau on October 21, 1965. We hit the beaches with our duffle bags and no ammunition. It was like an island resort. It was beautiful. No hint whatsoever of any kind of hostilities or war. After two days, our tanks arrived. We went by monstrous convoy across Vietnam.

Bypassing Saigon, we went straight up to the Iron Triangle, a triangular-shaped densely jungled area near Cambodia, controlled by the VC. We built a base camp [brigade-sized military base] in a rubber-tree plantation at Lai Khe. All the while we set up our base camp, we went out on operations.

The villages were pretty gross. The poverty was real bad. But I loved the kids and I loved the culture. The farmers were the best, as far as I'm concerned. No matter what country they come from, farmers only want to till the soil. They don't want a hassle from anybody.

The first night we were in the triangle, the VC tried to probe our perimeter. We killed a couple who tried to infiltrate our lines. The first time I ever saw any of our own guys get it was on our third patrol. I was walking point [lead man] and Lenny and Steve were behind me. A mine went off and wiped out the eleven guys behind them.

The guys in my unit were absolutely enraged because for the previous year we had all been very close. Every weekend our families would visit. We knew guys' wives, mothers, and fathers, their kids. And when they died it enraged us. We wanted to find the VC and kill them. But at that point it was very difficult to find them. They were ghosts. They would hit us with a mortar, plant a booby trap or mine. But you'd never see anybody.

The first time we saw them was a battle going on at a South Vietnamese Popular Forces camp. We went out in the morning. I was walking point for the battalion and was the first person into the area. The VC regiment had run over the camp and killed three hundred South Vietnamese. And there were about four hundred Viet Cong dead. So seven hundred to a thousand bodies were spewed all over the ground. I was pretty numbed by it all.

I had seen every World War II movie as a kid and loved them all. But walking amongst the bodies that were intertwined the way they died in hand-to-hand fighting... A Viet Cong with a bayonet in his chest clutching a South Vietnamese with bullets in his back... Hundreds and hundreds of bodies. The Vietnamese came with a bulldozer and made a great big ditch. We dragged all the bodies into the ditch, threw lime on them, and left. That was my first real shocker.

Our first real battle was in the Michelin Rubber Plantation. Our whole brigade was sitting in helicopters waiting for a sister battalion to get hit, so we could immediately pull into the fight. The VC came with a human-wave attack. And we landed behind them, around the outside of the American perimeter. It was a VC regiment. They wore black pajamas or just regular clothes. But they had all kinds of Chinese and Russian weapons—flamethrowers, rocket launchers. They were being pretty well supplied by North Vietnam through Cambodia.

We surrounded the VC, with the battalion camp in the middle. The Americans didn't even have foxholes. But fortunately, they only lost around seven guys. The VC body count was supposed to have been eight hundred, but I thought it was more. It was the first time I had ever killed anybody.

Just before dark, our platoon had to go about a mile into the jungle to an area where a bomb had killed a bunch of Viet Cong. They had brand-new U.S. Army .50-caliber machine guns that we had to confiscate. The guns were brand-new, still had the bluing on them [factory packing]. That really pissed me off.

That year seemed to get worse and worse. Never a rest, never a moment's break, never anything but insanity. At night the VC would hit our perimeter with mortars at times, sometimes snipers. They also had people trying to probe our lines . . . until we got starlight scopes [night-vision devices]. Then they didn't blatantly walk up to the wire anymore. Because we'd blow them away.

We went to Vietnam with the M-14 rifle, by the way. They made us switch to the M-16 during our tour. I liked the fourteens much better. The sixteens were unreliable, like a Mattel toy. Within a week I was carrying a Communist AK-47. The AK shoots a similar size round as the M-14. The smaller M-14 round would fit in the AK, but the AK ammo could not fit in the 14, giving the Communists an advantage in using captured ammunition.

We worked some with the Vietnamese army. Initially I had no respect for the ARVN at all. They were undisciplined, unmilitary. They didn't give a shit about doing a job. They didn't care about combat. It was like they were a defeated army, like they didn't care. But later in my year, I gained a lot of respect for the Vietnamese army. Not the regular ARVN, but I spent time with the Rangers and the Airborne. They gave me a whole new experience. They were tough people. Most of the Rangers were from North Vietnam. I still have a photo on my wall of a guy named Nu. We were at the Ranger camp for three weeks and he told me his whole life story.

I asked Nu where he was from. He said, "Hanoi." It was a shock to meet somebody from Hanoi. But his story was parallel to my story. He was a young patriotic boy who loved his country. In North Vietnam there were posters on the trees that said: Join the Army. Go down south to drive the Americans out, who invaded. Nu joined the army, trained for a year, then came with an NVA unit down the Ho Chi Minh Trail. As soon as they got into South Vietnam they got hit by a B-52 air strike, which scattered everybody.

Later he hooked up with a VC unit. They'd go into villages and kill the chiefs, rape the women, and impound the young boys . . . chain them to weapons and all. This all blew his mind—he had joined the army to drive the Americans out. Instead he was killing fellow Vietnamese.

He couldn't take it anymore, so he went over to the South Vietnamese side. And the South Vietnamese put all the guys like him into the Rangers and gave them the worst combat duty. They were tough, tough guys. I loved them. Spirit—they'd fight to the end. They had the same kind of esprit de corps that we had, they really believed.

People think that Vietnam was just one horrible mess of insanity. And it was. But there were some great funny moments—with the guys, with the local people. Just joking to stay alive. Once my platoon was pinned down by a VC ambush. They had a lot of firepower and had us pinned down for about fifteen minutes. I got so mad. Because I was laying in this wet rice paddy, soakin' and smellin' after so many days in the bush. I had a can of warm beer in my pack.

So I jumped up on top of this dike and I started screaming, "Why don't you bastards give us a break?" And I'm holding up this can of beer. And the VC stopped firing. I heard everyone yelling, "Get down. Get down!" All of a sudden everyone started laughing. And I just sat on the mound and drank the beer.

We went there thinking that we could win it in a year or two. But within the first three months I became very disillusioned because of the lack of decisive military actions. I mean, chasing a VC regiment right up to the Cambodian border and having to stop was insanity. I kept remembering the old phrase that no immobile army can win a war. And that's what we were—immobile.

We could only travel to the border and we had to stop. That gave the enemy the advantage of striking us anytime they wanted to. So, we were at a total disadvantage of being a target. Later, when Nixon went into Cambodia in 1970 it enraged me because we should have done it in 'sixty-five. In 'seventy it was too late. By then the press had turned the public against the war. But when I went, everyone was for us being there.

The realities of the war in 'sixty-five were trying to drive the insurgents back to the North and arrest all the Viet Cong. I have gone into villages where the VC had taken the young men, where they had killed the chiefs, where they had tortured the women. One woman, they took two water buffalos and tied the woman's one leg and one arm to one buffalo and her other leg and arm to the other buffalo. And they just split her apart. One leg had ripped off and by the time she died, her chest was torn wide open. I still have nightmares about this.

The villagers were horrified because they couldn't win at all. If they didn't submit to the Viet Cong and pay their bounty, the chiefs were killed or the young men or women taken away. And then here we come along or the South Vietnamese troops. And they'd have to submit to our will at the same time. So they didn't have a chance. I pitied them.

It's like Christmastime . . . Supposedly there was a truce. We went into the village to get a truckload of kids to bring them out to our camp and have a party for them. Truce. A VC company ambushed us. And I remember this one sergeant with a bullet in his gut, laying there on the ground saying, "Some Christmas, huh Frank." Some kids got wounded by shrapnel. It was sick. Really sick. That's when I really got disillusioned. Because we weren't fighting the war the way I knew we had to.

I had been in the army for four years. I had been in Korea on the DMZ. I had been in the 101st Airborne. I had seen the military from all kinds of perspectives. I knew that we were going into Vietnam with a tremendous fighting armada, with the greatest fighting power in the world. We were ready to march to Hanoi or Peking if we had to. But the way we had to sit there . . . I couldn't understand what was going on. Of course, I didn't know what was happening in the States. There was no antiwar movement when I went to Vietnam. I learned all that when I got back.

After I got hit the fourth time, they sent me to Saigon. My last three months I was a security guard with MACV [Military Assistance Command Vietnam]. I'd just gone shell-crazy. After being wiped out a couple of times, there were only six guys left of the original thirty-two in our platoon. And I'd known these guys very close. Plus my wife didn't write for six months. And then I got thirteen letters all at once telling me she was leaving.

But Saigon in 1965–66 was the Paris of the Orient. It was nightclubs, restaurants, hustling, bustling—nobody carried guns except MPs and security forces. The generals lived like kings. And I'd just sit at the entrance to their quarters, with a couple of White Mice—Vietnamese Police. And I had a ball. I had a good speaking knowledge of Vietnamese. So I had a great time.

Just as I arrived in Saigon, student demonstrations started. A Buddhist monk set himself on fire to protest the war. And a couple of weeks later I left.

I landed at Travis Air Force Base in California. I did the traditional things, kiss the ground when I got off the plane, and all that. I was so happy that I had survived. And I had a thirty-day leave. It was March 1967.

I didn't spend any money in Vietnam, so I had a lot of money. My brother was living in Berkeley at the time. So I figured I would take a cab to visit my brother before I went back to Philadelphia to see my family. As I'm riding down Telegraph Avenue I told the cab driver that I wanted to walk. It was sunny and beautiful, all these bright colors and people. And the cab driver said, "Are you sure you want to get out here?" Well, of course, I didn't know what was going on. I got out of the cab. I was in my Class A uniform.

I was spit on. This gang of guys walking behind me threw peanuts at me. I went into a bar and phoned my brother. I almost didn't make it out of there. The real shock of coming back was in that bar. These guys weren't going to let me out. They wanted to kick my ass. Calling, "You kill any women? You kill any kids?"

These guys were long-haired, long-bearded. And my brother and Nicky and about five other guys came and busted into the bar. There was a big hassle and I stopped them from fighting. I just wanted to get out. My brother drove me to his home and told me what the score was because I didn't understand. I just didn't know.

We went out to a dance that night. All I had was my Class A uniform. And boy, it was such a shock. People looking at me like, "You scum." They'd walk by and spit on the ground. And I got this tremendous feeling that I had done something wrong. It was like I wasn't supposed to have survived.

# THE GATHERING STORM

**Ken Moorefield**

*Military Advisor*
*21st ARVN Division*
*Mekong Delta*

*May 1967–April 1968*

I grew up in a military family. My father was a colonel in the infantry and had been a highly decorated battalion commander in World War II. I had always been impressed by him and what he accomplished. And I grew up all over the world.

In the 1950s, when I was ten, eleven, twelve years old, we lived in Europe and traveled from north to south. We must have been easily to twelve or fifteen countries. I saw the big role the U.S. had in rebuilding and reshaping Europe. So I grew up with this sense of purpose and responsibility.

When I graduated from West Point in 1965, my graduating class realized that Vietnam was going to be our war. When I was a junior at the academy, Bernard Fall, who wrote *Street Without Joy*, lectured in one of my political science courses. I can remember the sense of drama with which he laid out what was unfolding in South Vietnam: the extent to which the Viet Cong, supported by the North Vietnamese, had made dramatic inroads in controlling even down to the hamlet level of the country, assassinating village chiefs. He put a map of South Vietnam on the board. Everywhere he placed a red pin, a hamlet or village chief had been assassinated in the previous twelve months. It looked like all South Vietnam had a case of the measles. I remember thinking that here was the gathering storm.

I arrived in Vietnam in the spring of 1967. I was assigned as an advisor to a Vietnamese infantry battalion of the

110

21st ARVN Division. We were in the extreme southern part of South Vietnam, in the Ca Mau Peninsula. An Xuyen Province had traditionally been a highly contested area. The average villager never had a chance to choose, in the sense that we think of choice. His life was shaped by forces that were so clearly dominant that the most he could hope to do was sway with the wind and survive.

Government forces controlled district towns, provincial capitals, certain hamlets. But the Viet Cong had the ability to operate out of the Nam Can and U Minh forests. In motorized sampans they could hit anything from the center of the province by nightfall. Everyone was vulnerable.

We had a small four-man American advisory team: a captain, a first lieutenant (myself), and two noncommissioned officers. I rarely saw another American soldier in the ten and a half months that I was in the field. The 21st ARVN Division was covering a tremendous tactical area. We were widely dispersed and rarely saw other South Vietnamese units except for local militia.

Our war was our battalion spending days at a time in some far-flung area of the U Minh or Nam Can forest hunting for reinforced VC regiments. The morale was generally quite high, although I think there was a certain fatalism. And I felt a bit awkward. Here I was an advisor coming over to fight my year. But I wasn't there for the duration. Next year some clone of myself would arrive for a mere twelve months.

Well, the deputy battalion commander had been fighting for five years and the battalion commander for six or seven years. The recon platoon leader, who was a sergeant, had fought with the Viet Minh against the French. He crossed over to the government side and had been fighting the Communists ever since. This guy had been wounded fifteen or twenty times. He was absolutely marvelous. I couldn't have respected the man more. And we had talks, God knows. When you're out in the field in war, there are many nights when you're just sitting and waiting. There's nothing to do but reminisce with your friends.

I remember one Vietnamese first lieutenant who became a captain and a battalion commander while I was still there. He had two children. He had been a mathematics and physics teacher in high-school level before the war. He told me, "If I ever determined that the Communists were going to take over Vietnam, I will take my family and flee to Cambodia or to Thailand." Of course, in those days Cambodia still seemed safe. But he had no intention of permitting his family to be raised under Communist rule. I had tremendous respect for this man. Unfortunately, he died.

We Americans had a lot of pride, a lot of conviction in ourselves. And the better South Vietnamese units had that same conviction. The 1st ARVN Division, the paratroopers, and the Rangers had been up against the best that the North Vietnamese had, quite successfully. And in my own experience, we gained that confidence through our day in, day out performance. We knew if we got trapped we were going to have to fight it out. There was no way to get another South Vietnamese unit to us in time.

Most of the time when we got into shoot-outs we spent the day fighting it out completely on our own. There was a certain resiliency and determination that came as a result of knowing that we were the equal of the very skillful and determined Viet Cong main-force units.

In December 1967, while my battalion was providing security for Ca Mau Province headquarters, the Viet Cong launched a surprise attack from the fringe of the U Minh forest. They attacked around midnight with several battalions swarming our positions, wave after wave. We fought all night long. They almost wiped out our battalion command post, but we beat them off.

At daybreak we were still fighting nose to nose, literally. It became obvious that they had no withdrawal plan as the battle continued during the course of the day. We counterattacked very aggressively, giving them a serious setback.

At Tet, a month later, they came again with several regiments. During the early phases of the attack they took over a good portion of the city. They had control of the police station, the province hospital, Buddhist temple. They had penetrated the city fairly well with the help of fifth-column elements who guided them.

The battle lasted several days. We got to the point where

we were perilously close to running out of ammunition. American logistical resupply was tied down to the north and could not assist us. But our division fought valorously. And I hate to refer to a body count because it does not always reflect whether you have broken the will of the enemy, or whether or not they will be prepared to fight again. But at Tet, it was an indicator that we had given them a decisive defeat. Killing three to four hundred of them.

Later, intelligence reports indicated that they had told their troops, "This will be the great victory we have been waiting for." And the VC troops were not provided with any withdrawal plan. This insured that they would be hurt even more than they needed to be.

From the second and third day of the battle, using artillery and U.S. Air Force support, we really stuck it to them. Hands down, there is no question that we really kicked their ass.

# WHAT IS BEAUTIFUL

## Gen. Lu Mong Lan

*Deputy Chief, Operations and Training*
*Joint General Staff*
*Republic of Vietnam Armed Forces*
*1958–1962*

I remember in 1955 when I was Operations Officer of the 1st Field Division, I went to Phu Bai Airport to meet my first American advisor. To communicate we used sign language. At first, the U.S. army assigned its very best officers, who were both soldiers and diplomats. But this was the first time they were in touch with an armed force that had no previous training.

The Vietnamese word for "American" is *Mỹ*, which is also a synonym for "what is beautiful." When I was twenty years old, if I wore a very nice belt, people would say, "That belt looks very American." Anything that looked nice, we would say, "That is very American."

Secondly, the impression Vietnam had of America was "America is a hero." We were all very aware of what happened in World War II: the Normandy landing, the liberation of Europe, the capitulation of the Japanese. We'd say, "The Americans are great." We had lived almost one hundred years under French domination. We'd say, "The French are also Occidental, but they are not civilized. They are not the hero of liberty like the Americans."

But frankly, we did have a lot of conflict with American advisors. Americans were the victorious heroes after World War II, very proud of themselves. They came to Vietnam and it was our impression that American people looked down on those who did not speak English; on those people who do not have the same culture; on those people who are not good-looking... small, dark.

So naturally, having a partner like that, we could not

114

expect that the Americans would have full respect for us. But Americans said, "This is a nice country, a young country, a poor country. We want to make it become democratic and prosperous."

If we did not have a war, the relationship between the Americans and the Vietnamese would have been perfect. But the war began, and the American advisors said, "The American army has never been defeated in the past two hundred years. We won Guadalcanal. So the best and only way to build the South Vietnamese army is to copy us. We'll equip your army like the U.S. Army. And you plan it the American way."

And certainly, we South Vietnamese officers did not agree a hundred percent with the Americans. I spoke with my advisor. He said, "You have fought this Indochina war for years, and we see what the Viet Minh have been doing. We strongly believe that in the future conflict will happen again in this land. It will be tactically the same as the previous conflict. This is a war of lieutenants, captains; this is not a war of generals."

I remember President Diem called me to his palace and said, "Colonel Lu, now the American government proposes to give us advisors down to the district and battalion level. What do you think about this?" I said, "Excellent." Because at that time we had very poor communications equipment. I said, "Any advisor will have very powerful radio equipment. And I would be happy to be able to call any battalion throughout the country."

But President Diem looked forlorn and said, "You will lose your Vietnamese personality. And it will be hard to convince your counterparts to understand the Vietnam war."

I reflected on the Vietnamese captains or majors commanding battalions at age forty-five or fifty. Some of them had served as soldiers in the French army. Sometimes they dye their teeth black like the North Vietnamese to prevent tooth cavities. And his counterpart is a very sophisticated American captain who graduated from West Point a few years ago. He had an impressive background in mathematics, calculus, understanding the fallout pattern of nuclear bombs, and other sophisticated things. He comes to Vietnam and he wants to communicate with his counterpart, the forty-seven-year-old Vietnamese who does not speak any English. And what is the impression of that young American captain when he looks at that Vietnamese battalion commander with the blackened teeth?

The American captain will consciously say, "I should take care of this battalion. I should help Vietnam. But I cannot communicate with my counterpart." And in that unit there is a Vietnamese sergeant who acts as the translator. And the American captain would say, "This sergeant is better than the major. He communicates easily with me in English."

The major is impatient to explain the whole Vietnamese history of the war, fighting the VC: guerilla warfare, all the tactics of sabotage and subversion. And the American captain gets an order from his superior who wants a "body count." And puts a lot of pressure on what this young captain should achieve in his battalion. This created big problems. No superior anticipated or taught the young captain to adapt to our situation and cultural environment.

The American might have attended some briefings before he came to Vietnam. But when he saw the real war, he is shaken. He had no idea of what was really going on in Vietnam. It was not solely a military war. As declared by North Vietnam, it is a "total war." Political, economical, cultural, propaganda, intrigue . . . everything. And the enemy was infiltrating our society at the highest level.

Sometimes students speaking English would approach GIs at beaches like Nha Trang and talk about politics. They would denounce the Diem regime and couch their arguments in terms that would sway Americans who were naive to the whole situation in Vietnam and isolated from the Vietnamese society because they could not speak the language. The first person who would communicate with these Americans was a prepositioned VC underground agent claiming to be an ordinary student. And before this, the major with the blackened teeth could not communicate with the sophisticated captain from West Point.

The American advisor was under pressure from his superiors, so he would make ridiculous intrigues to control his Vietnamese counterparts and take over control of the battalion, as if it were his toy. And he played for one year.

And at his farewell party, when his year's tour of duty was over, he was very sad. He'd say, "Major Hoan, I'm sorry. It's only now that I understand what this war is about. I tried to do my best. Now I'm sorry for all my advice of the past year. Good luck." And he would get on a plane and take off.

Then, another year begins. And another American advisor arrives for this battalion and does exactly the same thing as the young captain he replaced. That is the history of advisors. American people have good will, but they are impatient. They want everything done yesterday, not tomorrow.

# SELF-DECEPTION

### Edward Brady

*Combat Operations and Intelligence Advisor*
*Military Assistance Command Vietnam*
*Central Highlands and Saigon*

*1965–1970*

My first introduction to the Vietnamese military system
I served as a young, naive lieutenant advising a South
Vietnamese Ranger battalion in 1965. Even before I entered the service academy, when I was sixteen years old,
I started reading things like T. E. Lawrence's *Seven Pil-
lars of Wisdom* and Mao Tse-tung. So I thought I knew
a lot about guerilla warfare and insurgency movements
and what it takes to put one down. But I had not really
thought about or been exposed to the power of culture.

My first exposure to reality in Vietnam was through a
second lieutenant who was a company commander in the
Ranger battalion. My first reaction on meeting him was
that at his age he must be incompetent to only be a second
lieutenant. But as I began to learn the Vietnamese language from a corporal, who was my radio operator and
cook, I began to converse with this lieutenant. I discovered that he had seven Gallantry Crosses and he had
fought in every significant battle in the highlands for the
past five years. And he was a graduate of the Military
Academy. He had this enormous combat experience and
he was very successful and extremely brave. I could not
figure out why he had never been promoted.

After time, as we became close friends, he told me that
all of his classmates were majors. But he didn't want to
discuss why. One time we went to Pleiku to visit the II
Corps command staff. The assistant operations officer,
his former classmate, threw money around and bought
everybody dinner. He was obviously quite well off as a

major. So, driving back to our camp, I asked my friend, "Why is it that you live in a run-down hut with your wife and three kids and command a company unit?" He told me that was because he had never had a staff assignment. His family hadn't the political connections to obtain any for him. The major, his classmate, had a well-connected family, so after graduating from the academy he became General Vinh's aide. Within a few years he had become a major without ever being in a combat unit or in a battle. And he got a certain amount of money from the privileges he was able to exercise.

For example, the whole region would be controlled by the army for physical access because of guerillas and North Vietnamese military forces moving through the area. So a civilian needed a permit, for example, to be a logger. And he would pay the military for a permit.

But my friend was in a combat unit. Therefore he had none of that power or privilege, thus got no money. But he didn't mind because he was patriotic and he wanted to fight the war. But the real reason was his family had no connections. Combat units like the Rangers were not looked upon with favor by anyone seeking to advance themselves, their families, or their fortune.

In my area, the ARVN division commanders were something like Chinese warlords. They had certain political and geographical responsibilities in addition to being military commanders. Whole companies or battalions of regular units would be raised from local villages, much like our National Guard. If they got into a really bad battle, these home-grown units were not risked to suffer heavy casualties. Because the warlord would lose his political support in the villages.

On the other hand, the Ranger battalion I was in was commanded by a guy who had been a political prisoner after the Diem coup. The parachute and Ranger troops were often press-ganged off city streets, destitute people who were forced into the military. When you assign them out to a place like II Corps, our three Ranger units had no ties with the local villages. And if five or six hundred were killed in a single battle it didn't affect the status of the local warlord. These three Ranger battalions were called the Corps Strategic Reserve. It became customary that whenever there was a serious military action in the region they were the ones thrown into the breach.

When there would be hot engagements, like a U.S. Special Forces camp along the Laotian border would get surrounded by a North Vietnamese regiment... they'd call in the Rangers. Or when a regular ARVN infantry division would run into stiff resistance, they'd pull back and send in the Rangers. Typically, my unit would get heli-lifted into another province and thrown into battle to make a frontal assault on a North Vietnamese unit.

Once we had broken through, the regular ARVN would come in for the mop-up operation. We would go into a battle with maybe four hundred to five hundred people if we were up to strength. We'd maybe take a couple hundred killed and wounded and come out half-strength. But that didn't jeopardize the political support of the local division commander warlord. In fact, he'd take credit for the victory and pass out medals and other awards to the local units for their participation.

Survivors in the Ranger units, like the lieutenant who had been in engagements of this kind for more than five years, became very adept, very savvy military commanders. These men had experienced more combat engagements than ninety-five percent of the ARVN commanders. They were constantly thrown into battle and either killed because they were brave leaders out in front, or survived and developed great skill.

My friend was killed in the spring or summer of 'sixty-six. We went into an area in Ban Me Thuot against several North Vietnamese regiments. The local ARVN unit had been rebuffed and thrown back down this hill, so they called for us. The helicopters descended into the jungle in the wrong place. That night we were overrun. He and I were listed MIA together for three days as we crawled in the jungle through a North Vietnamese regiment, only moving a few hundred yards the first night and day.

Three days after we reached the ARVN lines, he predicted on the map where we would be ambushed as the units tried to return to Ban Me Thuot. But the local division commander wouldn't listen... we took another 120 killed during the day. That night there was a skirmish and we linked up with a South Vietnamese armor unit. Armor had an institutional life and a system all its own. The

Vietnamese very much valued these tanks and to lose one was a big disgrace. Their typical procedure when attacked was to throw hand grenades out the hatch, close the hatch down, and fire all around themselves on a 360-degree perimeter, starting a hundred feet out.

Well, we were there protecting them. And the tanks fired right through my unit, killing my friend. He took a .50-caliber bullet through his side. And because it was a heavy battle, the U.S. medevac helicopters wouldn't land. I held him for about five hours while he bled to death.

But I didn't really understand corruption while I was in the Ranger battalion. There was obviously corruption in the way the military system worked, what you did to get promoted. It was clear to me that this was not the way to build morale and leadership.

It was when I was assigned to a province headquarters in late 1966 and got involved in province operations that I began to see how corruption in the military actually worked: district chiefs would get a supply of rice. They would sell half, then send half to the military outposts. So the National Guard and village militia would be on half-rations for a month.

I was fluent in Vietnamese and drove all over the province—me and two bodyguards. I would go to outposts and talk to troops and commanders to find out what the hell they were doing. I discovered that there had not been widows' pensions paid in four and a half years. These women were out in remote hamlets where it was a two- or three-day journey by foot to get to the province headquarters to complain. They were illiterate. They had no ability to operate against the powerful system. The top man knew they would never try to get their money, so he would just take it.

So morale was piss-poor. The soldiers realized that if they were killed, their families wouldn't be paid their pensions, their kids would go hungry with no means of support. So the troops were not going to risk their lives. If the Communists attacked an outpost, you'd damn sure have to fight. But you don't go chasing them into the bush when they pull back. You don't conduct aggressive operations. You only defend your camp. This is the mentality that evolved.

And later when I was assigned to the General Staff in

Saigon I found that you could buy and sell promotions and assignments to major units. Being a police chief was an enormously lucrative job. The police controlled all the licenses for fishing, logging, restaurants, everything.

Positions were bought and sold daily. The key wives of the key General Staff members were very heavily engaged in that. I saw many promotion lists go into one very high-ranking general. He would take a list home at night and in the morning give it back to his confidential aide, who was a close friend of mine. You could see the handwriting of the general's wife down the side of the page with names scratched off—"No. No. No."—and who she wanted handwritten in instead. These were positions that had been bought, but he was just doing what everyone else did.

Like in most Third World countries, I don't know if we could have done anything about this corruption. But it was doubly damaging in Vietnam when there was a war going on, and a need for a certain amount of efficiency. In countries in Africa or South America, if you want to start an import business you can go into a local ministry and quickly find out whom you've got to pay off to get your import license. But in Vietnam you couldn't do that because it would be an enormous loss of face for an official to admit he's corrupt. So there's all these networks of go-betweens. Often you had to pay two or three times falsely until you got the right connection. And almost all of that was handled by the women.

I was very close to a number of mistresses of general officers. The arrangement was that they supported themselves this way, through corruption and the selling of influence. Everything was a cash economy, they had no checking system. So they would carry bags of cash between people. I frequently drove generals' mistresses from one place to another and watched these transactions. And incredibly enough, many American senior advisors and officials were very naive about this.

I once read a report John Paul Vann wrote where he scathingly attacked some U.S. official who had suggested that one particular general, whom Vann was advising at the time, was corrupt. This was incredible. I had been to this general's house many times. I knew a number of his girlfriends. I had been to Vung Tau the week before with the general and two of his mistresses. And Vann said that his general was a loyal, upright family man, who had never had any association with anyone other than his wife. And that Vann had just recently been to the general's home in Tu Duc for dinner and it was a very modest home. Well, that was the general's third mistress' home. I mean, Vann had no idea of how the culture operated or what was really going on. Other advisors would also rebuff evidence and feel insulted that anybody would suggest that their Vietnamese counterparts were corrupt.

The highest-level people clearly had some sense of the risk they were running, otherwise why would they have salted their money away in Switzerland, Hong Kong, or Singapore? They always had in the backs of their minds that they could flee. They had their own helicopters. They had their own airplanes. They could load their families on and escape.

But when you got down to the regimental commander, the battalion commander, the district chief . . . they had no idea of ever being able to flee if there was a disaster. They had known war all of their lives. They had been born in it, grown up in it. They thought that a seesaw kind of guerilla warfare would go on forever. It was a way of life.

There would be a skirmish here, an attack there. If you were unfortunate enough to be at one of those locations, you might be killed or wounded. But fundamentally, this was a chance to make money. There was enormous inflation because of the presence of five hundred thousand American troops, the whole U.S. AID program, and all that money. The Vietnamese knew that this wouldn't continue forever, and the war seemed like it would. So the priority became making money, because now was the time to do it.

If you were a military officer, you could fundamentally change the whole status of your family. And in the extended-family concept you probably would have been considered sinful not to take advantage of the opportunity to help your family. There was strong impetus and pressure on them to do it, even if they themselves didn't want to. And they didn't, in a sense. One of the corrupt generals would tell you, "I never sold a commission." And he didn't ... his wife and mistresses did. They divorced themselves from that reality. The Vietnamese are great at that. They have this mental ability to disassociate themselves and claim innocence in a way that allows them to tolerate the reality. But they always really did know what they should have been doing.

# THE CHERRY
--------

## Rufus Phillips

*Military and Civilian Advisor*
*South Vietnam*

*1954–1968*

## Jonathan Polansky

*Rifleman*
*101st Airborne Division*
*I Corps*

*November 1968–November 1969*

PHILLIPS: If you were to pick a guy who had been in an American combat unit and pick a guy who had been an advisor, and you asked them, "What was Vietnam like? What do you know about the Vietnamese?" you'd have two different countries. It would be like two different worlds.

POLANSKY: I was drafted in May 1968. By November I had finished my training and found myself in Vietnam, assigned to the 101st Airborne Division. I was sent up north to Camp Eagle, near the DMZ.

The supply sergeant gave us all gear and told us to pack up: "You're going out this afternoon." The morning I arrived at Eagle, the platoon I was assigned to had come by chopper onto a hilltop. Unfortunately, between twenty and thirty U.S. Marine Bouncing Betty mines [explosive devices that bounce up and explode waist-high] were left unmarked. Three-quarters of the platoon got wiped away. So all these rumors were going around Eagle.

All I knew was that I had this big knapsack and all these things to put into it. I had no idea how to pack this monstrous thing. Older guys who were getting ready to go home were telling me, "You'd better take more water than that ... you better carry extra grenades ... fuck the food, man. Take ammo." And every now and then Top (first sergeant) comes by and says, "You guys ready in there yet?" There were five of us getting ready to go. I must've been white as a sheet because I felt so scared. I thought

I was immediately going to get killed.

So I packed everything as best as I could and hopped on the chopper. This was the first time I had really seen Vietnam. The countryside was lush and rolling rice paddies and all the fine diagrams on the land created by the dikes, thatched grass houses. It was a settling feeling. The most beautiful land I'd ever seen.

From the chopper it looked so beautiful. But at the same time I was scared to death because I thought I was going to get killed. They dropped us off in a grassy area at the base of a hill. There were a couple of guys there to meet us in muddy fatigues [uniforms]. Their hair was longish, they were unshaven, and some of them have bandanas on and writing all over their helmets. Guns on their shoulders and bandoliers across their chest. I'm thinking, "WHOA. Where am I? This is unreal." And these people who have been there and have experienced a little bit of everything look at you with that discerning, "You'll learn."

We had to climb up to the top of the hill. I had this pack on my back which weighed forty or fifty pounds. I weighed 112. About fifty feet up the mountain I realize that I can't carry this monster. My breathing starts getting heavier and I'm struggling. I start to lose my footing because it's slippery and I start to fall. I pick myself up but I'm panicking because I don't want to look like I can't handle it.

I started to get so tired that I got a pain in my chest. This big guy about six-two, also a new recruit, is trying to push me up from the back. By the time I got to the top of the hill, I realized for sure that I could not do this. I was willing to die right there, anything.

I was taken to the company commander, a big strong strapping guy with about eight days' growth of beard and blond hair straight back. The platoon sergeant was this big black guy, equally as big. I was awed by these men and the guys with the dirty clothes. I was in my brand-new little green fatigues and my boots were still shiny. I looked about twelve years old with my bald head and helmet that was too big swimming on me. And they just kind of looked at me and laughed.

My heart fell. I can't ever remember feeling so intimidated, so weak, so ineffectual. And the captain just looked at me and said, "Go over there." I felt like a kid that just wasn't wanted. So I struggled over to a few people who were settling down. I introduced myself and they said, "You'll be in our squad." The squad had just three people. Of course, nobody is too excited about anything because they've all lost friends that day—to U.S. Marine mines, which is twice as aggravating. And nobody wanted to see me because I was a new guy. Nobody wanted a "cherry" out there. Especially this skinny kid who was obviously going to fuck up.

I was aware of how horrible it was. How was I going to get out of it? So I sat up that night. I didn't sleep and I didn't eat. I just sort of laid there crying and scared, thinking about home. How wonderful home was—and really wanted to be there. I didn't want to be in this war. I thought, "What am I going to do?"

Just before dawn everyone was still asleep. I'm sitting in the dew watching the dawn from the top of this mountain. All of a sudden in the distance I could hear, pumf—pumf. Close by somebody shouted, "Why the fuck...I told you to dig in." We were getting mortared. And nobody had dug in because we were all too tired. People were screaming, "INCOMING!" And somebody was yelling at a lieutenant, "Get the motherfuckers. Can't you find them?" trying to call artillery in on them. And other people laughing.

I was wedged between a rock and a tree. I didn't even know where my weapon was. All I knew was that I was scared. Three rounds came in and it was over. People were picking up their bags and were pissed off.

We started back down the hill to get into choppers to fly back to Camp Eagle. I'm wondering, "Why did they fly me out here and make me climb this motherfucking mountain, to get these motherfucking things shot at me, to go back down the mountain to go back to Eagle." All of a sudden—crack-crack—"AK-47." We were being sniped at. All of a sudden forty or fifty guys start firing. Bullets and bangs and explosions going on all around me. I thought, "This is it, World War II, now I'm in the war." I'm not firing my weapon. I'm scared to death.

It's over as soon as it starts. It's silent. And this big

sharp captain and big sergeant come running up the line: "Let's go check it out." All of a sudden everything starts moving fast: Some guys go out this way and some go that way, some are laying down. And one guy's calling in on the radio. I sit there watching all of this going on.

When it was over, everybody loaded onto choppers and we were taken to a railroad stop near Camp Eagle, to set up for the night. As soon as we got there, I went to see the captain. I walk up and he's sitting there with the platoon sergeant. And he says, "Yeah?" I said, "I can't do this." He looked up and said to me, "What?" I said, "When I went out yesterday and tried to climb up the mountain with the thing on my back, I couldn't do it. And I don't think I'll be able to do it." I seriously thought that by telling him this, something okay was going to happen.

So he says, "What do you mean you can't do it?" I was stuttering and very nervous. "I don't weigh that much and I just can't do this. I was wondering if there was some other job that I could have. I'll do anything to get out of the field."

He looked at me and said, "I should kick your ass." The big sergeant starts laughing. And the captain says, "I'll tell you what. You're not only going to carry that pack, I'm going to give you more to carry. Do you think that I would give a punk like you an easy fucking job when there are men out here breaking their fucking asses, risking their lives, getting shot at day in and day out for weeks and months? If you think that I'm going to give you an easy fucking job before any one of them, you've got another think coming. Now get out of my sight."

I just looked at him. There were more deserving people than me for an easy job. So I took a deep breath, turned around, and walked out. I didn't know what I was going to do. But at that time I realized that there was no way out.

The next morning we walked along the train tracks for about two hours until we came to the base of the hill. We had to go up the mountain. We knew that the platoon that had gone up this mountain yesterday had run into booby traps, every hundred yards or so a lot of people had gotten wounded. The word was to be as cautious as possible. As we started up this mountain, I was the last person.

The mountain was much worse than the one we had
had to climb the day before. It was one of those monsters
that keeps going up. So I just took an attitude like the
story of the Little Engine That Could: "I think I can, I
think I can." And after about two hours of climbing up
this mountain and web of trails, I realized that I could do
it. I'd grab for trees to pull myself up. I'd lose my footing
but refind it. I found the position for the rucksack on my
back so that it felt a little bit better.

I saw other people falling out on the trail, while I didn't
feel nearly as bad as I had felt the day before. I seemed
to be stronger for some reason.

We spent the entire day climbing up this mountain. And
at the end of the day I felt fantastic. I felt that I would
survive. Third day in country, I knew I would make it. I
didn't know how, but I knew I would.

# CARE PACKAGES

## Jim Noonan

*Communications*
*1st Shore Party Battalion*
*Chu Lai*

*September 1966 – October 1967*

I was born in Brooklyn Hospital and educated at Brooklyn College. Still live in Brooklyn. I only left Brooklyn once in my life—that was to Vietnam. And they were shooting at me, so I decided to never leave Brooklyn again.

I got out of high school a year before I joined the Marine Corps. I was not a very promising student and didn't have any college prospects. I was working. And the normal thing for a kid in my neighborhood to do if you weren't in college, you went into the service.

I was deferred because I was the sole support of my mother. My father died when I was fourteen years old and she raised me alone. But it really seemed like it was my duty to go. So on March 2, 1966, I joined the Marine Corps. I enlisted on a buddy plan with George Hankin, who is now a cop in New York City, and Richie Radcliffe. We all went down to Parris Island together.

Richie and I wound up going to Vietnam. But George hurt his arm—he had already broken it playing football—and he didn't go. He was pretty bitter about that because his cousin had been killed in Vietnam. And it was a holy mission for George.

I went to communications school as a message center man, learning to operate teletypes and things like that. From there, I was sent to Vietnam in late September 1966. I was assigned to the 1st Shore Party Battalion in Chu Lai. I remember it was the rainy season. The truck that took us to our outfit couldn't make it in the mud. So they left me out with my seabag over my shoulder. And I hiked

130

the last mile through mud that at times was up to my waist.

I reported to the company office in our base-camp area and they assigned me a bunk. Several months later, when the sun came out, was the next time anything was dry. Mud was just everywhere. We had no electricity. The only reason we had showers was because we found a fuel tank that had fallen off a jet.

I had contact with Vietnamese people in the villages nearby. I have this crazy theory that sanity stops at about the age of eight and begins again at sixty-five. So the children, no matter where you were in Vietnam, provided a certain buffer against insanity.

My mother, my two sisters, and my sister-in-law were always sending me "care packages." I would then hitch-hike to this orphanage and give them the canned food from home and play with the kids. In Chu Lai we had Vietnamese working in our base camp. That was something not all of us were comfortable with, but we grew accustomed to it.

One thing that made a dynamic impression on me was the place where these Vietnamese lived. They would come in from the hills to work at the base. Trucks would pick them up and bring them back. They lived in places surrounded by Cyclone fences, with barbed wire on the top. Their huts were fashioned out of flattened beer cans and cardboard boxes. Each night these people would take our garbage. And they didn't take it to make compost—they took it for their dinner. They were transients, refugees. And in a difficult time, they were the ones who had the fewest rights. That made a pretty big impression on me.

Right now, I don't have to close my eyes to get a vision of the children's hospital . . . and a particular kid I probably spent twenty minutes staring at with my mouth open. The wounds on his back and the backs of his legs and buttocks were opened, festering with flies. No mosquito netting, no bandages, he lay on a dirt floor. It was nothing more than a tent.

My last year in college I worked as a medical technician for New York City's lead poisoning program. I would take kids' blood in tenement buildings. And I had difficulties.

The kids in Bedford-Stuyvesant called me "Dracula." I saw serious poverty. I remember walking up to the top floor of a four-story tenement. I wore a white clinical coat because I looked so young that nobody would believe I was able to stick a needle in a kid's arm.

When I reached the top of the stairs, my coat was drenched with sweat. I sat down in front of the kid and I thought I was going to faint. The wall across the room appeared to be moving. It was covered with cockroaches. Thousands of them! It was an ill-lit apartment and the wall was coming in and out, like breathing. But it was the cockroaches crawling all over each other, just festering on there. I saw that kind of poverty. But even still, I've never seen anything like the Vietnamese people gathering our garbage, protecting it like it was precious stones.

In the Chu Lai base camp I lived a relatively secure life. But the worst three days I had in Vietnam was when we were hit with 122-mm Russian rockets and just about everything else the North Vietnamese could throw at us. It was absolutely extraordinary. Everywhere you looked, it was tracer bullets. Every light bulb in our hootches [huts] was shot out. The air mattresses were flattened . . . bullets went through just about everything. And then the 122-mm rockets came in. There's a slight second between the banshee whistling and the explosion. During one of those slight seconds, I just about bit through my lip. It was terrifying.

I came home on Halloween 1967. I arrived at Kennedy Airport with all my nieces and nephews waiting in their Halloween costumes. It was wonderful seeing my mother, my brother, my sisters, and all the kids. My nephew Chip was standing there in a skeleton costume.

My Uncle Jim, my mother's brother, died the day before I came home. He had been sick for a long time, so my nieces and nephews didn't know that he existed. And my nephew Chip heard his mother say, "Uncle Jim died." Now the only Uncle Jim he knew was me. He was very upset. My sister asked him what was wrong. And he said I was dead. She said, "No, no."

When I came home that night, Chip handed me a note that said, "Dear Uncle Jim, I'm glad you're not dead. Love, Chip." It had little American flags, soldiers, a stick-men kind of drawing. You know, the art of a child that age. It was a wonderful note. I couldn't have agreed with him more. So I kept it, and to this day, keep it in my little area for precious things that can't ever be replaced.

# LEATHERNECK SQUARE

## Adolphus Stuart

*Scout*
*Special Landing Force Alpha*
*1st Battalion, 3rd Marines*
*I Corps*

*April 1967–March 1968*

My mother died when I was three years old. My father remarried and I had trouble with my stepmother. I was treated like the proverbial stepchild, the Cinderfellow-type story.

It affected my schooling. I wasn't a failing student, but I know I could have done a lot better. In September 1964, on my seventeenth birthday, I made a decision. I asked my father to sign me into the Marine Corps. And he did.

I went to Vietnam in 1967. I was assigned as a scout with the battalion landing team, a very mobile task group. All-inclusive: land, sea, and air. As a battalion scout, my job was to be a liaison between battalion intelligence and the company I was attached to. I would prepare maps and issue them to the company commanders and platoon commanders. And I would travel with the company commanders and radio people. On platoon- or squad-sized patrols, I would make records of whatever we found, like enemy bunkers.

They coined a phrase, "Leatherneck Square," for the area we worked in—Dong Ha, Quang Tri, Hue, Cam Lo, the DMZ—all up north. Vietnam was the hottest place I've ever been. All day, all night, usually above a hundred degrees. Guys were passing out from heatstroke like flies. We lost our fair share of people from "short rounds"— friendly fire—just plain fuckups. A guy calls artillery on the wrong place and we get hit while the enemy is getting away. And air strikes... I've seen 250-pound bombs dropped on friendly positions. It's a mistake, but a lot of guys got wasted [killed]. And when somebody I knew got waxed in an ambush or firefight, I can't express the rage I felt and remain civilized.

There was a guy who joined the scout unit at the same time I did. We went through California and trained in Okinawa together. He was killed the very first operation. He was shot in the neck and died from the loss of blood ... helicopters were unable to extract the wounded in time. I can remember being very hurt at the death of my friend. He was white, by the way. But I cried like a baby. The way he died made it even worse. I had nightmares out there in the field, dreaming about killing a bunch of people in Saigon. I've never seen the place, but in my dreams I would go to the heart of where the shit is, the nation's capital, and cause havoc.

I was feeling very bad. And the unit was getting ready to move to better locations, helicopters were flying in. And we began getting mortared and receiving automatic-weapons fire. A feeling of total helplessness—there was nothing you could do. Pray! That feeling of helplessness I have felt since such encounters in Vietnam. That feeling of "What am I going to do now?" There's nobody there to stop it when you want it to stop. You got to fight ... to have that madness stop. And all the time you're wondering what was coming down. Will it come down on me?

Adrenaline? Phew! I stayed scared thirteen months. Without a doubt, stayed scared. In June 1967 the 1st Battalion, 9th Marines, walked into a very bad situation. They were known as "the walking dead." And our mission was to retrieve the bodies. This was near Cam Lo, way up north in a place called "the Trace." Which was "McNamara's Line." Named after Secretary of Defense Robert McNamara's idea to create a physical barrier across Vietnam.

It was a joke, about seven hundred meters wide and thirteen miles long. Barren ... it looked like something out of a World War I movie. I was afraid of it. I knew that there was something bad in there. It was a haunted place. This was the DMZ. Barren and bombed out, with big craters. It looked like nothing real. Six hundred meters to my rear were banana trees and tea plantations. I mean, just a few hundred yards and you were in hell.

We had to cross the Trace to retrieve the bodies. We were immediately hit with artillery from North Vietnam. They were shooting everything they had in their arsenal—rockets, mortars, recoilless rifles, automatic weapons, and gas. They were trying to employ chemical warfare, CS gas. But it didn't work because the wind blew it back on them.

We were able to move within sixty to seventy yards of them, about a city block away. We could see the NVA massing their troops. We didn't need binoculars. And at that time people back in the States were saying there were no North Vietnamese in South Vietnam. I can remember seeing an American newspaper questioning the validity of American being inside the DMZ. The NVA would mass their troops at a departure point, and we would run a patrol maybe a hundred yards, the length of a football field. That's as far as we could go. There was very little cover.

On the third day, my company was on one of these patrols. We moved in front of the battalion perimeter to set up an outpost. It was hot, dry, dusty. We carried five-gallon water cans. During the afternoon, we were called back to man our positions on the perimeter. As we were moving through Bravo Company's sector, we got hit with the largest artillery barrage outside of the siege of Khe Sanh. We were out in the open, without foxholes—nothing. Jesus Christ, it rained artillery. I was scared to death. I was praying some serious prayers.

We had to get up and move when the North Vietnamese were reloading their guns. It's not a good feeling. But in the craziest situations, I found some things to be very comical. I was running and jumped in what appeared to be a tiny Vietnamese-built fighting hole—two feet by two feet. And this huge Hawaiian gunnery sergeant, Kikohana, says, "Get out of that hole, Stuart. That's mine." He's standing up to direct traffic as these fucking artillery explosions are going on all around us. And he's telling me, "Go find your own hole, goddamn it, that's mine."

I had to make a mad dash to another position while hearing the POP of artillery coming in. It's, "Oh no, in a few seconds they'll be here." And the closer they came, the louder the sound—you can hear them whistling right in on you. It didn't help my sanity.

I have pictures of bodies on tanks that we helped retrieve from McNamara's Line. A high percentage of the
bodies were black. But I still didn't think anything about
a racial imbalance because I was in an all-white unit. I
didn't know how many blacks were out there, even in my
own battalion.

My first racial incident in the field amazed and shocked
me. I was in a tent in base camp. We had just pulled from
an operation. Everybody's stinky and dirty, and there was
no shower. We were so tired, we only wanted a place to
crash. A corpsman comes into the tent and says, "Jesus
Christ, it's blacker than the nigger's asshole." And as he
lit a candle, I thought, "I'm the nigger in the tent. The
only one." And he sheepishly apologized and said, "I
didn't realize." But I realized, "Okay, this is what is in
the back of your head. This is what you think." I really
lost a little respect at that point. But once we were in the
field, there was no trouble. There was no color.

I put my life on the line many a time trying to stop a
white fool from doing something that he was told not to
do. And as a result of getting hurt, he exposed me to more
danger. I hated that. And fortunately I was never in a
position where someone had to do that for me. But I'm
quite sure that they would have done the same for me.

Out in the field, everybody put their ass on the line.
And I don't think you'll find as much diversity and difference of opinion amongst Vietnam veteran peers, black
and white, as you'll find with people who did not participate or in the generation before us.

After the operation in McNamara's Line, I wrote my
minister and asked him to forward the letter to my congressman. I knew that if I sent the letter direct it would
be censored. So my pastor sent my letter to the congressman. And the congressman wrote back to me. I received
that letter in January 1968, just before Tet. And it was
censored. It was opened when I received it.

My letter questioned the tactics that were being used
in Vietnam. I grew up in an era of combat on television:
TV series, John Wayne in the movies, World War II, and
Korea, where they didn't fight like we were fighting. Going
into the same area over and over again, like playing chess.
Our maps were broken up into thousand-meter grid
squares.

I would place my unit in one grid and then follow our action. A lot of times I'd use a piece of tracing paper overlaid on the map to make sense of what was going on, in conjunction with what other scouts had brought back from the field. I found that it was like playing chess. Some of the moves in chess were like some of the moves made in Vietnam. Like a knight would move—up one, over two. You're at an LZ [landing zone] and the next day's operation is up one grid, over two. And after the game was over, they set up the board and played the same game again. Up one, over two—on the same area.

I couldn't understand how that was going to win a war. And I was just a twenty-year-old kid with limited knowledge. But I saw that it wasn't going to work. And I questioned it. And my congressman's response was, in essence, "We know what we're doing. This is the way the war has to be fought." Just a blanket statement that sounded like it was mass-produced and rubber-stamped off to the guys. I didn't expect that kind of an answer.

I was trying to figure out why I had to lose so many comrades in an area where I had lost comrades previously. It became a real joke. The villagers would know you. I'd see the same old mamasan whom I'd seen five or six weeks earlier. She'd remember me. And it was like, "What's going on?"

# RULES OF ENGAGEMENT

## Mark Berent

*Fighter Pilot*
*U.S. Air Force*
*Vietnam, Thailand, and Cambodia*

*1965—1973*

My first tour in Vietnam began in December 1965. I was stationed at the air force base at Bien Hoa, flying F-100s, more than two hundred missions. My second tour began in late 'sixty-eight, flying F-4s out of Ubon, Thailand. I was in the Night Owls, flying over the Ho Chi Minh Trail for the first seven months. And the last five months I was commander of the Wolf FAC [ Forward Air Control]. They were very fast FACs, covering the Ho Chi Minh Trail in Laos all the way to North Vietnam. This was during the period of Johnson's bombing halt. So some missions were sanctioned, others unsanctioned—which weren't clandestinely approved. Some of us just did it on our own.

The first tour, my motivation was, "I'm a fighter pilot. I've trained to do this all my life. Can I really hack it?" Mixed in with, "The country's at war. You go." I gave no thought to the politics of it whatsoever. They didn't concern me in the least. All I knew was, here was combat and I had to be there.

I got a couple of surprises in Vietnam. One was that I received medals. On one occasion I turned down a Purple Heart because a Special Forces friend of mine had just walked twenty-six kilometers at night, with a .51-caliber bullet in one arm and a wounded Viet under the other—that's Purple Heart stuff. All I had was some junk in my eyes from taking a hit in the cockpit.

I completed my year tour and was assigned back to Systems Command in California. The air force was determined to get their pound of flesh out of me, having sent me through college to get an engineering degree. I had a fat-cat job and lived right on the beach with the 69th Tactical Fornication Squadron—living the good life. But every time I would pick up the paper, another buddy had been shot down or killed.

So I arranged to be upgraded to fly F-4s, to go back over there. There was no way that I could stay in the United States when the war was going on and my friends were still there. Some captured, some dead, someone being shot down every day. So I went back.

The first seven months of flying F-4s out of Ubon, I was in the Night Owls. The Johnson bombing halt started a month before I arrived, so we couldn't go to North Vietnam. All we could do was hum up and down the Laotian segment of the Ho Chi Minh Trail at night, which was the Karst Mountains. And if you're trying to knock out North Vietnamese supply trucks taking full advantage of the bombing halt by going to South Vietnam—you can't do it with only F-4s. We flew through the overcast. One ship [jet] pops some flares while the other ship looks for trucks.

The first thing the truck drivers do when they see the flares is say, "Here come those dummy Americans. Let's pull over to the side of the road and watch them fly into the Karst." And we lost an awful lot of airplanes flying smack into the mountains. Because we didn't have night eyeballs. We didn't kill any trucks...it was a bullshit mission.

The only time it became any good was when they brought in Spectre—AC-130 gunships that had night-observation devices. Low-light TV, infrared, and Black Crow that could read a truck's emissions. They had the eyeballs.

We linked up with Spectre to do two things. One was suppression of the antiaircraft guns that would open up on us. Spectre was a lot more vulnerable, slower and bigger, than we were. And second, direct us to our targets. And we started killing trucks. I remember one night I personally got fourteen.

Spectre could see them and mark them for us different ways. They would shoot with rapid-fire 20-mm cannons and say, "That's where they are down there." Or they would throw out airborne flares to illuminate the convoy and we would roll in to dive-bomb. Or they would throw out a "log"—a great big hunk of material that would burn and glow in the dark for fifteen or twenty minutes. They'd put one log in front of the column and one log at the other end, and say, "Okay, hit between the two." And then we'd start killing trucks. And eventually, the Ho Chi Minh Trail did get bottled up. We damn near won the bloody war militarily.

But during the bombing halt that began in November 'sixty-eight we were pissed. I went through many bombing halts over there. And each time we were really pissed. Because it let down everything we had been gaining.

For instance, during 1966–67 our buddies were flying F-105s and F-4s over a very high-threat area in North Vietnam where the latest SAMs [surface-to-air missiles] and radar the Russians had were deployed. But under the Rules of Engagement [political restrictions on military operations], we were forced to fight the war with a hand tied behind our back, one eye blinded, and only half a pocket full of ammunition.

Officials like Robert Strange McNamara, Secretary of Defense, were saying that there was no bomb shortage in Vietnam. There was very definitely a bomb and ammunition shortage, at least for the air force. We had guys going north into worse flak than World War II, with two 250- or 500-pound bombs, or two cans of napalm for a rail cut. You can't cut railheads with napalm—you burn down weeds along the tracks, that's all. It was criminal. And I know some very sharp officers during this period who seriously considered refusing to fly, to invite a court martial to expose this.

Bureaucrats got around it by saying, "There is no bomb shortage in Vietnam." But in Saigon, American merchant marines chartered to bring the bombs over were backed up in the harbor. The ammo was aboard those ships and could not be unloaded. The harbor had never been enlarged, so you couldn't get the boats in on time. Furthermore, we had to pay the Vietnamese harbor fees to off-load the boats. And we had to look the other way when materials such as small arms and medical supplies went to the Viet Cong. Because we were "guests in their country."

At that time, I was still thinking, "Well, people in Saigon and the 7th Air Force know what they're doing." But I was beginning to perceive, "Things are going well. But it doesn't look like we are going to be allowed to win the war." Because of the Washington-imposed Rules of Engagement.

We'd be flying up in the Plaine des Jarres in Laos supporting Vang Pao's Hmong [hill tribe] who were fighting the North Vietnamese and their Pathet Lao Communists. And there were things we weren't allowed to hit, like within one meter of a pagoda. Well, the Pathet Lao would load a pagoda up with ammo and whatnot. And sometimes they'd be stupid and shoot at you from inside it. And then somehow you just might slide over the pagoda and— POW—it would cook off and the ammo inside it would explode for a couple of hours.

There's a famous story of a Chinese cultural center up in the Plaine des Jarres. We weren't allowed to drop a bomb within three kilometers of this place. Well, one night somebody who will remain nameless, with a terrific crew, said they had had enough of this shit. And they put some right in the middle of the Chinese cultural center. And the ammo stored there cooked off for a week.

After November 'sixty-eight, when the bombing halt was on over North Vietnam, we could not hit the North Vietnamese trucks until they got on the Ho Chi Minh Trail in Laos at night. Then the antiaircraft guns would come out and our guys would fly into the Karst Mountains. One day I stopped counting at one hundred trucks lined up bumper to bumper at Mu Gia Pass in North Vietnam. They were waiting for dark to start down the trail. And we weren't allowed to hit them. Just like our guys who flew north between 'sixty-six and 'sixty-nine, who would see SAM sites being built. But they couldn't take these out until after missiles were shot at them. They would see MIG [Soviet jet fighters] airfields being built with extended runways. But they could not hit them until MIGs were taking off and shooting at them. Rules of Engagement.

We could not hit the rail lines bringing supplies from China into North Vietnam. We could not mine Haiphong Harbor . . . everything Nixon wound up doing in 1972 that brought Hanoi around. And to stop the supplies before they reached the goddamned battlefield in South Vietnam.

The primary role of the tactical United States Air Force is to stop the enemy's logistical capability before it gets the bullets, the artillery, the mortar rounds, the guns, onto the battlefield. That's called "interdiction." And the only reason for the air force is to support the army. The reason you bomb the factories is so they don't manufacture the weapons and ammunition to kill American soldiers. The reason to give close air support is to help the soldiers kill the bad guys. The reason we have transports, the whole business, is to support the army.

In Vietnam we weren't allowed to practice effective interdiction. And where the hell do you think all the POWs came from? Eighty percent of the POWs were aircrews. And they were shot down by SAM sites and MIG sites that they had watched being built. And in South Vietnam, the movement of supplies and troops from North Vietnam contributed to American deaths on the battlefield.

We could see the trucks in broad daylight, bumper to bumper, brand-new. They belonged to the 559th Transportation Squadron out of Hanoi. Now there were some people who said "Fuck this shit." We'd radio Invert, our radar control:

"INVERT. . . THIS IS SO-AND-SO. I'M GOING TO BE DOWN BEHIND THE KARST FOR A WHILE, SO YOU WON'T BE PAINTING ME. I'LL GIVE YOU A HOLLER WHEN I COME BACK UP."

We'd fly over these trucks and give them a little heart failure by popping our afterburners or maybe hose off a rocket or two. But we couldn't bring a strike flight in there. I was by myself. Now had I got caught doing this, I would have been court-martialed. But I knew that the North Vietnamese were sending weapons on that trail to kill U.S. soldiers and South Vietnamese civilians.

I remember a South Vietnamese Montagnard village the NVA went into with the flamethrowers. They burned out everyone . . . women, children. Because the villagers would not do whatever the North Vietnamese wanted.

# SOLDIER OF THE REVOLUTION

--------

## Nguyen Tuong Lai

*Guerilla Leader*
*Viet Cong*
*1954–1968*

In 1963 I was vice-commander of Regiment 1410, operating in the six southernmost provinces of Vietnam. I was wounded in a battle at Vung Tau. And afterwards I was sent to attend the military academy in North Vietnam. But because of the changing situation in the South following the Diem assassination, I was sent back in April 1964 to take command of the 28th Special Commando Battalion of the 9th [Viet Cong] Division.

In 1967 I was made a regimental commander in the Iron Triangle area, north of Saigon. The area was an intense battlefield during the American operations. Attleboro and Junction City. My troops never stayed in one place. We remained mobile, attacking from one district to another.

Fighting against the Americans was easy because of the restrictions they imposed on themselves. But the South Vietnamese army was a much different matter because they would cross the Cambodian border and come in after us. And sometimes the American air force went a little bit beyond the boundaries. When my unit heard the sound of helicopters coming we were damned scared and would hide in our shelters.

During the Tet offensive of 1968, we attacked the Bien Hoa Airport. Tet was a great loss for the NLF forces. Our army had to be restructured afterward. There were three phases of fighting during the offensive: During the first phase in my area the NLF forces did the fighting. We lost too many men and in the second phase had to be reinforced by North Vietnamese units. And in the third phase, the fighting was done exclusively by North Vietnamese units, even in Tay Ninh and Saigon. The southern forces were decimated . . . and from that time on mostly served as intelligence, logistics, and saboteurs for the northerners.

In June 1968, I was assigned to attend the Tran Phu School of the Central Committee of the Communist Party at COSVN (North Vietnamese/NLF Headquarters) in Tay Ninh Province. During this time the American leadership changed from General Westmoreland to General Abrams. And due to our Tet losses and a change in American tactics, all of our units had to retreat into Cambodia. During this time the war was fought on the border. Our orders were to launch all of our attacks from Cambodia, to which we could retreat and remain safely.

We knew that the American commanders had strict orders from their higher echelon to respect the Cambodian border. That's why we abused Cambodia's neutrality. Whenever we were chased by the enemy, we knew we could retreat across the frontier demarcation into the safe zone and get some rest. We were protected by international law. Also, we knew there was a large antiwar movement in America who would not allow the American army to cross over the border.

We had to live in miserable conditions in the jungle. We were cold, wet, caught malaria, and did not have enough food when the supply section was delayed or disrupted. For example, in the Ma Da area of Binh Duong Province, for three months we had no rice. So we had to eat leaves and roots in the jungle—whatever we could find for survival.

We would spy on the American fire bases [temporary large artillery bases]. And when they would pull out, they left behind C-ration cans and wasted food. We would gather their leftovers. This helped us a great deal.

The most effective American units were the Special Forces and Marine Reconnaissance, who operated across the border to the Ho Chi Minh Trail. Operating in small groups with Mike Forces [indigenous tribal units] and ARVN Special Forces, they effectively attacked and captured our soldiers and disrupted our supply lines. This weakened our forces and hurt our morale. Because we could not stop these attacks. We understood that these American soldiers were very skillful and very brave in their tactics to disrupt infiltration from the North.

# PROJECT DELTA

## Chuck Allen

*Commanding Officer*
*U.S. Special Forces Project Delta*
*I Corps*

*December 1966–December 1968*

Project Delta was a strategic reconnaissance operation. We had a support force of around 900 to 1,100 people, drawing upon Korean troops, Australian troops, U.S. Marines and Air Force, an almost self-sustaining little army. The 281st Assault Helicopter Company was in direct support of us. And we had the only ARVN Airborne Ranger battalion. They were all in direct support of us, under U.S. and Vietnamese joint command. And we were primarily U.S. Special Forces, Vietnamese Special Forces, a company of Nungs, and the Roadrunners.

The Roadrunners were made up of all the ethnic groups—Montagnards, Cambodians, Laotians, and Vietnamese. Their mission was to be inserted into our operations area [OA] wearing enemy uniforms and a cover story, to join up with enemy units and gather intelligence. Then they would fade off into the bushes and call in air strikes.

They were quite successful in a lot of operations, but in some they were not. One particular Roadrunner team linked up with an NVA unit. While they were sitting around talking and gathering information, one of our little guys pulled an orange out of his pack and started eating it. And when he did that, he gave himself away ... the NVA didn't have Sunkist oranges.

We had to search them just two minutes prior to putting them on an aircraft because we would find Hershey bars and Salem cigarettes. They'd be in complete NVA or VC uniforms and we'd have to strip them down and take various items away from them.

When I first took over Delta, I was classified as "advisor to the CO [Commander] of Project Delta Training Center," who was a Vietnamese major. We found out after a while that this was not satisfactory. I would have to visit General Quang, commanding general of the Vietnamese Special Forces. I'd bring him a new .38 pistol because he needed one for his brother, or a radio or a tape recorder, then we'd discuss operations. And his back channel down to the Project Delta commander would say, "Go ahead with whatever the crazy Americans want to do." It ran very successfully that way. It cost us a lot of money and a lot of bribing to get them to completely cooperate, but it worked.

This does not reflect upon the troops in Project Delta, who were highly motivated. But bribes were necessary for the higher-ranking commanders who were political appointees. Who they knew in the high command is how they got their job. But one of the things that contributed to the success of Project Delta was that the entire Vietnamese operational staff had been to Fort Benning or Fort Bragg. They were high-caliber soldiers. And most of them spoke a little bit of English and were a whole lot easier to work with.

Once we more or less assumed command, we could generally do what we wanted. Plan our operations and the Vietnamese commander would say, "It sounds good to me." But we had to do that initially in an abrupt way. One Vietnamese commander didn't want to go out on an operation. So I said, "Fuck you." I took about sixty Nung ethnic tribesmen—who worked directly for me and hated the Vietnamese . . . and were better soldiers—and went out into the field. We had a very successful operation— took a couple of POWs and captured a bunch of weapons. When word of that got back to the Vietnamese high command, things started to fall into place. They found out that we weren't playing games. And, by God, we were going to do it right.

At that time I was about forty–forty-two years old. I wasn't a kid, but I wasn't an old man. And in retrospect, when I look back, I did an awful lot of extremely foolish things in doing my job. In one situation, I sent a recon team into an area. The team leader saw some NVA on a hill and wouldn't get out of his helicopter, he got scared. I was in the C and C [Command and Control] ship. So I pulled my ship down to the LZ, jumped out, and sent my ship back into orbit, ordering this other ship to land.

When that other ship came in and landed, I walked over to the team leader and said, "Get the fuck out of your ship and do your mission." Needless to say, it scared the shit out of him to see me standing there by myself with a lot of NVA over on the hillside, a hundred meters away. They could have had my ass in a minute. It was a foolish thing to do, but at that time it was correct.

In retrospect I think, "I've got a wife and six kids at home. Why should I jump out to an LZ deep in the Ashau Valley?" But it's that combat high—where you're only thinking about getting the job done. You don't think about anything else.

A lot of times we went into landing zones with a small C and C ship to check things out when we shouldn't have. We probably exposed the ship to destruction many times, but you don't think about that at the time. You think about getting the job done and not what's going to happen to you. I personally knew that I was coming back alive. Never gave it a second thought. I was not one of those who kept all my shit tidy back in base camp so they could ship it home easily if I was killed.

But you get into combat and after the first few minutes of a firefight, you're wrapped up in the situation. So your fears are gone or they're pushed to the back of your mind. And if you're well trained, you go ahead and do your job. And when combat continues day after day, there comes a point where the initial fears are not even there. It's kind of a high . . . I don't know how the hell to explain it. You don't think about the people back home. You're just concerned about what you're doing. In periods I'd make in some days fourteen to sixteen hours in the air in ten or fifteen different chopper flights making inserts and extractions. In all that there was no fear. But I still had this excitement about what I was doing.

I finally realized I was on this combat high, if you want to call it that, after I got back home. It took me a month or so to get down off that high. And it's not anything to be ashamed of or comical. But if a car backfired, the hair on the back of my neck stood up during that period while I was coming down.

Special Forces people have more training than anybody else. And that does make a difference. You can see people do things in a combat or highly hazardous situation almost automatically. Sometimes they don't even realize they're doing it. That's a direct result of repetitive training. It's automatically knowing what to do in a firefight, which way to turn in the woods when you're map-reading or in a dead-reckoning situation. The better a man is trained, the better he will act in a combat situation. No question about it. You can't train enough.

In Project Delta, some of our recon trainers had been through basic Delta training six or eight times. Every time we would come back to our base camp for a stand-down and assign a new man to a recon team, it was my policy that the entire team went through the training cycle to help train that one man. They didn't like it, but they did it. Because that team trained as a unit and worked to bring that new man up to their standards. And that's probably why we took so few casualties.

Political restrictions did not filter down to Project Delta. We didn't have the political ramifications that the infantry had to contend with. Our orders came right out of West-moreland's shop. We were given an operational area that sometimes was eight hundred square miles. We had the resources and personnel and equipment to go into that area and saturate it with reconnaissance patrols. And we had the fire support behind us whenever we needed it. So we could tie up ninety-five percent of enemy movement in that entire operational area.

If you've got an enemy moving through an area who doesn't know they're being watched and before they know it bombs are falling out of the sky on him, this slows down his movement and operations. And we in fact tied up all of the enemy's movement, which limits the use of enemy force and what he can do, how he can move, how he can operate. We tied up the entire 325th NVA Division for months on end.

Special operations, if done right, can tie up a large

enemy force or paralyze guerilla operations with a few small teams. It's an economy of force. You can tie up one province with an outfit like Project Delta with only thirty or forty Americans in it. And that's all you're exposing to the enemy. You demoralize them and beat them on their own turf.

# COUNTERTERROR

## Gen. Lu Mong Lan

*Commandant*
*Command and General Staff College*
*Dalat*

*1966–1967*

At the U.S. Army War College today, people look back at Vietnam and ask the question, "What should we have done?" Now they realize that they should have used the Vietnamese forces on a territorial mission and U.S. forces on the DMZ and Ho Chi Minh Trail to stop resupply from the North. This way the U.S. forces would have had no conflict with civilians and no confusion.

I used to tell my soldiers, "The minute you harm an innocent person, you put the whole family in the hands of the Communists." The North Vietnamese didn't care. They have always said, "It is better to eliminate ten innocent people than to miss one enemy." This is Party policy, even today. But I told my soldiers, "For our side to adopt such a policy would be catastrophic. Our job must be to win over the hearts and minds of the people. And that should be kept in mind all the time. You should always respect the villagers."

There were some ARVN officers who had the wrong concept because they began by serving in the French Intelligence Bureau. They used to torture people and would cut dead VC's ears or noses off. They would feel that this made them courageous people. A wrong concept of mostly illiterates. We used to tell them not to do this, but we had no control over them.

Some of them were court-martialed when they did it much too openly. But some of the generals like Duong Van Minh [Big Minh] had as his aide-de-camp a man who emerged from this group. This major killed President Diem.

But he was killed by his fellow paratroopers during the second coup.

It was our mistake to keep these people because they were a danger in themselves. They would go out on a long patrol, kill a VC and cut off his ears. They'd bring them back to the unit commander, who would chastise them but not seriously. So these men would think it was a good thing. And the next time they would go out and do it again. They would feel like heroes, but it was wrong.

When the VC did this, it was done as a part of their strategy. Done selectively in a village to make their point. And then they would keep a presence to enforce it. Our forces should not have done anything similar. Because even if your forces are spread thin, as ours were in many areas, the more respect you show people and the better example you set, the better chance that they will be on your side. Or more importantly, they will consider you on their side.

I would never allow my men to do actions that would put us in a light worse than the Communists. If we could not be there to stop the Communists from killing the local schoolteachers or putting mines in the road that blow up busloads of farmers, at least we were in a better light in the eyes of the people. And the people would see us as someone to protect them rather than someone they had to be equally afraid of.

In areas close to their sanctuaries in Cambodia, the North Vietnamese were never more than a two-day march from any village. There was always a fear of reprisal among people who cooperated with our forces. And with our forces unable to keep a presence in every village, it was important to be especially polite to people who always lived in fear of the Communists. And there were well-informed VC agents who monitored every villager's activities.

One time I found a diary on the body of a North Vietnamese soldier. In the diary he said that he was educated every other day while infiltrating through Laos and Cambodia to South Vietnam: "My commissar teaches me that so far we operate in the jungle area. We have the trees as our camouflage. Now we prepare to infiltrate the populated areas of South Vietnam. We should now consider the people as trees to camouflage us."

I understood what they wanted to accomplish. Because I fought as a guerilla against the French. You feel good when you are among the population. I was armed with only a shotgun, but I feel very confident. So this is a very important target to win over the population.

But during the North Vietnamese offensives of 1968, 'seventy-two, and even 'seventy-five, this popular support never happened. There was no popular uprising. And, to the contrary, the Communists exposed themselves as terrorists. Unfortunately, the Vietnamese people understood this, but the Western public opinion was deluded into believing the complete opposite. Terrorists were honored as martyrs by the news media.

No Western reporter ever asked the South Vietnamese soldiers, "How do you like fighting in the city?" Whether it be Saigon, Cholon, Ben Tre, or Hue. It was very hard on us emotionally. We tried to use a public-address system to warn our civilian population where to hide and what to do. But the North Vietnamese and Viet Cong acted like bandits robbing a bank, using the civilians as hostages. Just like the PLO did in Beirut. This is a very old tactic.

It is very important to distinguish the friendly people from the enemy. Each month, when I was a corps commander, I issued a map of my area to all American and Korean units. It had the name of each hamlet and the hamlet chief. And I used to assign one Popular Forces or Regional Forces leader to the U.S. 4th Infantry Division in Pleiku to accompany each American unit on operations. It was impossible for Americans to distinguish among our people: "How can we tell these Vietnamese apart? They all wear black pajamas. If they wear white, does this mean that they are on our side?" And if they killed somebody thinking he was VC, a hamlet chief might come to see me crying, "He was my nephew. And he was anti-Communist."

The Americans would get completely confused. For example, I understand what could have happened to Lieutenant Calley at My Lai. I served in Quang Nai when I was a second lieutenant, back in 'fifty-one and 'fifty-two. At that time I was fighting against the Viet Minh because the Communists had killed off most of the nationalist leadership in the resistance. I know all the tactics the VC used to harass you. To push you to the point where you lose your mind. And the population is used as a shield by them. This is a deliberate tactic. They had used it for many years, but the Americans had no understanding of this. And in Calley's case, it broke him under the pressure.

For instance, the Americans deploy a force on an operation. Now, the enemy does not confront you. But he harasses you every night to give you the impression that all the people around you are hostile. Everybody becomes your enemy. But in reality it is only the same five or six VC who come back every night. And they plant the punji pits, the booby traps, land mines, propaganda leaflets on the roads.

There are also villages in the area. The VC make you nervous to the point that you lose your patience and say, "I want to be finished with this." And you have fallen into their trap. You kill the wrong people because your mind has snapped.

In a guerilla war, an army should always be aware of this.

# THE DESERTED VILLAGE

*Scout*
*Special Landing Force Alpha*
*1st Battalion, 3rd Marines*
*I Corps*

*April 1967–March 1968*

I was involved in an incident where I wanted to kill a
woman. We had just come through a very dangerous area.
We entered a village and there were no men, none whatsoever. And I had an interpreter with me. We asked this
lady, "Where are the men? What's going on?" She said,
"I don't know. I don't know." The same old bullshit that
we always got from the sympathizers and supporters of
the Viet Cong and North Vietnamese.

We knew that the lady was lying. And we had just come
through an area that was heavily booby-trapped. Guys
got hurt. We knew the VC were around. We just couldn't
find them. So I took this lady outside the hootch. I drew
my bayonet. I grabbed her by the hair, pulling her head
back with the bayonet in her back. And I'm thinking,
"How many more people are going to get hurt because
she doesn't want to say anything?"

And when I couldn't intimidate her . . . I let her go.

# THE SHADOW

## Nguyen Tuong Lai

*Commander, Counterintelligence*
*Viet Cong Southern Security Section*

*1971–1975*

In 1971 I was promoted to a command position in the NLF army reconnaissance [counterintelligence] of the Southern Security Section. My unit was responsible for seeking out and attacking the American and South Vietnamese intelligence systems.

I had three special units in the Saigon–Bien Hoa area. When we received special orders from the higher authorities to eliminate a particular target in the American or RVN secret service, I would activate the counterintelligence service that was under deep cover in Saigon.

After the 1968 Tet offensive, our sabotage section in Saigon was feeble because we didn't have cadre left to do terrorist actions. An exception was Miss Do Thi Hang, who did assassinations in District 10 in Saigon. We usually received orders to attack house no. 3 on Bach Dang Street and house no. 11A on Hai Ba Trung Street, American intelligence offices.

I would usually stay in the bush outside Saigon. But at times I would come in disguised as a cyclo [taxi] driver to survey targets we were intending to attack.

My most important success was capturing an American in the My Tho area. I had received information from the higher level that he was a CIA agent disguised as a businessman. My second greatest victory was to kill a priest, named Nguyen Van Man, in Tay Ninh. We believed he was an intelligence officer. I put an antitank mine in his car on a Sunday morning before he went to perform a church service. The people thought it was the South Vietnamese government who did the killing.

Between 1965 and 1969 we did not capture many Americans in our area. Even when we did, usually they would not obey our orders and we had to eliminate them. In 1969, we received orders from Hanoi that any prisoners or bodies of Americans must be sent immediately to the North. And after 1969, there was the antiwar movement, so some of the Americans we captured cooperated with our army.

# THE RELEASE

## Dan Pitzer

*Prisoner of War*
*U Minh Forest*

*October 1963–November 1967*

By September 1967, I had been a prisoner of the Viet Cong for four years. Nick Rowe and I were held in isolation in the U Minh forest the entire time. We did not get the true picture of what was going on in the world, only the propaganda the VC gave us. After the war escalated, we kept seeing the aircraft change. We often wondered how many Americans were in Vietnam.

The local little grocery store up the canal had copies of the American GI newspaper, *Stars and Stripes*, that they wrapped their sugar and everything else in. The guards would bring it back to the camp and toss it away. I picked up a piece of this paper one day. It had the total amount and name of every American unit in Vietnam. We couldn't believe it. We counted five hundred thousand people. We said, "What the hell are we still doing in this prison camp? This war should be over with."

Every night we had to listen to Radio Hanoi. It was a ritual facilitated by the camp interpreter. It played some decent music and a lot of comical commentary—though not intentionally comic. They'd air antiwar statements by different people. I heard Robert Garwood [a turncoat who returned to the U.S. from Vietnam in 1979]. They tried to get us to say something like: "The war is bad. American soldiers go home. Join the Liberation Front and they'll have a lenient policy toward you."

The interrogators told us that if we did not repent we would be tried as criminals and treated accordingly. But the most frightening thing was how they tried to manip-

159

ulate our behavior through Thought Reform, which they did to their own people to maintain political control. For the Viet Cong cadre there was no reason to understand their orders. They just repeated it, memorized it, and believed it. Dissent was not allowed. That is the key to Communist order. Democracy, the ability to question, is diametrically opposed to their system.

It is ironic that they played up the antiwar protests in our country, because in their own system that kind of public dissent is forbidden. It would be dealt with severely, the way the Viet Cong brutally eliminated opposition in the local villages. Self-criticism and peer pressure is the way they police their own actions. Nobody has any privacy—someone is always watching over you and taking notes. I have listened and watched as cadre verbally flayed young kids alive and reduced them to tears. Except for the physical torture, they controlled their own people similar to the way they treated us.

One way they conducted psychological warfare was to show us reports from *The New York Times*, the *Washington Post*, news magazines, and the *Congressional Record*, displaying the antiwar sentiments at home. It was hard to drive ourselves on day after day when the guards showed us newspaper stories of protesters flying the VC and North Vietnamese flags around the Washington Monument, while students burned American flags.

The interrogator, Major Bai, would say, "Look, this is your Capitol. Look where our flag is, look where your flag is. Why do you resist? Your own country looks at the people who support our cause as heroes. Why do you stay here and suffer?"

What was being published in the U.S. was much better propaganda than anything the Viet Cong could write. And while it was disheartening for us, it was a real boost to their self-confidence.

In October 1967 there were four of us in the prison camp: Nick Rowe, myself, and Jackson and Johnson, who were black. The VC based a lot of their propaganda on what the American people were doing. So when Martin Luther King marched on Washington, D.C., the Viet Cong made an announcement. To show appreciation to the black Americans for protesting the war, they would release some black prisoners. The VC believed that any protest in the U.S. was a protest against the war. And though this black march on Washington was just a civil rights demonstration, the Communists saw it as an opportune time. So they prepared these two blacks and myself, because I was a medic.

One of the blacks, Johnson, was dying. He was a little older than the rest of us and he was getting into trouble mentally. He was scared to death the whole time he was there, so the VC took advantage of him. They called him "Da Den"—"Black Skin"—and picked on him a lot. Johnson was about ready to die. I was told, "You keep Johnson alive until we reach a 'neutral country.'" Well, what neutral country was it but Cambodia.

It took about thirty days to move us. Walking, but mostly on the canals at night by sampan. I sat there with a coolie hat on watching thousands and thousands of sampans moving south during the night from the VC sanctuaries in Cambodia. Once we got into Cambodia we saw cache after cache of weapons, huge stockpiles.

They kept us for about two weeks on the border. They fed us—I was down to about ninety-five pounds. I might've gained ten pounds during just that short time on the border.

Jackson and I literally dragged Johnson home. I was told that this man had to live until we got to Phnom Penh, "or else." That man ate more rice than he ever anticipated eating. Johnson was so sick that they were not going to release him. In Phnom Penh I argued with the Communists that he was not well enough to go before the cameras, which was another bunch of Communist bullcrap. They said, "Well, then, we'll just leave him here in the hospital and he won't go on the flight." Jackson and I protested and got him out.

In Phnom Penh the only people we saw were Communists. No free world representatives or press people there. They tried to put us in front of the cameras for the propaganda thing that they had set up. And they showed us a telegram with Martin Luther King's, Ralph Abernathy's, and everybody's name on it from the peace movement. And Tom Hayden was there waiting for us in Phnom Penh. We immediately told him what we thought of him.

We were put on a Czechoslovakian airliner. Johnson was out of it and Jackson was pretty busy taking care of him. And Tom Hayden sat with me. Hayden said, "I'm over here to pick you guys up." I said, "Well, what do you do?" And he couldn't explain. We got into some hot and heavy arguments. Hayden was telling me how bad the war was. And I said, "Have you been over there in combat?" He said, "No." Finally I just said, "If I could get the door open, I would shove your ass out."

Two Cubans and two Russians were on the plane to see that we got where we had to go. They pretended to be innocent bystanders. Hayden was not cooperating with these people. I'm not protecting Hayden—I just think that he was as dumb and ignorant about what was going on as we were. Except that as a representative of the peace movement of the United States, he was supposed to take us to Prague, Czechoslovakia, to participate in a big demonstration with Communist-type propaganda: In solidarity we support the Viet Cong. Here are three prisoners of war that are coming home. This is the lenient policy of the National Liberation Front.

And there were rumors that they would move us to Moscow for the same thing.

From Prague or Moscow, Martin Luther King and his associates were to meet the two blacks in Paris. From there they would escort the prisoners into New York.

We stopped in Bombay and Kuwait. Every time we landed, the Russians and Cubans would make us get into the plane's bathroom. But this one worker came through the aircraft, spraying for insect control. I asked him, "Do you speak English?" He said, "Yes." I asked him, "Would you get a note out to the American Embassy for me?" The note said we were three Americans with no passports or identification flying on a Communist aircraft.

When we touched down in Beirut, Lebanon, a big guy got on the plane. I'll never forget him, his name was Art Beaton. He was with U.S. Federal Aviation. He flashed his credentials and walked right over to us. He stood between us and the Russians and Cubans. He said, "Would you guys like to get off the aircraft?" I think we made our own door.

When we were rescued in Beirut, we had no credentials

whatsoever. And Tom Hayden had none. We all received temporary passports. We were put up in the Hotel Fenizia that night. Yeah, Tom Hayden and I bunked together.

The U.S. Marine guards at the embassy donated clothes for me to wear. Because all I had was that damned pair of Viet Cong black pajamas.

The guy from Federal Aviation volunteered to come back to the States with us. He baby-sat us all the way back, keeping reporters away. When we landed in New York, I'll never forget, two guys in black trench coats picked up Tom Hayden. I don't think his feet touched the ground all the way to the terminal. That's the last I ever heard of Tom Hayden until recently.

During the last election time, Hayden called me up, wrote me letters wanting me to help him on his election. He said, "I did have something to do with the release of you prisoners." I said, "No you didn't." He said, "But I was there when you guys were released." And he said, "All I'm asking from you is a statement that I had something to do with your release."

And at that time I found an old picture of Jane Fonda sitting at antiaircraft guns in Hanoi during the war, wearing a North Vietnamese Army helmet. I bundled up two of those, mailed them to him, and put a note on it: "My grandmother has an old saying, 'Sleep with the dogs, you wake up with the fleas.' Sorry, I can't help you."

I still suffer from the aftereffects of captivity. I came back with a beriberi heart that put me out of the service on a medical discharge. I've got to watch what I do. But I think if a guy can sit down and accept the fact that he's not the physical being that he was before, fine.

I look back at those four years and think, "I could have done something else. I could have gone to college or four years anywhere." Before my discharge, I put in four more years in the service, because I believed that was lost time I owed my government. I regret it, not necessarily because of the lost time, but because of my health. That four years in 'Nam may have shortened my life ten or fifteen years.

Some prisoners had understanding wives they came home to. But a lot of guys had problems. I'm a divorcé. I came home and tried to make a go of it. But the four years I was a prisoner, taken out of the family, taken out of the home ... when I came back I felt that "I'm not needed anymore except for one thing." That was for monetary reasons to hold the family together.

I've talked to other prisoners about this. And I'm not blaming this on a wife who was greedy or anything like that. But it was difficult for a woman to take over a household, raising kids, for as much as seven years. The oldest son has been running the show. And all of a sudden here comes Dad back. They've got to find a place for him in the house. I felt that happened to me. We tried to get along. And when I think back to those days, maybe if I would have asked for some counseling it would have worked.

Even today I find it difficult. Immediately after I was out of the service, I went to work for the navy at the Survival Center, where I was needed. But I left California because the pace of living was too fast. I decided to come back to North Carolina.

Now, I don't know if it's because of my physical problems but I'm having a difficult time finding a job. Not that I need it—I have a sizable retirement check and my wife is working. But I need to work, for my own sanity, just to have something to do. I'm fifty-one years old. How many times can you putter around the house, mow the yard, or wash your car?

# PSYCHOLOGICAL WARFARE

--------

## Truong Nhu Tang

*Minister of Justice*
*National Liberation Front*

*1960–1976*

As a Central Committee member of the NLF before 1968,
I shared responsibility for mobilizing the population in the
towns. And although I became the minister of justice in
the PRG in 1968, my main job was always psychological
warfare actions.

Psychological warfare is an integral part of the "popular
war," which mobilizes all political, economical, psychological, military, and diplomatic fields. Psychological warfare is the principal decisive arm of the popular war.
Another section of the NLF was responsible for working
with groups in the West opposed to the war, and Western
media to weaken the resolve of the American government.
This is also an important aspect of psychological warfare.

Our aim was to present ourselves to the world as a large
representation of the South's population. And the American media is easily open to suggestion and false information given by the Communist agents. The society is
completely hypnotized by the media. (For example, Pham
Xuan An manipulated several important American reporters in Vietnam for years. Today An is a high-ranking
officer in Communist intelligence in Ho Chi Minh City.)

The tragedy was that the PRG told international and
Vietnamese public opinion that our movement is a nationalist movement, with our end to create a democratic
Vietnam. And that our political regime would not be Communist.

At that time it was very easy to mobilize people in the
United States because the U.S. was overengaged. Thou-

sands of American boys were in Vietnam and there were
anti-U.S. demonstrations in Washington. In South Vietnam, religious organizations, like Buddhists or Catholic,
protested against the regime. But behind them were always some political activists who were Communists. This
is a tactic we call "the watermelon"—green on the outside
and red on the inside. These tactics were used in South
Vietnam before 1975. This is a tactic of the Soviet bloc
for propaganda against the free world.

The aim is not so much to achieve direct support of
Soviet goals, but to make opposition to the policy of the
free world. Like with Vietnam, we were not so much
looking for supporters, but rather for opponents to the
American and Saigon regimes in order to create a crisis
among allied governments of the free world. And paralyze
them so that they cannot act. And to isolate the U.S.
government from its people.

Another big problem is the way the Communists twist
ideology. They always use words like: freedom, peace,
democracy. And the better impulses of people who truly
want peace are manipulated into a popular movement
against the free world's defenses. While in the Soviet bloc,
no such movement is tolerated. And they continue to build
their offensive military capabilities and continue acts of
aggression by themselves or their surrogates.

Now, this is not to say that America did not make mistakes in Vietnam, or that war is anything but a horrible
thing. But I can assure you that not only were the South
Vietnamese and American public lied to by the Communists. Even those of us who lived in the jungle and
sacrificed and fought for true independence and concord
were made victims of the Communists' lies and deceit.

# RINGS OF STEEL

## Rufus Phillips

*Consultant*
*U.S. State Department*
*South Vietnam*

*Summer Visits, 1965–1968*

I visited Vietnam in the summer of 1967. In Saigon I ran
into Pham, a Vietnamese friend. We were just chatting
about what was going on. And he said, "An incident oc-
curred yesterday, right outside of Saigon. The area is in-
secure as hell."

I said, "Jesus, the ARVN supposedly had this big op-
eration with Rings of Steel and all, for security around
Saigon." And he said, "There is a post about four miles
outside Cholon where the local militia got decimated.
Maybe you would like to go out and see it." And I said,
"Sure. I'll go with you."

Pham had a little Renault car. We drove out there. And
Jesus, it had been a massacre. And the worst part of it
was, it had taken six hours for any relief to come. I asked
survivors why. They said reinforcements came from way
across the rice fields from the Long An provincial headquarters. I asked why. They explained, "We don't communicate with Saigon. We communicate with Long An."
And I said, "That's the damndest thing I've ever heard.
What the hell kind of security around Saigon is this?"

So I wrote this up and Ed Lansdale, special assistant
to the ambassador, took it into the embassy counsel meeting. And, God, Westmoreland went through the roof and
said, "This couldn't be so."

They sent Brigadier General Freund to see me. And I
said, "All right, I'll get Pham and we'll go out there tomorrow." So the general showed up wearing civvies, with
a .45 under his arm. Pham showed up in a taxi, his car

had broken down. I said, "How do you feel about this, Fritz?" And he said, "Well, I guess it's all right." So we went out in a taxicab.

He interviewed the same guys, got the same information, came back, wrote up a report. And not a goddamned thing happened. And if you want to know how the hell the VC were able to bring in those units during the Tet offensive, that's how they got them into Saigon.

The South Vietnamese government kept special battalions and special security units in control of Saigon. But they wanted to keep them decentralized politically. So a huge no-man's-land developed where nobody had responsibility.

# THE DUCK POND
--------

## David Sciacchitano

*Mechanic*
*U.S. Air Force*
*Quang Tri*
*1967–1968*

During the Tet offensive, I was at a small MACV compound in Quang Tri, sixty or seventy people. We had a small air force contingent. And there were some army and marines.

I was a mechanic at the landing strip. But we all had to stand guard duty. I hated it. It was always when you were in bed that the bad stuff started happening. It never happened when there was an alert. The intelligence was always wrong.

Tet 1968 came around and I was told, "We're all going to be in the bunkers." And I was so tired and I hadn't eaten. All I wanted to do was get cleaned up and go to bed. Then the news came that Hue had fallen. Everybody panicked.

There was a Vietnamese army fort across the road. They started firing and some army guy along our line started firing. There was absolutely no discipline except for the marines and officers. The enlisted guys were mostly typists—totally undependable. They began shooting and the guy next to me begins blasting away.

I was on top of a flat bunker with an M-60 machine gun. We didn't have time to put sandbags up. Of course, I didn't think anything was going to happen. I thought it was all bullshit. But that night we did come under attack. The guy next to me had no idea what to do. He was carrying a knife, a .45 pistol, an M-2 rifle, and he had an AK-47 with no ammunition. I gave him my M-16. And he lost that as soon as fairly heavy shelling began coming in.

He instantly panicked and tried to jump off the bunker. A truck right next to us blew up. Mortars were hitting a couple of feet away. The bunkers on both sides of us were hit. A guy was killed on a bunker near mine. So it wasn't the situation where you'd want to jump off the bunker and run. I had to grab him and hold him on the bunker.

Another guy who panicked was an army first sergeant, a tough-talking guy. There was this little pond in front of our compound where a dozen ducks lived with claymore mines around it. As panic started, claymores went off, bullets were flying, incoming mortars were slamming in. A lot of ducks were running around quacking. I was amazed when dawn came and all the ducks poked their heads out of their wings. Not a single one had been hit.

And there was a house across the way. Six o'clock every morning a woman came out to sweep the porch. The morning after this battle was no exception. The army sergeant jumps up with his rifle and tries to shoot her. He ordered a marine on a .50-caliber machine gun to shoot her. He said she was a Viet Cong.

At the same time, there were some refugees who in the light of day packed up their belongings and were running down the road. The North Vietnamese had hit the town from three sides: one regiment got lost; one was decimated; and the other hit an ARVN airborne company. So fighting in the area was quite heavy.

As the refugees were streaming down the road the sergeant wanted the machine-gunner to fire on them. This was a young marine, but he knew better than to shoot people trundling their goods down the road in handcarts and bicycles. So the sergeant grabbed a rifle and tried to kill this woman on the porch. Her house was already full of holes—it looked like Swiss cheese. I don't know how anybody survived inside that house. But luckily, somebody grabbed him and prevented him from shooting.

And there was a young air force guy. He didn't know anything. He had an M-16 that he really didn't know how to shoot. And he was stuck in an unprotected area all by himself. He scooped out a hole with his hand to use as a foxhole. This same first sergeant came by before the attack started and said, "We don't need any sandbags." And kicked over this young guy's cover.

Well, the first bomb that came in landed right behind

that position and almost killed this kid. He was all full of holes. The sergeant got a little piece of shrapnel in his foot that he was later medevac'd for. He went on to a soft job in Danang with a nice Purple Heart.

The air force guy spent a couple of months in the hospital. Then he came back to the compound . . . For one reason: the air force was going to sue him. He'd left his M-16 behind when he was wounded. After the explosion, he yelled for a medic. A navy nurse ran over, grabbed him, and dragged him to safety. And he was medevac'd out. Of course, nobody knew whatever happened to his M-16. So the air force was going to charge him.

He came back to try to find out what happened to his M-16. The poor pathetic guy was running around looking for it. They wanted him to pay for his helmet and flak vest, too. They were going to charge him around four hundred bucks, which was a lot of money in those days. We were getting paid about one hundred fifty bucks a month or something. Not counting fifty-five dollars combat pay.

# THE CEASE-FIRE

## Tran Van Luu

*Student*
*Saigon*

*1960s*

The feeling among students in Saigon during the early to mid 1960s was very joyful, very naive, because they knew nothing much about the war. The war was outside of the city, in the villages. And the majority of the students only wished to have an easy life and didn't bother to engage in politics.

There were some students on the Left whose fathers were former members of the resistance faction dominated by the Communists. And there were some very anti-Communist students. But the majority of the students were neutral. But this all changed during the 1968 Tet offensive.

Tet has always been a very sacred time for Vietnamese families. People got very angry at the Viet Cong attack during this time. Even the military did not have a precaution against a possible attack. Because the majority of the soldiers were celebrating Tet with their families. Everybody was very shocked and surprised. Because the holiday cease-fire was first suggested by the VC. So the Viet Cong played a trick by asking for a longer cease-fire than in previous years. And they used this to launch the attack on the cities.

At first rumors were rampant during the offensive that the Americans had purposely let the VC into Saigon to test the will of our people. But after one or two days, we saw the Americans fighting against the Communists. At that time we realized the true danger. Because the enemy were not only in the villages, but right in the city. Then, in the second offensive, the Communists were shelling with 240-mm rockets all over the city. Can you imagine

*David Schiacchitano*, Vietnam

*Gen. Edward Lansdale* (standing center, tipping cap) Front row:
Gen. John O. Daniel (left), U.S. Ambassador G. F. Reinhardt,
President Ngo Dinh Diem

*Truong Nhu Tang*

EDDIE ADAMS

*Anne Miller* with
President Diem, Hue, 1955

USIA-USOM

HANK PASCAL

*Mrs. Le Thi Anh*

*Ha Thuc Ky* during his 1967 national presidential bid in South Vietnam

*Hoang Van Chi*

*Dan Pitzer* (left), Chuck Allen, Col. Nick Rowe

*Rufus Phillips*, Vietnam, 1955

CINDY BURNHAM

*Chuck Allen* (left) outside Khe Sanh, 1963

*Gen. Lu Mong Lan* welcoming Viet Cong "Hoi Chanh" defectors, 1965

*Ken Moorefield* (second from right),
anti-piracy patrol, Thailand, 1983

*Frank McCarthy*, Vietnam

*Edward Brady* (right) receiving Bronze Star, Vietnam

*Jim Noonan*

*Jonathan Polansky,* Vietnam

*Adolphus Stuart,* Vietnam

*Mark Berent,* Cambodia, 1973

*Tan Van Luu*

*Peter Braestrup,*
Khe Sanh, 1968

*Col. Harry Summers,*
Sergeant, Korean War

*Dr. Yang Dao*

*Berta Romero* (second from left),
Thailand, 1978

*Chhang Song*

*Eddie Adams*, Israel, October War, 1973

*Al Santoli,*
Ban Vinai Refugee Camp,
Thailand 1983

*Doan Van Toai* with author Henry Miller

*Nguyen Cong Hoan*

*Mrs. Keo Vey* (center)

*Kassie Neou*

*Dr. Erwin Parson*

*Eve Burton* (center), Songkhla Refugee Camp, Thailand

*Kay Bosiljevac*

Capt. Michael Bosiljevac,
Missing in Action in Vietnam since 1972

that? It was just like raining bombs for two or three days. I had friends and neighbors who were killed.

Around my house was a small wall. And beyond the wall one man was killed. His leg was cut off by the fragments of a rocket. Another rocket fell into our yard. It was in the morning. My mother saw something orange-colored in the yard. She touched it and got her hand burned. An explosion immediately woke me up. I didn't know what happened.

To see the smoke ... and the noise ... it was terrible. The most terrible time.

# TACTICAL VICTORY, STRATEGIC DEFEAT

--------

## Col. Harry Summers

*Political Military Action Officer*
*U.S. Army General Staff*
*Pentagon*

*1971–1973*

In war, to differentiate between the tactical level and the strategic level can sometimes be quite contradictory. The classic case in Vietnam was the Tet offensive.

Tactically, the American and South Vietnamese armies were enormously successful in destroying the Viet Cong during the Tet offensive. Even the Viet Cong leaders admit that they were decimated during Tet. But on the strategic level, Tet was a disastrous defeat for the United States, probably the culminating defeat of the Vietnam War. Because of what it did to public opinion, that had been led to believe that the end of the war was in sight.

Of course, the news media played a part in this. Because they didn't see it as a tactical success either. They were reporting on the instant and in too many cases did not leave Saigon. And some newspeople, even today, hold the North Vietnamese General Giap as the model to emulate. But Giap by his own admission took six hundred thousand battlefield deaths during the period 1964–68— the equivalent of seven million American casualties—and to no immediate effect.

One of the things a newspaper article said about him was that Giap really tricked General Westmoreland by the feint at Khe Sanh to open the way for Tet. But both Khe Sanh and Tet were disasters for the North Vietnamese at a tactical level, in terms of casualties and results. But they did have the strategic effect on the home front of the United States. Probably the greatest strategic effect was on President Johnson.

It's ironic that from Tet on, we and the South Vietnamese—to give them the credit they never received—were quite successful in rooting out the Viet Cong. There's been studies done on this by academics that point out that after Tet 'sixty-eight, the Viet Cong were perceived by Vietnamese peasantry as losers. And by 1974–75 the guerilla threat wasn't there. People were driving from Saigon to Vung Tau and up and down the coastal highway without fear.

Everybody hears about the U.S. inflation of body counts. But there also was a gross inflation of body counts by the Communists, fabricating all the great successes they had. And evidently, their leaders back up the pike said, "Since you're doing so great, do it again." So in case after case, they'd attack U.S. positions and we'd stack them up in rows. Because of the immense firepower that we could bring to bear.

There was no case where U.S. forces were defeated in a major battle by the North Vietnamese or the Viet Cong. We won every one of the battles. Our problem was, as Clausewitz pointed out 150 years ago, that successful battles in and of themselves are meaningless, unless they're directed to a strategic end.

Public opinion at home turned when the average citizen perceived that we didn't know what the hell we were doing. That we had no plan to end the war. And we didn't know what constituted victory. By 1968, the public had given us four years, their money, and their sons. So I don't blame the American people. I do blame the national leadership, including the military leadership, for not setting clear and definable goals and objectives.

We had some of our top military leaders appearing before Congress saying, "We're not trying to achieve a victory in Vietnam like Appomattox or World War II." And the obvious question of the guy on the street was, "What the hell are we doing there, then?"

Meanwhile, the North Vietnamese goals were very clearly expressed. They very clearly said that they were fighting the second *Indochina* War. So their use of Laos and Cambodia was never hidden. They called Cambodia's Parrot's Beak area "Kennedy's Garden." Because it was the United States that permitted them to use the sanctuaries.

It's amazing what we did. It was a self-inflicted wound. Primarily because of the misreading of what a "limited war" means. The only meaning of limited war that makes any sense is that it's a war fought for limited political objectives—which most wars have always been throughout history. But it's not necessarily limited in terms of territory. Especially when your adversary is using Cambodia and Laos.

Some people say that the Vietnam War was doomed to fail to begin with. But that is a cop-out. Alexander Solzhenitsyn has said, "We shouldn't hide under fate's petticoats." It wasn't "dialectical materialism" that conquered Vietnam, it was four North Vietnamese armored corps.

# GRASPING STRAWS

## Peter Braestrup
*Bureau Chief*
*Washington Post*
*Saigon*

*January 1968–February 1969*

I took over as Saigon bureau chief for the *Washington Post* on January 15, 1968. Tet caught a lot of news organizations in Vietnam, on January 31, 1968, with one shoe on and one shoe off. A lot of people were changing over reporters at that time. Saigon was supposed to be off-limits. And the VC had declared a two-week truce that we thought for PR reasons they would carry on.

The siege of Khe Sanh had begun. And that's where I was when Tet began. But even there the guns stopped for a whole day. I was able to tour all of Hill 881 and the outposts by helicopter. I had a cigarette and it was a beautiful day. And that night, the shit hit the fan.

I remember going through the city of Hue right before Tet. There were all these Vietnamese going to visit relatives, all dressed up in bright colors. Little did they know that two days later they would be caught in the middle of a big fight. After Hue was retaken, mass graves were found where the Communists had executed or buried alive 2,800 civilians. And another 2,000 Hue residents remained missing.

In Vietnam, before Tet, a reporter could pick and choose his battle or war. And if you didn't want to go, you stayed in Saigon or Danang or Nha Trang to enjoy the beautiful beaches. It was a very shocking experience to have the war come right in on them.

In Saigon at that time, the whole press corps was kind of living day to day. Newsmen don't have objectives, they act off their instinct: what's a story, what isn't a story, what interests you. And combat reporting in Vietnam was unlike that in Korea or World War II because of the helicopter. Television crews could not film at night, so the incentive to spend the night in the field was limited. They wanted to come in, do their film, and get out. The helicopter was a corrupting influence. You could fly in and get a feature story without ever understanding what the soldiers had been through before you got there or what happened after you left.

And many of these reporters were inexperienced in military operations or in the tactics of the Communists. Particularly the television people had no real grip on the football game. They could go out and take pictures of the players and the drama. But they were like sportswriters who had no concept of the game they were covering.

They could see the human suffering, the dramatic image. They could show people shooting, usually our people. Then at Tet, they started showing our people getting wounded. The pictures largely showed American troops ducking, under pressure and at the mercy of the other side. Which was misleading.

One of the big problems for war reporters is that they can't be everywhere. Like an infantryman, your war is what is going on in your immediate area—if you get badly cut up, then you think the whole war is going badly. This is the same for a reporter or cameraman. One of the great limitations of Vietnam reporting was that there were very few pieces of intelligent journalism that related the individual incident that was described or filmed to the overall picture.

This was partly because nobody knew what was coming next. The siege at Khe Sanh became the big story after the recapture of Hue, on February 24. "What was the next drama?" There was an important drama going on—the Viet Cong were retreating all over the country. But instead, the press corps switched to the Khe Sanh melodrama. And Khe Sanh was portrayed as being under extreme pressure long after the North Vietnamese, in fact, had started to withdraw. And long after they had sustained heavy casualties.

We couldn't get into their areas to see, so nobody could report this. But what could have been told after March

1, when the weather cleared up, was that the North Vietnamese shelling was very inaccurate for the volume of artillery and rockets that were thrown at the marines. There was relatively little hardware poured into the place compared to Dien Bien Phu. And we kept calling it "another Dien Bien Phu." And in terms of the total number of men engaged and the number of casualties, some of the marine companies and battalions at Khe Sanh took a beating. But as a whole they suffered less than other American units in the field elsewhere.

Few reporters bothered to go out with Vietnamese or Cambodian units to see what was going on in what was supposed to be "the real war." The big headache was that the South Vietnamese didn't know how to handle the American press. Nobody does, particularly in Asia. If you had a Vietnamese friend, you could get out with them. But it was a big pain in the neck. It was easier to go out with American advisors.

During the Tet offensive at Hue, I spent a lot of time doing after-action reports with the South Vietnamese. Some print reporters did. The TV reporters tended to focus on the Americans. It was ethnocentricity. Reporters did the same thing in World War II, concentrating on the Americans but not the British or our other allies. It was an important flaw because the key to the whole American effort obviously was the performance of the Vietnamese. And we correspondents really didn't force our editors to take that into consideration.

If anything, the South Vietnamese were generally portrayed as victims, incompetents, or crooks. No one, even today, mentions that more than two hundred thousand Vietnamese soldiers died during the war. None of their units ever went over to the other side. There were far more Viet Cong defecting to our side. That never got across.

And the other scapegoat of the war was the American veteran. There are a lot of veterans who, because of the reception they received, had a difficult time of it when they returned home. And the media are as much to blame as anybody. They maintained and sustained the negative stereotype, with hardly a good word said about the veteran for many years after "peace with honor."

The press, in terms of themes they convey, are a reflective institution. They have cultural biases and there are trends and fashions. But on the big issues, the president of the United States dominates when he wants to. Why did the media press the panic button at Tet? President Lyndon Johnson seemed to have been struck by a kind of immobility. He had just had the Pueblo affair with North Korea. And suddenly Tet comes.

Johnson knew that something big was coming because General Westmoreland had told him. He had sent reinforcements ahead of time—the 11th Infantry Brigade from Hawaii and two brigades of the 101st Airborne.

But Johnson never mentioned this in his State of the Union Address. He was doing everything possible to downplay the idea of war—and, with an election year in progress, upgrade the idea of peace negotiations. So he failed to prepare the public or the press.

From the start, the President had failed to define a clear strategy for winning the war. He failed to mobilize the country or decide how we were going to end the war. He was grasping for straws and buying time, hoping something would turn up. Public opinion—the man on the street—doesn't quite know what's going on, but he's not satisfied with this. So Lyndon brought home the famous "progress campaign" of 1967. Everybody was brought in from Vietnam, including General Westmoreland, to say, "We're making progress." That was short-term relief in the Gallup polls for Lyndon. Then comes Tet.

All of a sudden, everybody is saying, "We can't go on like this." The hawks are saying it behind closed doors, the doves are saying it out loud. And Johnson isn't saying anything. For two months he doesn't say anything and takes no decisive action. He did not do what Richard Nixon did in the 1972 election year—send in the B-52s and mine Haiphong Harbor—take a forceful retaliatory posture against the North Vietnamese. Nixon's popularity went up. And though he wasn't popular with the press, his policy was coherent. They understood that he had a scenario. He did not leave a vacuum. He was a decisive, forceful president in a time of crisis. That is what the public looks to. And that is what the press looks to also.

At Tet, Lyndon Johnson in effect got into his bunker.

He left the political debate and furor in the hands of his critics and to the press. Johnson was in a crisis of his own making. The press will aggravate any president's problems. If the President is nervous or indecisive, the press will make it worse. And more of his critics will come out of the woodwork.

The press, in effect, becomes a prism. Concentrating the heat on the White House. But the President starts the demoralization himself. He's like the platoon leader. If they run into an ambush, all the troops look to the platoon leader to take charge. If he's lying on the ground for ten, twenty, a hundred seconds, the troops get demoralized. That's what happened at Tet. One trooper, like Walter Cronkite, who's a little shook, will say, "Let's get the hell out of here." Panic will start. And the press will overreact to everything. That's the way they are.

Add to that problem the fact that for every American who went to Vietnam, the war began the day you got there and ended the day you went home. Very few reporters stayed with the story. The war changed every year, and it depended on where you went and what your editors were interested in. And you've got to remember, a reporter can always leave the battlefield. That's the big difference between a reporter and a soldier.

That a reporter could experience what an infantryman experiences, nobody but a wacko would think possible. But a lot of these people in Vietnam were so egocentric that they in effect claimed to be doing that. "Bringing the war into your living room." In reality, they showed edited images of isolated events. And nothing lies better than a camera.

# THE TET PHOTO

--------

## Eddie Adams

*Photographer*
*Associated Press*
*Vietnam*

*1965–1975*

In Vietnam you had two different kinds of newsmen. You
had the guys who covered the war, and the guys who
covered the briefings. Among the very few guys who actually went out to the field there was a hard core. We
didn't have respect for the people in Saigon.

Where the whole thing really turned around was the
Tet offensive. The situation in Saigon was covered mostly
by people who had never gone out to the field. I've never
seen panic like this. I couldn't believe it. Someone came
running up to the AP office with all kinds of guns, telling
me, "You'd better get a gun, you'd better get a gun."

I just looked at these people. I mean, it was really sad.
Some were well respected—I could name names. These
were the heroes, you know, writing all the stories.

I was there before the marines. I first got to Vietnam
the end of January or beginning of February 'sixty-five.
A couple months later, I covered the marines coming in,
with all the girls with flowers waiting on shore. That was
a riot.

When I went into the field with American advisors, one
out of six operations we would get shot at. It was a big
deal to get shot at then. You'd walk in the jungle with
advisors for a few days and really get pissed off if you
didn't get shot at. Because there wasn't any story then.
And when the marines first made contact [against the
enemy] in Vietnam, I was the only press guy with them.
So I had the banner headline all over the world.

It was a marine reconnaissance unit. There was a lieutenant, Sean del Grosso, who is now a full colonel in

China. I'll never forget this as long as I live: They start getting incoming fire. And del Grosso says, "Fix bayonets." I thought, "Son of a bitch, like the movies, man." I was so excited. Everybody drew their bayonets. And I'm going apeshit with these pictures. It was unreal.

I watched the war all through the different stages during the years I was there. And the war correspondents in Vietnam never referred to ourselves as Americans. We would say, "The Americans did this" and "The Americans did that." I mean, all of us were Americans. But it was very strange that so many times I'd find myself doing this when I'd be talking to somebody.

I did very little in Saigon. Not more than a dozen photographs in all the time I was there. When Tet first hit, I took off immediately for Nha Trang. Because that was the first area where the North Vietnamese were reported moving in. Little did I know that Saigon would be hit. So I was stuck in Nha Trang for a day or two while everything else was blowing up at other places. Nha Trang sucked— there was nothing there.

I flew back to Saigon because things were still going on. AP and NBC were next door to each other. We used to work together a lot. Because if a story moved on the wire, they knew they would get the story on TV. We heard this battle was taking place at the An Quang pagoda. So we all teamed up in one car.

The North Vietnamese or the Viet Cong were inside the pagoda, shooting at the South Vietnamese army, the police, and whoever else. So we come into the fighting— a lot of people were caught in the cross fire, the typical little battle. At about the same time, we all decided that we had seen enough. As we were heading back to the car, we saw the police walking out of a building with this prisoner. His hands were tied and they were walking him down the street. So like any newsman, you photograph him in case he trips and falls or somebody takes a swing at him, until they load him on the wagon and drive off. It was just a routine thing.

We get to the corner of the street. And all of a sudden, out of nowhere, comes General Loan, the national police chief. I was about five feet away from him, and I see him reach for his pistol. I thought he was going to threaten the prisoner. So as quick as he brought his pistol up, I took a picture. But it turned out he shot him. And the speed of my shutter . . . the bullet hadn't left his head yet. It was just coming out the other end. There was no blood until he was on the ground—whoosh. That's when I turned my back and wouldn't take a picture. There's a limit, certain times you don't take pictures.

I thought absolutely nothing of it. He shot him, so what? Because people die in fuckin' war. And I just happened to be there this time. This is not an unusual occurrence. I could tell you lots of stories—heads being chopped off, all kinds of hairy stuff.

And I didn't find this out until much later, but the prisoner who was killed had himself killed a police major who was one of Loan's best friends, and knifed his entire family. The wife, six kids . . . the whole family. When they captured this guy, I didn't know that. I just happened to be there and took the picture. And all of a sudden I destroy a guy's life. I'm talking about the general, not the Viet Cong—he would have gotten shot if I was there or not. Look, that's what I was there for. And I'd do it again tomorrow. But I don't like destroying people's lives from a picture for the wrong reason.

And later I heard from a lot of people, "Why didn't you stop him from shooting?" I said, "Come on, man. This is war." Right after he shot the guy, Loan walked over to me and the NBC people. All he said was, "They killed many of my men and many of your people." And walked away.

I'm not saying what he did was right or wrong. But I ask, "If you were the general, and they killed your people and their children, how do you know what you would have done?"

In the next couple of days, I started getting telexes. I thought, "What the hell?" Because when I sent the film in, I didn't even say that it should be processed. I said, "I think I've got some guy from the police shooting some Viet Cong." And I went out to eat lunch, I was hungry. And I thought absolutely nothing of it.

I didn't know until a couple of days later when I started getting these playback reports from all over the world. The photo was all over the front pages. Full page in Germany, different newspapers all over the world and America. I had no idea . . . But it was very one-sided. I didn't have a picture of that Viet Cong blowing away the family. It was very detrimental—perfect propaganda for North Vietnam.

When I arrived in Vietnam in 1983, a Vietnamese government journalist greets me. He says, "You've got to come to our war museum. We have your photograph on very big display." I never went to the fuckin' place. He wanted to interview me. And I didn't want to seem rude because I was a guest in their country. So I kept saying, "We'll try to fit it in." But each time he tried to reach me, I said, "Oh jeez, I have to go to . . ." So I never got interviewed. And I never went to that war museum either.

So I tell everybody, "Joe Rosenthal has a monument in Washington on Iwo Jima, for his famous pictures. I have one in Hanoi."

In 'sixty-eight, after the picture appeared and things were happening, I got a message from New York saying, "We need a story on who this guy Loan is and what he does." So I volunteered to do it. The guys in the AP office said, "Don't go near the guy. Stay away." And I said, "Fuck it, man. I want to do the story."

Every day for at least a week I'd go to Loan's office. I'd knock on the door and some colonel would answer. I'd say, "Can I see Colonel Loan?" [His rank at the time.] And the response would be, "No, he's all tied up. He doesn't have any time."

At the end of the week they said, "Okay." So I go in. And the first thing Loan says to me is, "The only reason I'm seeing you is because you're so persistent. Sit down." So I sat down. I never mentioned the picture at all. And I hoped he didn't know that I took it. I said, "Colonel, I'd like to do a story on you for the AP, and live with you and go around with you for a while." And he walks over to me. Pushed his nose up against mine. He said, "I know the Vietnamese who took that picture."

It was too much, man. He said, "Vietnamese." In other words, he wasn't blaming me. Then he sat down and said, "You know, after that happened, my wife gave me hell for not taking the film from the photographer. She thinks that all I had to worry about was some photographer's film."

# PLAYER DRAMATIC TEAMS

## Ron Norris

*Military Intelligence Advisor*
*Military Assistance Command Vietnam (MACV)*
*Vinh Long Province*

*May 1968–December 1969*

In May 1968 I was assigned as an advisor to South Vietnamese military intelligence in Vinh Long Province, in the middle of the Mekong Delta. In our area during Tet, the main-force VC units had been decimated. But the most effective weapon the liberation front still had was psyops—psychological warfare. So that's what we chose to combat. It was very, very difficult.

I was receiving newspapers from home, Greenville, South Carolina. Surprisingly, the U.S. media accounts of how we "lost" Tet were reaching Vinh Long through Hanoi before I would receive my paper. And of course, the local people, knowing it was the American press, asked, "Why would the Americans say they lost if they had won?"

The problem was the lack of communication with the government in Saigon. And the people could not see what was happening in the rest of the country, or even in the outlying areas around their districts. So we worked on that.

We developed our own little psy-ops theater teams, Player Dramatic Teams, that went out and entertained people. Read the newspaper to them during lunch breaks, over loudspeaker systems. So that they could know what the various newspapers in Saigon were saying. And that the VC were indeed defeated. It took a while, but we were fairly successful.

The Player Dramatic Teams had a lot of young girls, high school students, who wanted to participate. Traditional Player Dramatic Teams had existed for centuries in Vietnam. Minstrel troupes that would sing and present little skits. Basically we wore black pajamas, no costumes as such. We performed traditional skits and songs that had existed for years and were appreciated by the country people.

Besides the Player Dramatic Teams, we also worked on programs to improve conditions in the villages. One particular incident always sticks in my mind. We built, through U.S. funds, a five-room schoolhouse. The villagers were all involved. The schoolhouse was completed and we had a dedication scheduled. Five o'clock that morning, the VC blew up the school.

I walked down to the site as the children arrived for their first day and found they didn't have a school. So they had an impromptu demonstration up to the district town. No teachers involved. These were grade-school children. They made little posters denouncing the VC for destroying their right to education.

Even in this rural part of the Delta, the Vietnamese treasured education. It was a big thing to them.

# TICKET-PUNCHING

## Ken Moorefield

*Company Commander and Aide-de-camp*
*1st & 25th Infantry Divisions*
*III Corps*

*July 1969–July 1970*

What we called the second battle of Tet took place in
April 1968. I was still an advisor with the ARVN 21st
Division in the Delta. During Tet we had seriously dam-
aged the Viet Cong's ability to fight in An Xuyen Province. In the second battle, they were down to the twelve-
and thirteen-year-olds. They were scraping the bottom of
the barrel. So there was a great opportunity to press our
victory to its natural conclusion.

During this second battle, the VC tried to take Ca Mau
city again. The battle lasted three days. On the second
day, we were counterattacking and pushing the Viet Cong
battalions away from the city. Ca Mau was built like the
hub of a wagon wheel, the spokes being canals. We were
pushing the VC along one of these canals outside the city
and the battalion commander and myself were in front of
our troops. The VC were hiding behind a couple of foot-
high dikes in spider holes [small fighting holes] with overhead cover. They had set up a machine-gun position that
we could not knock out. We were taking tremendous casualties along our front line.

Our Cobra helicopter gunships couldn't determine where
they were. So I had to expose myself in the open to direct
the gunship fire. I took a bullet in my arm and sank into
the canal. Some Vietnamese soldiers grabbed me before
I drowned and pulled me onto the rice paddy behind the
dike. In the next hour we continued our counterattack
across the open rice paddy and drove the VC out of their
positions. A U.S. medevac helicopter took me to the U.S.

9th Division headquarters in Tan An. And subsequently, I was evacuated to Walter Reed Hospital in Washington, D.C.

I no sooner hit Washington than Martin Luther King was assassinated. I was sitting in the hospital watching Fourteenth Street and Sixteenth Street burning down. Troops protected the hospital. I thought, "My God, this is eerie. I left the battlefield in Vietnam. And now I find that my country is part of that battlefield."

I was shocked to find that the Tet offensive, which I had experienced as a tremendous victory in the classical military sense, was somehow being construed by the media as defeat. Aspects of the Tet battle, like the VC penetrating the embassy grounds in Saigon, had been sensationalized. While the fact that we had eliminated a good part of the VC infrastructure and decisively dominated them on the battlefield was completely missed by the press.

In May 1968, while I was still in Walter Reed, the army told me that I was going back to Vietnam. I called up army personnel and said, "In case you didn't know it, I'm sitting here in Walter Reed Hospital." They said, "Oh, we didn't know. But you're going back to Vietnam in twelve months." I said, "Okay." But with my experiences in the United States between 1968 and early 1969, I was going back with greater trepidation.

I realized that the American public's support was beginning to waver based on what they were getting from the press. And for an officer like myself, responsible for the sons of American mothers and fathers, I could see the task was going to be more and more challenging.

After I was in the hospital for about three months and had three operations on my arm, I was sent to the advanced infantry officer training course at Fort Benning, Georgia. And what we studied for a whole year was the land war on the plains of Europe. But ninety percent of us in the course were going straight back to Vietnam. I had to demand that the army send me to jungle warfare school before I went back to Vietnam. These guys wanted to put me into a nuclear-weapons course.

I said, "Listen, Major, I'm going to be a company commander in Vietnam. I've been in the hospital. And I've been sitting in that classroom for a year. I need to sharpen my skills before I go back to Vietnam, so I can do my job better." And after a shouting match, the guy finally agreed to send me to jungle warfare school in Panama for a few weeks.

Where was our focus? We never accepted that this was the war we had to fight. I'm not sure that the highest level of the armed forces ever accepted it. I didn't feel that those of us who were fighting the war, who had the obligation to lead young men into battle and ask them to die for their country, were getting the kind of support we needed from the senior officer corps. There were inevitable conflicts in command that were intensified by the very strategy, the very technology, that we used to fight the war.

I have been in situations in Vietnam where an infantry platoon or company was fighting on the ground, trying to attack across an open rice paddy in the hot sun of the day. The battalion commander and his operations officer were sitting in a helicopter at a thousand feet. The brigade commander was at fifteen hundred feet. The division commander was at twenty-five hundred feet. The corps commander was at three thousand feet. And I swear to God, one day I was in a battle where COMUS MACV [Commander of U.S. forces] was at thirty-five hundred feet—all of them over the same battle.

Now, I can assure you from the point of view of some infantryman who is down there sweating his ass off, facing hot lead at very close quarters, it's very difficult to respect or identify with his leadership sitting up in the clouds in starched fatigues. There wasn't a man, short of maybe the first sergeant or my platoon leaders, who knew the name of our battalion commander.

I learned that in an army which is not mainly composed of professionals, you have to earn the respect and support of the young soldiers. Just because you're a senior officer it does not mean that your authority is going to be sanctified.

I was a company commander in the 9th Infantry Division, 2nd Battalion of the 47th Infantry. Most of the men in my company were draftees or volunteers. Young men had been made sergeants during the first year to eighteen months of their military service. They were very bright, creative, and very determined. But there was no question that they were not going to follow someone into battle who they thought didn't have their best interest at heart.

I was governing them with their consent. And only as long as I proved that I was clearly providing the best responsible leadership for them. I told them, "The best chance that you have to survive here is to listen to me, follow me. Support the other men in the unit as best you can. That is going to enhance your chances of returning home to your families."

We had gone beyond the point of saying, "We're here to defend South Vietnamese freedom" or "We are here to defend democracy." The waters had been too politically muddied by then. And I'm not sure that in most wars by the time a man gets to the front lines that kind of appeal works. He'll die for the man on his left and his right, maybe for his platoon leader or company commander. What drives him on day to day, moment to moment, is the strength of personal bonds within the unit itself.

I did not waste lives needlessly. But I was not in any sense timid. My attitude about military operations is the best defense is a good offense. You're better off keeping the enemy off-balance, therefore at a disadvantage, rather than waiting for him to come to you. So at times my troops thought that I was a little bit crazy. Because I sought opportunities to pursue the enemy, even into their base-camp areas. However, we took very few casualties. And I think that as long as the men had pride in what they were doing, they accomplished their mission and had confidence in my judgment. We had fewer problems than in some other units.

There was no question that a barrier had sprung up between black and white soldiers. For example, blacks had their own club in the battalion base camp. Whites were not welcome there. I think blacks felt alienated and isolated. They were finding it harder and harder to identify with this war. Back in the United States, before they ever came into the army, the Black Power movement was emphasizing their differences. This was a "white man's war, not a black man's war."

Regardless of all this, the blacks in my company, whether

they were noncommissioned officers, platoon leaders, or enlisted men, fought just as well as any other man did. But I sensed a tremendous inner struggle tearing them apart.

After four months in the field, I was assigned to be aide-de-camp to the commanding general of the 25th Infantry Division. But after four months in this job I felt uncomfortable because my men were out there fighting. And I belonged with them.

I volunteered to go back to my unit. To my dismay I was told that though I was rated as a highly successful company commander and had more combat experience than any officer in the battalion, they had many new captains. And since most of them never had any combat and needed company command experience, they couldn't let me take a company. I was outraged. It was a decisive turning point in my decision not to continue fighting in Vietnam.

I remember saying at that point, "This war is not worth dying for if our attitude is locked into the career advancement approach. If that is the underlying ethic, then after two years of fighting this war, I am not going to waste my life."

My tour ended in July 1970. At that point I was assigned to the Presidential Honor Guard Battalion in Washington. This was right after Kent State. The next thing I knew, I was in the streets of Washington, providing security for the White House and other places threatened by riots that were still raging.

I felt trapped. I could not identify with the leadership that was running the war. And I couldn't identify with the antiwar people. Because I believed it was the right war, but I didn't believe in the way the war was being fought. I only felt close to other men who had fought the war and understood its problems.

I was a careerist. I was a West Pointer. I was theoretically committed in principle to fight any war to its natural conclusion. But I had lost confidence. I lost faith in the very methodology and the leadership who were executing this war.

I believed that our young men needed the best possible and best experienced leadership they could get. Well, the system was that you the officer went over, got your company-command ticket punched, then you went somewhere else. They put some new guy in as company commander with no experience. Obviously the guy is going to lose more lives while he learns. Maybe that was ultimately good for his career, but this wasn't the way to respect the lives of our young men or to fight a war.

# BODY COUNT

--------

## Col. Dennison Lane

*Military Advisor*
*Royal Thai Army Volunteer Force*
*Bear Cat, South Vietnam*
*1969–1970*

*The Royal Thai Army maintained a small infantry presence, between regimental and division size with U.S. advisors, in southern Vietnam from 1967 until 1972.*

We had this order from American II Field Force that if we made contact with the enemy at night, we had to do a sweep of the area to get a body-count afterwards. This seemed pretty damned stupid. One night the Command Post of the Thai battalion I was with was hit by a VC unit. After the fighting was over, an American order came down to get the Thai troops out on a body-count sweep.

I turned to my Thai counterpart, who was a grizzled old bear of a man. Perhaps he drank more than he should, but he was a hell of a field soldier. Very tough, very brave. I said, "Sir, please set your people to go out and sweep the area." He replied, very abruptly, "If you want to go out and sweep, go. But I don't see the point of sending my people out to find out if we've killed anybody and lose more people ourselves. If your people want to do it, that's fine. But we aren't going to."

He was absolutely right. And there was no sweep at night in that battalion ever again.

I learned about psychological operations from the Thais. We Americans taught and preached it, but I'd never actually seen it done. The Thais practiced it. And it was an impressive show. Our battalion ran a search-and-cordon operation in the Nho'n Trach Rubber Plantation, where casualties on both sides were minimal, but we had twenty

Viet Cong defectors, one Thai killed by a booby trap, and two VC dead.

The emphasis was on psychological operations, psy-war. Every night for five nights a psy-war C-47 aircraft flew overhead, playing the "wandering soul" tape to great advantage. And the Thais also demonstrated that when provoked they could fight very well. But they didn't necessarily go out spoiling for a fight.

# MAHARAJAS

## Gen. Edward Lansdale

*Senior American Liaison*
*American Embassy*
*Saigon*

*August 1965–June 1968*

I went back to Vietnam for the State Department in 1965. I was an assistant to the American ambassador—Lodge, then Bunker—and senior American liaison for the U.S. Mission to the Vietnamese.

There was sort of a mixed group working in the U.S. Embassy at that time. They all said they had feelings for the Vietnamese but they didn't act that way. There was an awful lot of ego. An awful lot of getting ahead at your own job, getting promoted, then getting the hell out of Vietnam. Letting somebody else come in and take over, while not getting your own career hurt by what happened in the country.

I remember in one mission meeting I was very angry at the self-seeking motives of two members of our mission consulate. They were criticizing what others were doing in an unselfish way to help our soldiers. So I bawled them out. And I said to Ambassador Lodge, who chaired the meeting, "Goddamn it, anybody sitting in this consulate doesn't have to face combat, which a lot of young Americans do. We should be working very hard, very unselfishly, to ease their job. Anybody sounding off the way these two guys are should be given the task of spending one day filling body bags with the bodies of our casualties. And let them learn what the hell Americans are doing in this country."

Lodge looked at me and said, "You sure get emotional. Are you sure you can handle your job here?" I looked at him and said, "All of us should be goddamned emotional that way. I'm never going to change."

Another big problem in Vietnam was that the army never understood the subtlety of how to communicate with their Vietnamese counterparts. When Westmoreland left and Creighton Abrams took over, he said, "Could we please have lunch together? I'd like you to give me some ideas."

So I told him how Westy would deal with the chief of staff of the Vietnamese army. Westy would go to visit him in the back seat of his sedan. His aides would sit in the front seat and a staff officer would sit in the back with him. He'd have a jeep full of MPs preceding him and a truck in back of his car with a machine gun mounted on it. Followed by two jeeps of MPs. And before and after each end of the column would be twelve policemen, heavily armed. Now, this isn't like a general—this is a ruling maharaja.

The caravan would get to the ARVN compound, where Cao Van Vien, the Vietnamese chief of staff, would be standing with a battalion of troops on the parade ground. And he'd snap to attention and give a salute as mighty Westmoreland got out—his aides jumping, running, opening doors for him.

Vietnam's whole national spirit is aroused by the sight. And Vien's smart to say just one thing: "Everything is going fine with us." So Westy never gets a single bit of the truth about what the Vietnamese army is really up to. Because he's made it impossible for the guy to tell him the truth.

So I told Abrams, "Why don't you drive your jeep out to see Vien. And when you get there, toss off a salute and say, 'Can I park this jeep around back?' And when you go inside, start by saying, 'Gosh, I'm a little bit worried. We had a problem yesterday.' And tell him the way U.S. forces goofed up on something. It doesn't have to be anything serious. And he'll say, 'Oh, you don't know anything. My people . . . ' He'll tell you a secret about ARVN. And between the two of you, maybe you can help solve a problem."

I used to beg Westy to change his ways. And he'd always ask me, "How do you find out these things about ARVN?" I said, "I approach them very differently than you do." For instance, President Thieu was very angry at the way the Americans tried to get his government organized after the 1968 Tet offensive—giving out orders to Thieu to put in people whom Westy and Robert Komer [head of CORDS, Civil Operations and Revolutionary Development Support] had picked to run things. I saw the list beforehand. And I said, "Thieu is going to see red. He's very jealous of these people. He'll probably comply because you're blackmailing him into this, but he'll never forgive you." Which he didn't.

I walked into Thieu's office after them. And Thieu was kicking over the traces a little bit. I said, "Did you hear what they're saying at the officers' club, the General Staff?" He loved gossip. And he would sit down on the couch and we would talk. And later, the ambassador would ask me, "How come Thieu told you this or that?" Well, it would be after one of these gossip sessions.

If Thieu was mad at some of his generals who were friends of mine, I would try to get him to put them in responsible spots. He put General Thang in command down in IV Corps [Mekong Delta] during the Tet offensive. And Thang straightened the area out in a hurry. But Thieu hated his guts because Thang was pointedly honest with him. Thang felt that Thieu was on the take and ruining the morale of the army with corruption. And he'd tell Thieu to his face. He'd tell Thieu, "I've looked over the commanders you've got in the Delta, who are loyal to you and you think highly of. Most of them aren't worth a damn but two of them are. Here's their names. Make one of them the commander down there. I quit. You don't know how to run an army."

So Thieu would get mad and call me. He said, "Your man is disloyal." And I said, "I imagine he's telling you the truth. You ought to listen to people like that, they are priceless. Thang is as honest as the day is long. He loves his country and wants to serve. He sure cleared up IV Corps in a hurry." And Thieu said, "He's a northerner, he's from Hanoi." But I said, "The southerners love this guy after watching him work."

The first ARVN commander down there had taken the province governor's house in Can Tho. He had tanks and barbed wire around the house, and then around the block, and then two blocks out. The center of the city was an armed fortress. When my friend, General Thang, got down there he said, "What the hell is all this? The people can't use their own streets. Get this barbed wire out of here." And he told his officers, "We're not inviting the enemy to come in and attack us here. We're going after him, out in the countryside."

He told his soldiers, "I've got an old truck here, and I'm going to sleep in the back of it. We're going out to find the enemy. And we'll chase them through these rice paddies." Which he did. He went out into the Hoa Hao areas. They hate northern generals. But their women's club had a meeting after Thang had been down there for a time. They said, "He's a northerner, but still, he's a good Vietnamese. He's a very honest man. We like him." And they told their husbands that. I made the mistake of telling Thieu about this. Because he got jealous and got rid of Thang.

Another good Vietnamese, the chief of police, was a highly motivated military officer. He had Boy Scout ideals of how to run a police force. But he wasn't strong enough to fight Thieu. So Thieu shifted him to run the NCO [noncommissioned officer] school at Nha Trang.

In 1967 when they had elections finally for the rewritten Constitution, my friend was telling the students at the NCO school to vote by conscience. He said, "It's a secret ballot, nobody will know what you wrote."

Thieu found out about it and arrested the guy. He said, "Tell them to vote for me, what's wrong with you?"

I went to visit Thieu—the Americans never knew this. I told him, "This guy's wife lives next door to me. I know you've got him in jail. I know why you arrested him. A bunch of foreign correspondents are coming to my house and asking questions about him. And I'm going to take them right up to the jail, so they can see you let him out. He can walk across the street to his home."

So Thieu rushed to this jail and turned my friend loose. And I had to run around to find a couple of correspondents to take over there, to make my threat look real.

# IN OUR OWN IMAGE
--------

**Edward Brady**

*Combat Operations and Intelligence Advisor
U.S. Army and Civilian
South Vietnam*

*1965–1974*

After the Tet attacks of 1968, the Army transferred me from the Joint General Staff in Saigon to advise the Special Branch of the national police. I was very much in favor of doing something constructive with the Hoa Hao and Cao Dai sects, who were very strong in certain areas. But that conjured up bad images in people's minds because they remembered the detrimental former political power of the sects.

But the basic reason in the American Embassy for not being supportive was that nobody knew any Hoa Hao leaders. Nobody knew any Cao Dai leaders. Fundamentally because none of them spoke English and they weren't about to learn it.

The Vietnamese we dealt with officially were either the French-speaking or English-speaking elites. We only had a couple of decent linguists in the whole country. We didn't have them in the political section, the economic section, and we didn't even have them in the CIA. And in a country that had gone through French domination and then Japanese occupation, learning a foreign language is something only a relatively few people do. And by dealing with only those who spoke our language, we automatically restricted ourselves to experiencing a very small percentage of the population.

The second problem was understanding Vietnamese social structure and organization. Our minds are part of Judeo-Christian philosophies and organization. But the Buddhists, Hoa Hao, and Cao Dai are not fundamentally organized that way. So an American would go to a meeting of Buddhist leaders and wouldn't be able to recognize an order and structure. When he went to a Catholic meeting he didn't have that problem. So it was clear to him who the country's leadership would be.

The early villages that the Diem government armed were all Catholic. Priests would be the leaders of the villages. We did that because we could relate to them. We didn't understand how monks ruled. We didn't understand the way non-Western cultures are organized and function. So we opted out of the majority of the Vietnamese population.

The true political nationalists in South Vietnam were fragmented into twenty-six political parties. Some represented long-term non-Communist nationalistic movements from back in the nineteenth century, who were never truly made a part of the South Vietnamese government. We never succeeded in co-opting them into it. We never appealed to them in a meaningful way.

Thieu was not somebody who appealed to them. Diem was not somebody who appealed to them. But on the contrary, in the Philippines Magsaysay was somebody who appealed to the village people. He was somebody they could relate to and identify with. The British did the same thing during the transition in Malaysia. We never did that in Vietnam. That was a fundamental flaw in our strategy. And it's because we didn't understand the culture.

I wrote the procedure for the special police operations based on the handwritten notes that Sir Robert Thompson gave me from his tenure as police commissioner in Malaysia. I took the Malaysian experience and worked with the Vietnamese to translate it to our situation. It became clear to me, dealing with Ed Lansdale once or twice and working with Sir Robert Thompson extensively, that they never fully understood Vietnam. And there were fundamental differences between the success of Lansdale in the Philippines and Thompson in Malaysia compared to the situation in Vietnam.

In the Philippines, many people spoke English. So an average American official could go many places and learn the attitudes of large segments of the population. In Viet-

nam you couldn't do that. We never broke through the
language barrier.

And in Malaysia, the Communist Party was comprised
of a racially identifiable element, the ethnic Chinese who
were about a third of the population. You could take the
repressive measures like cordoning off a village, changing
them into armed concentration camps, to cut off supplies
to the guerillas. And two-thirds of the population wouldn't
get upset about that. Very few Malays or Indians complained about the repressive measures taken against the
ethnic Chinese. That political flexibility didn't exist in
Vietnam.

Sir Robert Thompson often said to me, "How the hell
do you know who's who? How the hell do you know how
to isolate these people? How do you take methods that
I've told you and implement them? It beats the hell out
of me." Because the whole population were potential
Communists. There was no visual way to restrict whom
you were trying to concentrate on. And you had political
problems associated with trying to instill democratic values in the midst of a Communist attempt to take over.

It was a difficult task to walk the tightrope between
carrying out a police operation against the Communist
cadre and yet teaching people about the fundamental difference between a Communist and a democratic government. It's very hard to carry out secret covert operations
and repressive kinds of things in order to separate guerillas from the people—and then make a speech to them
about how their individual rights are so important.

But even with this confused situation, when there was
a chance for an uprising against the government, such as
the 'sixty-eight Tet offensive or the 'seventy-two Easter
offensive, the people chose not to rise up. Because the
Communists were always even less popular than the GVN
[Government of South Vietnam].

When I was an advisor with an ARVN ranger battalion
in 1965, I had a cook and radio operator who was fifty
years old. I asked, "Why are you so old and you're only
a corporal?" He said, "I've only been in the army for ten
years. " I asked, "Why would an old man volunteer to be
in the army?" He told me that he lived in a village near
Qhi Nhon. When the Communists began to infiltrate this

village, they came in every night for propaganda sessions. The villagers were leery of it and the elders were uncertain. But finally the VC were successful in persuading the villagers to let them live there permanently. They organized the village into an armed camp.

The old corporal told me, "I didn't mind that. But a few months after they had achieved this, they decided that everybody had to give up a shirt for the guerilla army. They collected all these shirts and sent them away. And about three weeks later we were told to give another shirt. Well, I only had two shirts. That was too much. So I told them no. And they beat me. That night I escaped from the village and joined the South Vietnamese army."

The GVN became popular in a sense during the 1960s and early 1970s because of agricultural and development programs like the introduction of "miracle rice." They used to call it "Honda rice" in the Delta because everybody earned enough money to buy a Honda motorbike by raising a second or third crop per year. That's a fundamental change in life. They formerly struggled to have enough money to buy a bicycle.

Land reform was successful in many areas. Different crops were introduced. There was a prosperity separate from American money. The South Vietnamese government and Thieu were identified with that. So there was the beginning of a popularity. And some real participation in elections.

There's an old Vietnamese proverb, "The writ of the government stops at the edge of the village." Which means that the national government's sway does not extend into the village. A village has its own council of elders, its own rules, its own traditional ways. The villages never looked upon a national government as anything that was good for them. The national government only taxed them, or took their kids away to work on canals or be in the army.

But the average person—and I talked to literally thousands of villagers in their own language—knew they were better off in a government hamlet. There was never any meaningful, popular desire to be communist. That was done through force to achieve the small minority the Communists needed.

Once they took over an area by force—you have to remember the Vietnamese Communist Party goes back to 1929 in some areas—success and the future for individuals are all tied up in the Communist system. So I wouldn't expect to go into a remote hard-core Communist area and say, "Wouldn't you rather switch to the other side?" It's been generations. That's the way it is in Russia. Even the people who don't like the repression have a difficult time conceiving of not being Communist. And I think that's the way it was in a few areas in Vietnam.

The insurgency war in Vietnam was fundamentally over in the late sixties. Everything that happened militarily thereafter was cut-and-dried military maneuvers by the North Vietnamese regular army. At that time there was not a guerilla army operating in South Vietnam, but a regular North Vietnamese army.

I got out of the army in August 1970, but I stayed in Vietnam as a Department of the Navy civilian intelligence specialist. I kept my same job, same desk. After 1968 I ran an extensive secret network of agents, so I know an enormous amount about what was going on among the Vietnamese.

I specialized in anti-American Vietnamese nationalists. I had contacts with people in the national police command, special assistants to the prime minister, special assistants to the commander of the South Vietnamese forces and a couple of civilian ministers—people who really didn't want much to do with Americans. They mostly spoke no English. And they had a fully different view of Americans, what we were doing and whether to trust us or not. These people would talk quite frankly and openly with me because I was known not to be sympathetic with U.S. policies. And they knew that I was some kind of conduit and channel of communication that they desperately wanted. But yet, they didn't want to be co-opted and identified with Americans.

Often I would go to dinner with one of my friends. They would operate by having big five- or six-hour dinners at Chinese restaurants. In essence, these guys would hold court. Their followers from all over the country would come in and tell them information on this and that, make a payoff to get another job, or ask for a reassignment.

They would joke with me that a CIA guy had come in to see them three days before and wanted to know the South Vietnamese government's position on a particular matter. They'd say—big joke—"Well, we told him a bunch of horse shit." And I'd see it in the U.S. cables the next day being reported to Washington.

I'd try to persuade the Americans that the information wasn't what the Vietnamese really thought or were going to do. And these people either thought I was insane or they refused to acknowledge that they had sent the wrong information.

The South Vietnamese, in reality, never were obliging little puppets. They would take our money and they were dependent on us, but they would play us for all we were worth. It's natural in their culture. And in Oriental culture there's a strong tendency to say what people want to hear—not to have controversy or confrontation. So they would say what they thought the Americans wanted. And if it wasn't what they were really going to do, there's no sense telling the Americans and getting them upset.

I had an argument with Robert Komer several times: Komer created this term, "revolutionary development support cadre." The idea was to wrest the image of revolution away from the Communists and give it to the GVN. But that is never what they were called in Vietnamese, never, never. In Vietnamese they were called "agricultural rehabilitation cadre."

This image that he had of revolution being co-opted by the Vietnamese government in the people's eyes was never translated to anybody outside of a half-dozen Vietnamese officers who were dealing with him. I told Komer, "Look, can you read Vietnamese? Get a translator. Read it. Here's the title. It doesn't say that." But he never cared about that.

Because of my Vietnamese friends whom I worked with (many of whom were among the potential coup makers), I had the *Good Housekeeping* Seal of Approval." So I could talk frankly with Vietnamese officials in the countryside. Like, "You have this procedure that I helped write several years ago that talks about 'neutralization operations' of Viet Cong cadre. Now, you have this well-known guerilla leader operating in this province. His wife lives

in this district town and she has four children spaced a
few years apart. So we know the guy comes back here
and sleeps with her periodically. It would be relatively
easy for you to have a surveillance operation and catch
him coming back to see her. I don't understand why you
don't do that?"

And they'd all have a big laugh, order another bowl of
soup. They said, "You don't understand. This is our country. Our children have to walk to school and back. Our
wives have to travel to market. They have to live a life
just like your family back in the United States. Don't you
think the VC know where our wives and kids are?"

The Vietnamese never felt that we were selling them
down the river until the 1973 peace accords. Before that
they thought we were dumb, but we were with them. The
General Staff—the average Vietnamese field-grade officer—had an enormously hard time coping with Americans. They could not understand our mentality or what
we wanted. One general said to me, "You guys spend a
billion dollars a day on this war. So how can you tell me
that you are not going to meddle in our affairs? What are
you people after?" He was very confused. He said, "You
know, we have been occupied and co-opted hundreds of
time in our existence. We understand what being directed
means. We relate to that. Why don't you tell us what you
want? Don't give us all this money, which obviously means
that you own me, and tell me that you don't own me and
I can do whatever I want."

On the surface we wanted the South Vietnamese to
win. We wanted to contain the Communist menace and
not lose another country. But then you got down to the
nitty-gritty of how we wanted them to do that: what was
allowable politically; what they could do in propagandizing the people; what they could do about North Vietnamese incursions into South Vietnam. Could they bomb
Hanoi? Could they run operations into the sanctuaries in
Laos and Cambodia? We told them "No" to so many
things that they lost the sense of how they were supposed
to win.

But some of our least-known programs did make sense.
The villagers, like people everywhere, wanted to have a
prosperous economy. If they could send their children to

school, pursue their religion, plant their crops, have a
good flow of material goods, fancy silk dresses for their
wives and little suits for the kids, Honda bikes and little
push Rototillers for the rice paddies—that was seventh
heaven.

The U.S. AID program of double- and triple-cropping
rice was very important. So much of the country began
triple-cropping that the average farmer came to greatly
resent having the Communists come in and take his sons
away. He needed the full-time farmhands year round. That
made a big difference in the guerilla army's ability to
press-gang people without getting a lot of resistance from
the people. Few thought of rice as a weapon to undermine
the VC. But we should have pursued it from the beginning.

When they only had a single crop and the land lay fallow
for six months, that's when the guerilla campaigns were.
So even though the people did not like the Viet Cong
taking their sons away, it wasn't a serious economic problem for them to be gone. But when they began double-
and triple-cropping, it would have greatly interfered with
the family's livelihood. And the way to get true democracy
is to introduce economic incentives.

We were always fallacious in our tactical priorities. There
was always a priority on military security and political
things, and lastly economics. But economics should have
been much more important because it changed the fundamental fabric of the nation, the people, and the deficiencies in the culture. This got common people involved
in national-level policies and resistant to the VC in a way
they weren't before.

# RICE

## Adolphus Stuart

*Scout*
*Special Landing Force Alpha*
*1st Battalion, 3rd Marines*
*I Corps*
*April 1967–March 1968*

I came back home after a year in Vietnam. My own sister didn't know what side I was fighting for. She asked me, "Who are you fighting for, the North Vietnamese or the other guys?"

I knew that nobody back here understood what was happening. Because if my own family didn't know, what hope did I have with somebody who didn't even know me?

The first meal my mother gave me, she serves me this big bowl of rice. Now, I'd been in the rice paddies with buffalo shit. I burned rice. I carried rice. I ate at least fifty tons of rice while I was there. I mean, the Vietnamese people's whole existence was about rice. That's what the war was about, it was about food. The North Vietnamese needed that rice basin in the South. Rice.

I get home, the very first meal I get was rice. I says, "Wait a minute! I don't want no rice. Jesus Christ!" My mother got upset. "What's the matter?" That was the first time that I had ever cursed at the table. I said, "I don't want rice. I just finished killing people in this stuff. I don't want to see rice."

People were dying in it . . . in the rice paddies. A two-foot, three-foot-high dike . . . and people were dying on the other side . . . and you can't even get to them. In fuckin' rice.

# VILLAGE DEVELOPMENT

--------

## Stephen Young

*Village Development Advisor*
*U.S. AID*
*South Vietnam*
*1968–1971*

In my freshman year at Harvard, 1963–64, we raised money for Martin Luther King. And when he came to Boston, I helped organize his march and argued with other students on behalf of civil rights. But I drew the line with friends over Vietnam who said Hanoi was right and Johnson was wrong. I couldn't accept such narrow-minded thinking about Southeast Asia, where the stakes for the people were so great.

I was worried that America was sending a lot of army lieutenants to Vietnam, but not enough people to get the rice planted. And that's where we were going to win or lose the war. So in 1966, I signed up for AID because they were where you could get the rice planted.

After graduating from Harvard in 'sixty-seven, I had a year of language training at the AID Vietnam Training Center. I arrived in Vietnam the first week of September 'sixty-eight. I spent a year as a village development advisor in Vinh Long Province, in the middle of the Mekong Delta. There were lots of tree-lined canals and tributaries of the Mekong River, wide-open stretches of rice paddy with all the houses lined up along the canals. Parts of the province were secure. Parts were no-man's-lands—like Tra On District had been VC since the late 'fifties.

In the fall of 'sixty-eight we began the Acceleration Pacification Campaign. We'd go into a village, build a mud fort, and station some Regional Force troops, and the VC apparatus—already weakened by their great losses at Tet—would collapse. They would come over through the

Chieu Hoi amnesty program. We'd send them off to train as government Popular Force platoons. And they would come back. In essence, the same guys now defended the village who used to be holding it for the Communists.

We began local elections. And as the Viet Cong apparatus collapsed and this network of mud forts and guards spread out over the rice fields, you could see prosperity return. Areas that had been abandoned and turned to weeds would grow rice. Roads opened up. Trucks came in. People could buy Hondas and tractors. By 1970–71, we introduced IR8, this new "miracle rice," so they could double their yield. At the same time, market opportunities were opening up to sell the rice. And consumer goods were being made available.

Schools were being built. You had a sense of a community coming alive. It was incredibly exciting. We saw Vietnamese hanging together in their own way, doing their own thing. They didn't do it quite the way Americans do things, and not everything got done with the sort of zip and dispatch we would like. But roads were being opened. Fields were being planted. Kids were going to school. The economy was growing. They had nice pigs [a staple meat] and good vegetables. Cultural life was coming back.

Tam Binh District in early 1969 was surrounded by Viet Cong. The B-52s had bombed near there. This was bad country. The roads had been cut. We went in there as part of the pacification program and opened a road. One day the new district chief and I drove to a village that had been the base area for the Viet Cong who attacked Vinh Long during Tet the previous year. We put in some mud forts; some VC had *chieu hoi'd*. It was being pacified.

As we were walking down the street, we ran into a wedding party. The young Vietnamese man was in the traditional long robe, dark crimson with black embroidery, carrying a bouquet of white flowers. His mother was in a blue *ao dai* [traditional silk dress], her hair drawn back. And his father was looking rather dour. In the typical Vietnamese wedding celebration, they were calling on the bride's family to take the bride back to his house.

What blew my mind was here, in this place that had housed a VC battalion the year before, a year later a wedding party had driven down from Saigon. Nobody had shot at them and a big feast was going on. It was like Vietnam was coming back to itself.

I took a picture of some old men at the wedding feast. And behind them, next to the family altar, were pictures and names of many of the great Vietnamese nationalist heroes and martyrs. Including men who had been murdered by the Communists, like Huynh Phu So, the great Hoa Hao leader. So whoever lived in that house was a nationalist. They may have lived under Communist rule for a long time, but they weren't Communists.

I remember going to Tra On District and the young kids, who had lived under Viet Cong control for a long time, came running up to me saying, "*Mỹ, Mỹ,*" which means "American." And when they found that I spoke Vietnamese, they were delighted. You could sense that there was something deep and very Vietnamese which was crying out to develop, to become itself with no war. They wanted peace, in order to be Vietnamese. But if peace meant Communism, many of them didn't want it. Because it was more important to be Vietnamese than to be a "New Socialist Man."

Communism as an ideology is inconsistent with being Vietnamese. Because Vietnameseness depends on two underlying traits: One is individualism. While Communism is collective, the Vietnamese are highly individualistic. As anybody who knows them can see, it's very hard to get them to work together. They believe that each of us has an individual fate. They don't believe in a collective approach or an overbearing government. So there's a fatal inconsistency between Communist beliefs and Vietnamese culture.

The second trait is that the Vietnamese believe in private property. Through the Buddhist notion of karma, to have property, lots of kids, and things going well for you is good fortune. No government or other person can legitimately take that away from you. So the Communist notion of collectivity and state control robs the Vietnamese of their religiously derived benefits and advantages in life. The Communists know this, so they have tried to stomp out traditional culture and religious beliefs.

The American value scheme, based on individualism and private property, is very close to Vietnameseness in some curious ways. There's also some remarkable parallels between the Vietnamese belief in fate and virtue and the old American Puritan notions of predestination.

By 'sixty-eight–'sixty-nine, there was the land reform program, Land to the Tiller, for which President Thieu deserves a lot of credit. Because he was pushing that further than the Americans were. It was very successful— we turned over most of the land in Vietnam by 'seventy-two–'seventy-three to the people farming it. These programs, like Land to the Tiller and village development, tapped into the Vietnamese tradition of local village communal government and responsibility, which goes back centuries. So we were dealing in terms the Vietnamese understood. Unlike Diem's strategic hamlets that forced people to reorganize and relocate, or the Communists' New Socialist Man concept, we took the existing community, wherever the people were, and organized them to achieve their own end. This was the important reason for success.

Some districts were more successful than others. It depended on the local leadership. It depended on the factors of geography, the quality of the local troops. The closer you were to North Vietnamese troops, the tougher it was to have development. So it was necessary to combine self-defense, self-development, and self-government.

We distributed guns to the villagers so that they could defend themselves. The South Vietnamese government worked closely with us, with our advice but under their own legal framework of the Constitution of 1967. We were decentralizing guns, money, and political power. The people organized political communities that wanted no part of the Viet Cong. So the VC either had to run away or come over and participate in these communities through the amnesty program.

In many cases, where local officials are corrupt, this kind of program is not easy to do. Basically you have to recognize the fact that there is corruption. And from that basic premise, you must create incentives for the officials to cooperate. You have to work with the top level of government to have a legal structure. We got one in Vietnam with the 1967 constitutional laws.

If you have incentives and a legal structure, even incompetent and corrupt officials cannot frustrate the gathering momentum of a community organization. And particularly, if you tie in local elections, they begin to see that it's much better to get along with the local community than to try to ride roughshod over it. Because that's votes in their district.

We worked with the Vietnamese to organize village elections and to set up local village financial accounts. I was working to change the budgeting process so village governments could collect taxes and spend their own money. They wouldn't have to go to higher authorities to set up village credit programs. They could loan out money to people in their local community, get the money back, and loan it out again the next year.

The land reform program worked through the village. The land was distributed to those people who farmed it by village committees, who handed out the titles. So what this did was decentralize the government's power.

One of the sad ironies was that during these very years of effective village development and land reform, the great cry of the antiwar movement was participatory democracy. Those who opposed the war didn't realize that we were doing more for participatory democracy in Vietnam than they were doing by protesting in the United States.

The antiwar premise was that we were taking up with corrupt landlords, while the Viet Cong were ridding the countryside of corrupt landlords and were going to give people private ownership of land. But in reality, we gave the land to the people. And when the Communists took power, they took it away and turned much of it into state collectives.

# PEACE POEMS

--------

## Mrs. Le Thi Anh

*Writer*
*Vietnamese Nationalist*
*Saigon and Sadec Province*

*1971–1975*

In 1964 I was secretary of South Vietnam's branch of
PEN [Poets, Essayists and Novelists]. I obtained a
UNESCO grant for writers to come to the U.S. for a
program of mutual appreciation of East-West cultural values. I didn't speak English, so they sent me to the University of Michigan to attend the English Language
Institute. At that time the U.S. was about to get more
deeply involved in Vietnam, just before the Gulf of Tonkin
incident.

I was not politically active at that time. But I didn't
think it was a good idea to send troops to Vietnam. Because I knew that the Vietnamese people, who had been
under colonial rule for one thousand years, were extremely sensitive to the presence of foreign troops. One
rule historically applies to Vietnam: Any government that
would be dependent on a foreign power or would invite
foreign military presence is doomed.

In 1971 I was teaching a course on Vietnamese culture
at the University of Michigan in Ann Arbor. I was quite
involved in the antiwar movement. My type of activity
was Ghandian nonviolence. I wrote antiwar poetry in English. And antiwar people invited me to rallies to read my
peace poems. That year I decided to go home because
my mother was very old and ill. I was afraid because of
my antiwar activities. Two years earlier the Thieu government had revoked my passport and I had received
orders for extradition. But Senator Philip Hart introduced
a bill to get a permanent resident visa and keep me in the
U.S.

In 1971, when I decided to go back to Vietnam, Senator Hart told me, "Every week go to the U.S. Embassy and report that you are safe." He was afraid that once I got home, Mr. Thieu would put me in jail. I was afraid, too. But no such thing happened.

I found out that so much had been exaggerated in the United States. The authoritarian regime of Mr. Thieu was not that bad. It was corrupt, yes. But it did allow quite a great deal more democratic liberties than we had seen under Mr. Diem or surely what we have not seen under the Communists.

The American press exaggerated all of Thieu's errors, failures, corruption, and imprisonment of political foes. When I went home I saw that the atmosphere was different than what I had been led to believe in the U.S. Nobody put me in jail. With all my antiwar activities and my failure to return home when I was ordered to, one would expect some punishment. But nobody bothered me.

Most of the time I stayed in the Mekong Delta, commuting from Saigon. I was teaching at the Hoa Hao University in the Long Xuyen area, where people were untouched by the war. Because the Hoa Hao [Buddhist sect] militia kept the Viet Cong out.

In the countryside I was so pleased that everybody had a motorized sampan [rivercraft]. Everybody was well-dressed and had radios and sewing machines. Everybody was well fed, happy and prosperous. Because thanks to the Land to the Tiller program, underwritten by the U.S., all of them owned their own land and had a stake in building democracy. And the Hoa Hao kept the Communists out. So the people had been able to enjoy the fruits of their labor.

It was so different from when I left in 1962. Then the countryside was not well equipped or well-to-do. There had been no electricity or many clinics or hospitals. But by 1971, everything had improved.

The rural areas especially enjoyed great benefits from the American presence. Telephones, new roads and bridges—we never had those kinds of things before. I went to visit the family cemetery of my father and ancestors. Before, we could never drive the car across the river. Now there were small bridges. I remembered my father had always dreamed of the day that we would have a road that would lead up to our home.

I entered the village school. It was much better than the village school I had attended under the French. And during the nine years I had been away, the U.S. aid provided the country with a basic structure from which to start economic growth. The country had developed greatly. The schoolchildren should have had the chance to grow up and enjoy a free and democratic society.

In 1973, when the Paris peace accord was signed, many people in Saigon told me it was a betrayal. Because Mr. Thieu had been forced to sign something that he did not feel comfortable with. He had been threatened with a cut in U.S. aid if he did not go along. But Mr. Thieu and his government were very concerned about the 150,000 North Vietnamese troops that were allowed to remain in place in South Vietnam by the dictates of the treaty.

But even with all of these Communist troops present, if the U.S. had not abruptly cut the aid and, instead, persevered with us . . . with U.S. troops withdrawn, we began to have the just cause with us. The republic began to emerge in the eyes of the people as a legitimate, genuine, independent sovereign government. We were beginning the winning trend.

From the time I came home in 1971, the people were rallying to the non-Communist side. But when the Communists and their supporters in the United States said, "Stop the aid to the corrupt regime," what they were really trying to do was dismantle a democratic order in the South. The corrupt Thieu regime was one thing. But democracy in South Vietnam was another. The vast majority of Vietnamese people supported democracy, even if they might not support Thieu.

But the U.S. Congress said, "Stop the aid to the corrupt regime." And the democratic system fell as a result. The democratic institution in the South was not perfect, but at least it was a beginning. A democratic institution was precious to us. But we didn't have the time or the security to build it.

# VIETNAMIZATION
--------

**Peter Braestrup**

*Correspondent*
*Washington Post*
*South Vietnam*

*1972*

There was a certain amount of overoptimism fostered by
Nixon for political reasons about the South Vietnamese
capacity to militarily hang on without us, the Vietnamization policy.

In 1972, the South Vietnamese army did a fine job of
repulsing the North Vietnamese Easter offensive. I was
running around in the field with U.S. marine advisors.
And I saw that the glue for the south Vietnamese dual-
command structure, say where the generals of the South
Vietnamese marines and airborne wouldn't talk to each
other, was the U.S. advisors. The U.S. marine advisor
and the U.S. airborne advisor would talk and get the job
done.

Without the advisors present, it would have been chaos.
They were the reinforcing rods in the cement. Partly because of the American firepower and logistics they could
bring in. But just as much because they supplied the vertebrae and command structure—the teamwork notion—
that the South Vietnamese, because of their fragmented
society and history, had not developed.

Oppositely, the North Vietnamese in 'seventy-two had
one command focus, concentration, abundant supplies.
The vertebrae were much stronger with the totalitarians,
who had an enforced, unified structure.

From 1971 to 1973, our logistics, airpower, and advisors—those three elements—offset the long-term strategic advantage of the North Vietnamese, which was the
sanctuaries in Laos and Cambodia and the Ho Chi Minh

Trail. If Laos and Cambodia had been truly neutral, there's no way that the South Vietnamese, with a little advisory help, couldn't have held on indefinitely. It was the geography. Even had the South Vietnamese army been the Israeli army, supplied the same way and with the same kind of leadership, the geography would have killed them.

With that six-hundred-mile frontier where the Communists had a free shot at South Vietnam, a safe place to retreat to, and a secure supply line on the Ho Chi Minh Trail, there was no way the South could hold. The geography was against them. And of course, Lyndon Johnson and Richard Nixon preferred to make us all think about the war as if South Vietnam was an island.

# THE PARIS AGREEMENT

## Edward Brady

*Combat Operations and Intelligence Advisor*
*U.S. Army and Civilian*
*South Vietnam*

*1965–1974*

In 1972, during the negotiations for the peace accords, I was head of a team in Saigon that provided input to the Kissinger team in Paris on what was going on in Vietnam.

The procedure in Paris was that each side spoke a monologue. One side gave some position or argued some case. Then the meeting would recess for twenty-four hours. And the next day, the other side spoke. They never had a dialogue or spoke at the same time in an official capacity. The rationale was that they needed time to translate and understand what had been said. But what really happened was that during that interim period, each side went world-wide for information. And there were teams all over the world supporting these negotiations.

The North Vietnamese would say things like, "In Tet 'sixty-eight, we destroyed 532 bridges, took possession of 78 villages, 2,000 hamlets, and we had the country locked up militarily. So we have the right to this much of South Vietnam." So Kissinger would send a message to us: "What did they really do?" I ran the thirty-person analysis group that supplied the input for all that. We maintained the control maps that showed the political and military status of each village.

In Paris the Americans would figure out how much area and population the GVN controlled. They would subtract that from one hundred percent, and give the rest to the North Vietnamese. So I suggested that was not the right way to go about this, and proposed a change. Kissinger sent a message back, saying it was the most startling revelation.

I knew we were in deep trouble when the guy who is running the negotiations doesn't know that thirty to forty percent of the country is not populated and not controlled by anyone. And many villages were not under either side's control. And he'd been conceptually giving all of this neutral territory to the North Vietnamese in the negotiations.

Then, when we read the drafts of the actual agreements they were working on—what we were prepared to give as concessions to the North Vietnamese—it was clear that there was no way the government of South Vietnam was going to be able to withstand the political subversion, infiltration, and propagandizing of their population prior to an election. The agreement was that the government of South Vietnam could not proselytize or enter Communist-controlled area. Whereas existing Communist cadre could remain in place in the government's areas.

Kissinger drew this boundary line and said, "Everything that has been occupied by the North Vietnamese Army in South Vietnam is a 'Third Vietnam.' And all Communist agents in the rest of the South may remain where they are."

Once I saw that, I knew that we were fully prepared to sell South Vietnam down the river. You can be charitable and say that we didn't care. Or you can be worse, and say that we wanted to give it to the other side. My South Vietnamese counterparts looked at these maps and said, "What are you doing to us? Is your government going to agree to this? My life is forfeit. My country is gone!"

I stayed on for two more years with these people, who knew we had sold them down the river. It was an enormous eroding of their national confidence and will. First because of the terms of the Paris agreement. And secondly, the U.S. Congress vote of nonsupport for Vietnam in 1974—no further military aid to supply logistics and ammunition; and never again would we fly air strikes if the North Vietnamese attacked.

Once Watergate happened, no Vietnamese of any political sophistication thought that we would pay any more attention to Vietnam. There was no way to reverse what our Congress had done.

I wrote a detailed position paper in the winter of 'seventy-three–'seventy-four. I stated that there would be a major North Vietnamese military attack. And the South Vietnamese government would crumble if we didn't support them. I spelled out which military commanders would fight and which would run. I gave this to my superior at five o'clock one night. The next morning he came in and said, "How many copies of this do you have?" I said, "Five." He said, "Give them all to me. It's going to be stamped Top Secret with restricted access." I said, "Who is going to read it?" He said, "Jacobson [an ambassadorial assistant] has read it and he's given it to the ambassador."

A couple of weeks later I asked, "Where's my paper? When are they going to circulate it?" He said, "You're better off forgetting about it."

# THE CLAIRVOYANT

---------

## Chhang Song

*Director*
*Ministry of Information*
*Republic of Cambodia*
*1970–1975*

*Prince Norodom Sihanouk was chief of state in Cambodia from 1941 until 1970, and was replaced by his prime minister, Lon Nol. Chhang Song served in both governments.*

I was an assistant in Sihanouk's private cabinet before the 1970 coup. Sihanouk had a lot of publications and I was his editorial assistant. Sihanouk was very convinced that he could never be overthrown. He was an invincible man.

But there was a problem. The North Vietnamese and Viet Cong occupied part of our country. Sihanouk had been telling the world that there were no Vietnamese troops in Cambodia. However, for many years he had an agreement with them where they would supply through our southern port, Sihanoukville. And that was monitored by his officers. I don't know how much money went to him, but they made a lot of money on this deal.

The Vietnamese Communists would receive supplies from Russia or China and then truck them to Phnom Penh at night. Then to the border areas. A bad feeling was spreading among many Cambodians that the Vietnamese would occupy our territory, take over our land, forever. The same thing they are doing today, and have been doing historically for centuries.

In addition, corrupted Cambodian military officers who controlled the territory sold rice to the Viet Cong directly. So the tax didn't come to the government. And the government didn't have any money in the bank. Sihanouk had nationalized the economy and the distribution of goods, which was an economic disaster. And prices soared.

Sihanouk was a prince, playboy, writer, politician. He directed movies—musicals, both traditional and with people dancing the twist. But he was not a good manager of the country. He's extremely charismatic, inspiring ... clairvoyant to some extent. But also, he dragged the country to its demise.

In 1970, before he was overthrown, Lon Nol presented Sihanouk with maps of the Viet Cong infiltration. Sihanouk was persuaded. He looked at the maps and said, *"C'est fini"* ["It is finished"].

From 1963, Sihanouk became fiercely anti-American. The American Embassy was closed down. And he allowed the Russians and Chinese to have a lot of personnel in their embassies. They were basically KGB types who helped the Khmer Rouge and Vietnamese. Later, when Sihanouk sentenced the Khmer Rouge to death, Khieu Samphan [ideological head of the KR] and his comrades were saved by the Chinese Embassy.

Sihanouk was convinced the Americans would lose. He did not think in military terms but political. He was convinced that the South Vietnamese leadership was too corrupt to stand up to the North Vietnamese, and that the Americans would not be there forever. He was convinced that the only peace he could make was to make friendship with the North Vietnamese and Chinese, in particular. He was among the first chiefs of state to recognize the Peking government.

I don't know if this is a clairvoyant policy or whether his fatalism precipitated the loss of Indochina. By allowing the North Vietnamese to use Cambodia as a staging area, he gave them the means by which they could defeat the South Vietnamese. And that played a pivotal role in the fall of Cambodia.

Of course, the U.S. made some mistakes. You can always blame the Americans. But you can only blame them so much. The Americans would not have bombed Cambodia if Sihanouk had not initially allowed the Vietnamese Communist troops to be there.

After the coup, Sihanouk tried to vindicate himself

against Lon Nol by giving the enemy side propaganda. The support Sihanouk accorded to the Khmer Rouge with his radio broadcasts from Peking was very tremendous among the population. He called to everybody to join the Khmer Rouge in the jungle to fight against the government. That had a lot of impact.

In modern Cambodia, the only leader who has dealt effectively with the peasants is Sihanouk.

# TRUST

## Col. Dennison Lane

*Secretary, Joint Staff*
*Military Equipment Delivery Team, Cambodia*
*American Embassy, Phnom Penh*

*December 1972–February 1974*

I arrived in Phnom Penh in December 1972. We were well into the process of pulling out of Vietnam. And we were restricted by Congress to a total embassy strength of not more than two hundred people in Cambodia. This included both military and political people. Phnom Penh was surrounded by the Khmer Rouge. Supplies had to be brought in either by boat or by air. There was no way to get out by land. And we were already hearing Khmer Rouge atrocity stories, which were seldom taken seriously.

As long as you weren't a refugee, Phnom Penh was a never-never land. We were living in another world. French wine and Camembert came in, mangoes were in season, and we had delicious coffee. Life went on. Meanwhile, people were being decimated in the provinces. Few people in the embassy really were in touch with that.

At this time, the administration of the Cambodian army was a disaster. I'm not sure that if the embassy had unlimited people and supplies it ultimately would have made a difference. There were Cambodian soldiers in the field with no equipment and insufficient food. There was no medical evacuation for the wounded, no doctors, no pensions for widows, no accountability and generally no leadership. Yet there was equipment in Phnom Penh.

I remember a Cambodian brigadier coming to see me. He said, "I went to see a logistics officer for a trivial amount of necessary supplies which I knew that he had. And he said I couldn't have it." To my great astonishment,

225

this guy was a brigadier general, for Christ's sake, and the logistics officer was a captain or a major. But he was from a good [society] family and the brigadier wasn't.

I said, "You take your general's baton and hit him right between the eyes. And you say, 'Goddamn it, give.'" And he said, "Oh no, it is not our custom, not our way to do this sort of thing." Which it wasn't. But, of course, he didn't get the supplies either. And his people suffered because of it.

The brigadier was a very nice, quiet little man. He had been a sergeant in the French army and all of a sudden he found himself wearing a star in the Cambodian army. He didn't have the education to go with it. But he had a marvelous family and three beautiful daughters . . . all of whom perished after the fall of Phnom Penh.

He was ambushed and killed on his way to Lovek in a jeep, just before the end. He was driving up that goddamned road by himself. He was a brave man. God, there were so many very brave people. The Cambodians really believed in us. I'm not so sure the Vietnamese did. That's why Cambodia troubles me more than Vietnam or Laos. The Cambodians were the most trusting.

# REPARATIONS

## Col. Harry Summers

*Military Negotiating Team*
*Saigon-Hanoi*
*1974–1975*

In 1974 I was detailed back out to Vietnam as a member of the military negotiating team that had been set up under the Paris accords. As part of this assignment, we traveled back and forth to Hanoi, negotiating with the North Vietnamese. Mostly on an informal basis because the formal negotiations were stalled. I had the opportunity to be in Hanoi five days before the fall of Saigon.

We knew that the North Vietnamese were going to give us their terms for the withdrawal of U.S. personnel from Vietnam. So I asked the people at the Saigon embassy what our position was. What should I say or not say. And the answer I received from them was, "Damned if I know." And I asked, "What am I supposed to do when I get to Hanoi?" The answer was, "Well, do the best you can."

I thought, "This is a helluva way to run a railroad." If I had told the North Vietnamese this, they would have said, "Oh, you clever Americans. You can't get us to believe that."

So I went to Hanoi on my own initiative. And they did give us the terms for withdrawal of U.S. personnel. And they told me that the military team that I was part of had to stay in the country. One of the reasons they wanted us to stay was because they had linked the return of American bodies to the reparations issue. They felt it was okay for themselves to break the Paris accord by invading South Vietnam. But they expected us to give them reparations.

In an earlier visit to Hanoi, they kept talking about how the U.S. had violated the Paris accords. I finally got sick of hearing this. And there was always a press conference when we got up to Hanoi. I said, "Well, I've got to admit you're right. We have violated the Paris accords." Of course this drew an enormous audience. I continued, "And the way we violated it most flagrantly is that we promised the South Vietnamese to maintain aid at a particular level. And we have not given them the aid that we promised." There was an uproar about that.

# THE FALL OF SAIGON

## Ken Moorefield

*Special Assistant to the Ambassador*
*American Embassy*
*Saigon*
*July 1973–April 1975*

I got out of the army in 1971 and immediately went into
a year of graduate school. Dissatisfied with the quality of
education I was receiving, I decided to drop out for a
while. I had been declared forty percent disabled by the
Veterans Administration and received a back stipend they
owed me. So I took that money, put on a backpack, and
took off for Europe. I planned on staying there for as long
as it took to clarify my thinking and decide what I was
going to do with my life.

However, before I left I found out about an advanced
degree program in the School of Foreign Service at
Georgetown University. The dean of the school, unlike
some academic administrators, believed in Vietnam veterans. So I told him to send a telegram to Greece if they
accepted me.

In June 1973, at the end of my second semester, I was
coincidentally introduced to Graham Martin, who had just
been appointed ambassador to South Vietnam. After several hours of discussion, he asked me to join him when
he departed for Saigon ten days later as his special assistant.

I didn't expect to go back to Vietnam. Nor was I planning or anticipating it. We had already signed the so-called
peace treaty that had sold out the South Vietnamese by
permitting the North Vietnamese Army to remain in the
South. And my two tours as an infantry officer in Vietnam
were a painful memory.

But when confronted with the opportunity to go back

at a high enough level where perhaps in some way, however modest, I could influence the outcome of our waning support of the South Vietnamese, I immediately accepted.

We flew on *Air Force One* to South Vietnam on my thirtieth birthday, the tenth of July, 1973. As special assistant to the ambassador I read all of the cable traffic that came into the embassy from throughout the country. The South Vietnamese ability to divert resources into economic reconstruction was substantially undermined by the presence of the North Vietnamese Army on southern territory. And the South Vietnamese were increasingly struggling to maintain the same level of military operations that they had been able to maintain while the Americans were there. Because we were starting to draw down the level of military resources that we were providing. While, if anything, the North Vietnamese were getting stronger, through logistical support from the Soviet Union. They were receiving more sophisticated tanks, communications, heavy artillery . . . it was tragic.

When Watergate ensued, the situation got even more cloudy. Because the one thing that had been the equalizer in the 1972 North Vietnamese offensive was the use of U.S. B-52 strikes. Now it appeared that any secret agreements between Nixon and the South Vietnamese would be abrogated by Congress. This had a profound psychological impact on the South Vietnamese army and political leadership. Because they realized that in contrast to the North Vietnamese, who still had steadfast allies in China and the Soviet Union, the United States was on the verge of abandoning the battlefield completely.

By July 1974, it became increasingly evident that the North Vietnamese were building up the road system in the western part of South Vietnam. And they had already begun attacks on vulnerable positions. The South Vietnamese ability to retaliate, and even more so America's intention to retaliate, just weren't there. This heightened the confidence of the North Vietnamese.

Saigon was physically isolated from the battlefield. South Vietnamese soldiers, except those in the hospital, were not permitted in Saigon. There was no active sense of a country at war. Occasionally you could hear or see the evidence of artillery in the distance. But by and large, we just read intelligence reports from outlying provinces. I asked to be relieved from my responsibilities as special assistant to the ambassador. Sitting in the ambassador's office reading reports, I didn't feel I was making enough of a contribution.

In July 1974 I was assigned to the consulate general in Nha Trang in Military Region II, the Central Highlands. And I'll give you an example of what I found happening: there was an attack on an old U.S. Special Forces camp northeast of Kontum. This was a strategic flashpoint where the North Vietnamese had attacked several times before. It was the vulnerable point to cut central Vietnam from southern Vietnam. And it was not heavily manned.

It was clear that the South Vietnamese forces were spread pretty thin in Military Region II [the Central Highlands]. They were complaining of lack of hand grenades, M-79 rounds, they were husbanding their ammunition. And they were not operating aggressively. So I went up to investigate the attack on the Special Forces camp.

I went into the hospital with an interpreter. We found a company commander and a platoon leader, recovering from wounds. Most of the camp had been overrun by a North Vietnamese regiment, decisively routed. They were outclassed, outmanned, and had not been properly equipped to defend the camp against the size of force they faced. And there had been no units sent to their rescue. Little pieces of evidence, all together, led me to conclude that the South Vietnamese were in an extremely precarious situation. The reality was the growing capability of the North Vietnamese to launch a major offensive. And the South Vietnamese could not prevent it.

In December I went back to Saigon and was detached to the United Nations–appointed International Commission of Controls and Supervision as a liaison officer. This was another charade. The ICCS could no more control and keep peace than the man in the moon. And there was a decisive split within the commission between personnel from the two Communist countries [Poland and Hungary] who we knew were in close coordination and contact with the North Vietnamese and Viet Cong, and personnel from the two countries [Indonesia and Canada, which was later replaced by Iran] who were non-Communist. The commission was paralyzed. It would not establish a condemnatory resolution about any aggression on the part of

Communist forces. The North Vietnamese were just bidding their time, waiting for the right moment to strike.

In February 1975, the handwriting was on the wall when the ARVN retreated from the Central Highlands. Around the early part of April I estimated that we probably had a month at best. I began speaking with friends at the midlevel of the embassy—in the defense attaché office, the CIA station, the political section, and various other agencies—to try to take action. To help those Vietnamese to whom we had a responsibility.

I withdrew from the ICCS liaison position as soon as I had prepared the non-Communist delegations—Indonesians and Iranians—for an orderly withdrawal from their outlying positions. Then I transferred over to the consular section.

On the eighteenth of April, I went out on my own to Tan Son Nhut Air Force Base to set up liaison with the defense attaché in preparation for the evacuation. Almost immediately we were faced with a series of problems. There had been thousands of people already fleeing the onrushing Communist forces. They had escaped from Danang, Hue, Nha Trang, and had lost documentation. They had picked up children who were not their own, but for whom they were responsible. And they had no legal papers for adoption.

In the Vietnamese extended family, there were cousins and nephews, all of whom could not be abandoned. But we had a mandate to take only Americans and their dependents. In the case of legally married Vietnamese wives, we could not take her extended family, who in many cases was completely dependent on the American husband.

Then there were hundreds of unmarried Vietnamese women with Amerasian children. Some carried wrinkled letters from the American fathers that they'd been treasuring for several years. Some had been responsibly sending money to them from the States. And I had no authority, mandate, or instructions how to cope with this. I concluded that I'd better take initiative on my own because we were running out of time. God, the first day I must've signed hundreds and hundreds of documents.

Initially, I even tried to get people married or adopt children. But almost immediately I got reports from downtown Saigon that the black-market rate on marriage or adoption papers was going up dramatically.

The people who were at the evacuation center were panicked already. Terribly panicked. They'd already escaped from some other part of the country in most cases. They had already suffered the traumatic and dynamic collapse of the northern part of the country.

The North Vietnamese forces had not captured the military positions north of Bien Hoa yet. The ARVN were retreating but they were still defending. And in some places, bitterly contested battles were being fought. But it was clear that the noose was drawing tighter and tighter around Saigon. And the tighter it drew, the more people were trying to get into this pressure-cooker environment that had been created around Tan Son Nhut Air Base and the evacuation center. Because this was the only way out of the country.

The first day there were only three to four hundred refugees, but we were quickly up to the thousands. With only four guys helping me. I would normally finish up late in the evening, somehow get back to my apartment to catch a few hours of sleep, and start again at daybreak. I was working off all my adrenaline. Because we knew this was a race to the death.

I finally just started marrying people and arranging for adoption papers that said: "They are hereby considered children of or wife of the following American." I was still in a sense fighting. Battling for whatever maneuver room was left to save people's lives.

At the embassy I saw many people in shock. There were only a few who took the initiative to operate and do what could be done. I don't condemn anybody for not knowing what they could do under those circumstances. Because some people were not prepared.

Some embassy people chose to protect themselves or defend their families rather than stand and fight. They didn't feel the sense of commitment to the Vietnamese. Maybe they never worked with them, lived with them, or felt that we had responsibility as an ally who had abandoned them.

The ambassador fought with all his energy until the end. He had a hell of a hard time accepting the fact that it was all over. I think that in his own mind, he was convinced that we would somehow turn it around. That we would be in a position to negotiate a coalition government of some sort. I didn't believe that for a second. There was no way that the North Vietnamese were going to give up at the conference table what it had taken them thirty years to win on the battlefield.

The afternoon of the twenty-eighth, we were working our ass off in the evacuation center. It was hotter than hell. And we had hundreds and hundreds of cases backed ed up. All of a sudden bombs started falling. The building shook. The lights fell out, crashed on our desk. The Vietnamese were yelling and screaming. And the American officers just kept working.

I had associates who had deeply suffered from the stress during that two-week period. The pressure was tremendous. We were deciding people's fates on a minute-to-minute basis. And naturally, people suffered what I would call "burnout." One guy just stood up and said, "I quit. I can't take it anymore." Another guy, a young foreign service officer on his first assignment, had never had any kind of experience that resembled this before.

I'm not sure that there are many people who could've stood up to it for very long. Unless they believed with all their heart that what they were doing was so important that their personal considerations had to be completely sacrificed for the good of the whole.

That night one rocket landed right in the gymnasium. But fortunately didn't explode. I got the Vietnamese organized in a protected building across the street and arranged for a mass feeding with the supplies that we had left. Around midnight I got back to my apartment in downtown Saigon. Two or three o'clock in the morning, the North Vietnamese began shelling the city. A round went through the roof of the Majestic Hotel, about two blocks away, and killed an American. I felt a little uneasy since I lived on the top floor of my apartment building. So I took a few of my weapons and a little escape bag, and went down to a lower floor and waited until dawn.

The air base was still being rocketed when I arrived there. Helicopters and airplanes were trying to get off the ground to escape. The few that could. I went straight to the evacuation headquarters. There were several thousand people still there.

The panic really started to set in at this point. People were ricocheting around the city frantically looking for a way out. The only way out was to somehow get into the grounds of the American Embassy or onto the air base. Or by river to get out to sea, but that was a precarious voyage.

The North Vietnamese rocketing continued. The city was in flames. And the Communists had the city surrounded with missiles. They were in a position to choke off any further evacuation by air. From the time we began the helicopter evacuation that day, we realized that we were down to hours, if not minutes.

There was no time to handle even the people who were under our immediate responsibility. A sense of desperation and impending doom. Not something you could think about, because we had so much to do and so little time.

I volunteered to help arrange convoys to get into the city and pick up the Americans. We assembled as many buses as we could find and grabbed as many people to drive as possible. I grabbed—volunteered—a Vietnamese, I never even found out who he was. I found him cowering in a ditch with the rest of the people. We still were receiving rocket fire. And I asked him if he could drive. I don't know how or why, but he drove one of the buses.

We were hurtling through the city, picking up people as quickly as we could. At every point we stopped, we had to turn people back. My section of the convoy only had three buses. The rest of the convoy was spread out because of the density of the traffic—confusion bordering on total chaos.

Vietnamese army officers came up to me with their families jammed in cars with all their baggage. And they were obviously armed, wanting to get on the bus. But there was no room. And I was not going to start taking people from the streets. My mission was to pick up Americans and their dependents.

There was no place to get gasoline. And the Vietnamese air force guards had sealed off the air base. I had a confrontation with the lieutenant who was in charge. They

locked and loaded their weapons. It was clear that they
were not going to let us back in.

At that point, we returned to the city. I was just trying
to find a place to deposit the convoy. The American Embassy was sealed off and surrounded by hundreds of
Vietnamese, maybe thousands. They were just patiently
waiting outside, pressed up against the gates. They were
hoping that somehow we were going to let them in. Some
even had documentation or American passports. But it
was very risky to open the gates for anybody at that point.

So I stood with the crowd in front of the embassy for
a while and tried to figure out what to do. It was a rather
vulnerable feeling standing out there as an American. Several people came up and asked me who I was. I said I
was a Canadian journalist.

Sometime in the late afternoon I finally pushed my way
through the crowd and got to the front gate. I caught he
attention of one of the marine guards, who opened the
gate for me. I slipped inside.

The rest of the afternoon and early evening, I looked
to see what needed to be done and helped pull some
people over the back wall. Evacuation by helicopter was
ongoing. I helped string up some lights along the upper
wall so helicopters could continue to land after nightfall.

I walked up to the helicopter pad and worked with a
marine to bring people up from the embassy stairwell into
the helicopters. We were dealing with a ninety-mile-per-
hour prop blast and there was no guardrail. For people
who were tired, fatigued, or disoriented, it was somewhat
dangerous. One of our marines had fallen off the helicopter pad onto the roof below and cracked his skull.

I spent the rest of the night up there. During the wee
hours of the morning I had plenty of time to think. It was
a rather calm and reflective opportunity. Even in my fa-
tigue—at that point it had been several days since I'd
slept hardly at all—there was an opportunity to survey
the full extent of our damage and our loss. Almost car-
nivallike, a political rally was being conducted in front of
the embassy. I could hear this Vietnamese orator stirring
up the crowd with anti-American invective. I watched
people looting and scattering what we'd left behind.

Finally, I went down into the embassy itself and walked

through each of the offices on the top floors. Friends of mine had already departed. I observed mementos left behind: books and pictures, a can of tobacco a friend of mine left. I borrowed it for my pipe, since I had run out. I picked up a book, appropriately on military strategy, which I thought might provide a bit of belated insight into where we'd gone wrong.

I had an opportunity to talk with Tom Polgar, the CIA station chief, a short, stocky, bald-headed Hungarian in his mid-fifties. He as obviously in great emotional pain and despair. He said, "If only we hadn't cut off their supplies. If only we'd continued to provide them the support they needed."

It must have been around four o'clock in the morning. The marine major who'd been sent over from Hong Kong to command the security forces at the embassy came into the hallway. He said that he had received direct orders from the president of the United States that only American staff from the embassy be evacuated from that moment forward.

A helicopter came in. I went out to talk with the pilot. He said that the ambassador had to leave on this helicopter. So I went to the stairwell and told the ambassador. I believe it was his intention to let some of the few remaining people leave before himself. But he agreed to go.

He looked haggard. Probably like the rest of us, but he looked particularly spent. He'd had bronchitis for several days. And truly beaten . . . but not cowed. He never looked cowed.

I escorted Ambassador Martin and the rest of the embassy staff—the political counselor, the deputy chief of mission, and several others—to the helicopter. And they left.

I was getting pretty lonely at the top of the embassy at that point. It was very subdued in the courtyard because no helicopters were coming in. Those four hundred to five hundred Vietnamese that still remained were all alone out there.

The next helicopter came in. I put the last remaining American civilians onto the helicopter. There was no one left. I decided at that point that my job was done. There was nothing left to do. I assumed the marines could get out on their own. I got on the helicopter and went.

As the helicopter flew over the city, the dawn was just beginning to break. The fires in the distance could have been Tan Son Nhut Air Base, could have been the MACV complex burning, or the fires further in the distance, Bien Hoa.

An almost eerie calm had descended over Saigon. There was very little, almost no noise at all. No sound of gunfire. No sense of what was about to take place . . . the dramatic change that was about to overcome that city and country.

Looking out to sea, as the sun began to come up, there were hundreds of small boats off the coast. It looked like an armada of refugee vessels, all sizes and shapes.

# SECTION IV

# NO WAR,
# NO PEACE

# PILOTS IN PAJAMAS

## Janis Dodge

*Wife of Prisoner of War*
*San Diego, California*

*September 1967–July 1981*

*Since the end of the Vietnam war, close to 2,500
American servicemen remain missing in action in Southeast Asia. Of these men, 166 are known to have been
captured alive. Their fate remains unknown. Year after
year, the families of these men have dwelled in the emotional netherworld between hope and mourning. Janis
Dodge is one of the wives who waited.*

The Hanoi newspaper made a big fuss the day my husband
was shot down. He was involved in an air attack on a
bridge in Quang Binh Province that day, May 17, 1967.
My son was only three years old, and my daughter was
five.

The navy was very good when they came to tell me
about Ron being captured. They were very kind and con-
siderate. A chaplain came with the wife of the squadron
leader. They told me, "Ron is not dead." And he was
immediately classified as a prisoner of war. He was never
classified as missing in action.

After Ron's parachute landed, he spoke to his wingmen
from the ground. He said, "I'm moving up the hill. I'm
being surrounded. I'm breaking up my radio." The navy
brought all of this over to me on the initial visit.

Then Ron's picture as a prisoner appeared three or four
months later in the September 9, 1967, issue of *Paris
Match*. The navy sent me a reproduction and asked me
to identify my husband. I agonized over that. I had never
seen that kind of expression on Ron's face before. And

241

shortly after this, he appeared in an East German propaganda film, *Pilots in Pajamas*.

Although I never received a letter from Ron, I assumed
that when Hanoi released the first list of prisoners' names
his name would be on it. I was in my children's school
cafeteria, working on a PTA meeting, when that first list
came out.

I was having a cup of coffee by myself and waiting for
the meeting to begin. I opened the newspaper and saw
the list. Ron's name wasn't on it. It didn't affect me too
emotionally because I thought that it wasn't a complete
list. And Hanoi had been so secretive all along. All of the
Christmas packages I had sent Ron were always returned
unopened. And they let information out in just little bits.
But this is when I got my first twinge of "God..."

As time went on I started thinking more and more,
"Maybe he isn't captured." My emotions were swaying.
Sometimes I thought of him as alive and sometimes as
dead. I believed our government was doing everything
possible. I was a tried-and-true navy wife, who quietly
believed everything I was told.

In 1970, I phoned the navy captain who was in charge
of the issue in Washington. I asked him, "You have a
picture of my husband. Why don't you try to find out
what happened?" And he replied, "Well, we're going to
wait and see what the North Vietnamese say. It will all
work out." It was, of course, the middle of the war.

Murphy Martin, who works for Ross Perot, was in Paris
at that time, during the peace negotiations. He had seen
Ron's picture and suggested that I go to Paris and try to
talk with the Vietnamese. I readily agreed. And Ross
Perot financed my trip in May 1971.

The North Vietnamese would not see me. I phoned
them. I went and stood in front of their embassy. I knocked
on their door and tried to get in...I put the magazine
picture through their mail slot. But they absolutely refused to talk with me.

So we stood outside the peace talks. And when the
North Vietnamese negotiators [Le Duc Tho and Nguyen
Co Thach, who is currently Vietnam's foreign minister
handling the MIA issue] came out, we confronted them.
I showed them the picture and said, "Here's my husband

in black and white. You have him." And they said, "If he's not on the list, we don't have him." This was devastating. I realized what I was up against. They were using my husband for something, and I didn't know what it was.

There was an antiwar activist, Cora Weiss, who was appointed by the North Vietnamese to be liaison between the prisoners in Hanoi and their families. She was absolutely horrible. She told me—and many other wives and mothers—that if I wanted to correspond with my husband I would have to go through her. And she wanted the families to make antiwar statements. I told her that I didn't want to talk to her.

When the war ended and the prisoners were released, my husband was not among them. So I spoke with the navy man in charge of POW/MIA affairs. I said, "Why don't you try to find something out? You've got an East German movie of my husband. And you say there's been no information over the years."

And he said, "Well, the best people who would know are in Hanoi. And we're going to let it go through proper channels. We don't have relations with East Germany. So there is no way we can find out."

It seemed to me that they were only sitting there, not trying to find out what happened to my husband. Out of all the prisoners, he was one of the few for whom they had something to go on.

After so many years of frustration, I began to realize that I could fight and demand answers. I became involved with the National League of POW/MIA Families in 1980. The league took advantage of Ron's *Paris Match* photo to publicize the MIA issue. And so did each congressional delegation that went to Hanoi, including the Woodcock Commission in 1979. I participated in a lot of media events to publicize Ron's story and the MIA issue.

Then in July 1981, Hanoi decided to return Ron's body.

The two other bodies released with Ron were similar cases. Richard Van Dyke was known to have been captured alive. And Stephen Musselman's body was photographed next to the wreckage of his aircraft.

It was a very emotional time for my children. We went to the funeral home and saw the casket for the first time.

And my boy looked at the casket. And he's thinking, "There's my father." Where before, he was just an ambiguous picture, an idea.

We were fortunate that Ron was returned. For most of the families, not knowing is a horrible thing to live with. I know they killed Ron. They killed him. And they kept it a secret that they ever had him for fourteen years. And he is just one of many hundreds.

# HOLOCAUST

## Berta Romero

*Refugee Processing Coordinator*
*U.S. Refugee Program*
*American Embassy*
*Thailand*

*1976–1982*

## Kassie Neou

*Cambodian Survivor*

*1975–1981*

BERTA ROMERO: I'm from northern New Mexico. A small place called Encinada, where everyone is related and predominantly Spanish-speaking. My family is Apache, Spanish, and Mexican. My father passed away before I was born. And when I was around six, my mother remarried and we moved to Denver.

By 1973, I was going to college full-time and working as a legal secretary for the Mexican-American Legal Defense and Education Fund. At that time there was a lot of controversy about the Denver police department. And the Chicano movement was very big. I was pretty fed up seeing friends or people I knew from school arrested and beaten up for driving under the influence.

My goal in life was always to travel and see the world. One day as I was walking through the university campus in Boulder, there was a Peace Corps recruitment sign. Being a very idealistic young woman, out to save the world, it was the most wonderful thing. I volunteered for the Peace Corps in 1973 and was sent to Thailand in February 1974. I worked in a school for the blind in the beautiful mountain town of Chiang Rai.

When Vietnam fell in 1975, I was in the Philippines on a brief vacation. A friend of mine was working near Clark Air Force Base, where a lot of Vietnamese refugees were being flown in during the evacuation of Saigon. Pretty soon Laos fell, and Cambodia had already fallen. I kept wondering if Thailand was going to fall, because it is only a two-hour drive from the Cambodian border to Bangkok.

In the spring of 1976, I was preparing to terminate my

two-year Peace Corps commitment. A sign was posted in the Peace Corps office by the American Embassy, looking for ex—Peace Corps volunteers to work in a refugee program. That's when I first met Lionel Rosenblatt.

Lionel was on temporary duty from the State Department in Washington. He had been instrumental in the evacuation of Saigon and had come back on his own money to travel the Thai border to find out what kind of people were coming out of Laos and Cambodia.

So Lionel recruited thirteen of us. We worked in a very small house. One room was the Laos section, one room the Cambodia section, and one room the Vietnamese section. We worked around the clock, seven days a week. The first few days I worked in the Cambodia section, typing visas. The guy I was working for was shipped out to the provinces to take a look at the Lao hill-tribe refugees because nobody knew how many there were. The guy flipped out. So Lionel called me up to his office. He said, "You're section chief." I had no idea what to do.

The Aranyaprathet Refugee Camp on the Cambodian border was located near an old temple site. Buildings were quickly constructed in a very small area. It was very crowded and conditions were poor. There were three thousand people there when I arrived. But people were coming in from different areas of Cambodia and sneaking into the camp. So the population was rapidly increasing and no one really knew exactly how many there were.

People would just crowd around you. Cambodians who spoke English or French would say, "Please get me out of here." It was a madhouse—just incredible. The desperation in their faces.

At that particular time, I didn't know what was going on inside Cambodia. Lionel had given us a briefing that the Khmer Rouge were killing people. But it didn't really click until day after day, hour after hour, I was sitting across the table from people talking about what the Khmer Rouge were doing. With ragged clothes on their backs, a dazed, hungry look in their eyes ... total disbelief as to what they were coming from. Our interpreters had also escaped from Cambodia. It was very emotional, people were crying, and the interpreters would get choked up. And all I could do was write.

People who had worked for the former government or

military were being slaughtered. Anybody who was a teacher was being killed. Nurses, doctors, any kind of professional . . . if you wore eyeglasses, you were beaten to death. Children were being separated from their parents. And the parents were going crazy because they didn't know where the Khmer Rouge were taking them. The children were being reeducated to be informants to talk against their parents or tell the Khmer Rouge what their parents did.

There was no food. And no water in certain areas. People were getting sick and doctors were being killed off. Prisons were full. People were hiding their identities, throwing away their eyeglasses, shedding their nice clothing, and burying any gold. They just wanted to escape. And they were asking us as they came out, "Why can't America do something about this? Why did the Americans abandon us?"

KASSIE NEOU: By late 1976, the Khmer Rouge were in power for a year and a half. Thousands and thousands of people were incarcerated in forests, clearing land for agriculture and building earthen roads. We worked in the rain, in the sun, long hours.

The Khmer Rouge used the term, "We don't have to rely on tools or supplies from anywhere else." We were assigned to clear land within a given period of time. And if someone complained about not having enough tools, that person would be taken to a "higher education center." In the morning, when we went to work, people would be lying on the side of the road, bludgeoned. They had disappeared the previous evening. Sometimes we would see the people being taken out.

In nightly meetings the Khmer Rouge would say, "We have defeated the imperialist Americans and their dog, Lon Nol. Now we save our bullets to kill more. If you do something wrong, we will not shoot you. We have other ways of punishment." They used axes or bamboo logs. Women were murdered this way, too. Babies . . . Sometimes they'd take the two legs and rip the baby in half. Or they would throw the baby against a tree. Normally when they executed a whole family, they started with the youngest first, so the parents could watch.

The camp where I was, the percentage of death by

starvation was forty to sixty percent. Because we were all city people, we didn't know how to survive. No Western-made medicine. A lot of malaria. A lot of diarrhea because of eating enhusked rice. But later on we gained more knowledge in trying to survive, so the percentage of terminal illness became less.

One good thing was that Cambodia is the land of food. Under dry crushed soil we have food—frogs, toads, crickets, snakes, snails. It's delicious. You wouldn't believe it. That's what we lived on.

Cambodia is such a rich country in resources that for people to starve under the Communists, whether it be Khmer Rouge or Vietnamese, is only because the government wants people to starve. It is easy to grow food in Cambodia. Especially when everyone was made a rice farmer.

While in captivity, each year we gathered crops enough to feed three years. But we were not allowed to quell our hunger. Can you guess where the food went? We saw Chinese experts traveling on long trains, loaded very heavily with rice.

The best way to survive was to shut our mouth, close our eyes, and block our ears: not to see, not to hear, not to talk. None of us became Communists. We kept hoping that one day we would be liberated. But anytime we went to the Khmer Rouge meetings we were forced to agree. We could not say no.

They tried to get us to believe that the *Angka* [Organization] is great: justice, fairness, equality. We were told the same things: Hate imperialism. You must not wear any colorful clothes. You must forget everything from the past. Anyone who tries to keep Western civilization will be punished.

BERTA ROMERO: Throughout 1976, we worked from sunlight until sunset in the Cambodian refugee camps. It was hot, hideous, and as the population of the camps swelled, we still weren't sure that we were going to get the immigration "numbers" to process people to the United States.

Lionel Rosenblatt was dealing with politics and the State Department and Congress. We finally got word that eleven thousand numbers had been approved for the U.S. program. Out of this figure came the allocation breakdown per Southeast Asian ethnic group. The ethnic Lao and hill tribes had priority. A lot of them had been direct employees of the U.S. government. And a lot of Vietnamese in the Guam camp qualified because they had been embassy personnel. When it came to the Cambodians, it was tragic.

There was this incredible massacre of humanity going on inside Cambodia. And when it came to negotiating admission numbers it just seemed so inhumane. How can people—the State Department—think only in terms of admission numbers when we're hearing about large numbers of people being killed for any kind of association with the government that the U.S. had direct involvement with? No bureaucrat wanted to admit that the U.S. had really supported the Lon Nol government. I was very emotionally involved with the Cambodian survivors. Coming back to Bangkok was like being hit with a baseball bat... "We can only take two thousand Khmers."

They were living in bamboo shacks, hastily constructed. A lot of missionary groups got involved in helping with the relief. That's when we first started seeing these missionary types who have wonderful intentions and are very good people, but they try to convert refugees when they are at their very lowest point. In exchange, they give them T-shirts or food. A lot of refugees converted to Christianity at that particular time because they wanted clothes and food for their kids. And some people were converted, of course, for the right reasons. But that's when we gave the term "Rice Christians" to those who basically converted to get clothes and more rice.

Many Khmer were still straggling over the border. In some districts they would be put in jail. One of my jobs was to go to provincial jails and talk with Thai officials and interview new arrivals. The jails were small cells, no more than four by six feet. There'd be about twenty people in there. And they were given bowls of boiled rice. You'd look in the cell and your stomach would fall to your feet. They were so emaciated. They were hungry. They had this desperate look in their eyes. But they couldn't speak and didn't know why they were in jail. The Thai didn't know what to do with these people.

There was very little press coverage. Nobody cared. I

have feelings about that. Because when I was in the States, I was part of the antiwar movement. It wasn't until I went to Southeast Asia and started working with refugees that I really got a good dose of what was going on. I learned what happened in Vietnam, Laos, and Cambodia through the refugees. But there was no press coverage. None of the human-rights groups even thought about getting involved.

People fleeing from the Khmer Rouge in 1975–76 were witnessing one of the greatest holocausts. And no one was focusing on it.

In the border camps in 1976, when many people in the U.S. were calling the stories coming out of Cambodia CIA propaganda, I spoke to thousands of refugees. And I believed them. How could so many people keep saying the same thing over and over again? And the look on their faces. You look at their eyes . . . there's nothing there.

I learned the word for "dead," "gone," or "starving"— *Slap.* I would interview people: Family tree? "Everybody's dead." Living relatives? "None." Every single story was the same, over and over again. That stayed with me when I returned to the States in 1977.

I tried to explain to my family and friends what I'd been doing. I had come back home after three years. With family, I was home for good as far as they were concerned. "Refugees?" They really didn't know about refugees. They'd see an occasional news clip on it or a TV program. They had no idea what it was like.

People could not understand what I was going through. I felt totally isolated. I thought, "There must be something wrong with me. I can't relate to people. I can't relate to my best friends." They want five minutes on where you've been—"Did you have a good time? But you still look the same." And that was it. "What are you going to do this weekend? Let's go out. Let's go hiking. Let's do this, let's do that." There were very few people whom I could share my experience with.

And being a Chicana [Mexican-American] in the Southwest is different, too. Because I left a very critical situation in Denver at the height of the Chicano movement. Going away from the needs of my own community to Southeast Asia. A lot of friends thought I was a sell-out.

When I came back, I tried to look them up. But they didn't understand.

I would talk about what the Cambodians were going through. There was no awareness—all that people knew about Cambodia was Kent State. That was it. I felt like I was at a dead end.

It's interesting to see the way that people here think that they have it so bad. As opposed to the brutality of the Khmer Rouge.

KASSIE NEOU: The Khmer Rouge that ran our camp assigned me to a ploughing team. On November 20, 1976, I was working with one of the team members who spoke French and English.

The day before he had lent his whip to a man on another ploughing team. And on this morning, he was ploughing in front of me. The tip of my plough hit his back several times. I said, "I'm sorry, brother. But your oxen are slow today. You should be faster." He said, "They were faster when I had the whip. But I lent it to a guy on the other team and he has not returned it to me."

And by mistake, I said in English, "That's your confidence in him, right?" Suddenly I heard a strange voice behind me: "Very good, brother. That's what we are looking for. You speak American language." I realized that I was in trouble.

That evening, the Khmer Rouge gave me an *assignment*. Before I left the village, I stepped into my house and called softly to my mother, "Mom..." And I didn't say anything because I didn't want to frighten her. I only said, "Look after my two kids." My son was still very sick. And my mother was sitting next to them. I didn't say another word. I pulled a scarf around my neck and left.

At the place where I had been told to go, three soldiers were waiting for me. They took a rope and bound my arms behind my back. Then they tied the rope around my neck and the loose end to the seat of a bicycle. They rode bikes, but I had to run behind—for fifteen kilometers. I fell down once or twice. And they stopped to smoke and talk twice.

When I got to the jail, they pulled me straight up to the

interrogation room. They didn't give me a chance to rest, because I was a "spy," speaking American language. The first question was, "Tell me the name of your American bosses." I said, "I don't have any American bosses." They said, "What were you then?" I said, "A cab driver." Something just happened to my mind to say "cab driver." I believe that this was from God. It saved me.

They kept beating me and saying, "You are a spy. You work for Americans." They beat me until I fainted. When I regained consciousness, I found my neck and two legs were chained with steel cuffs. An iron bar was through the leg cuffs and linked me with nine other prisoners. The Khmer Rouge called all of us "enemies."

Though my knowledge of the English language put me in prison, my knowledge of stories from the British Broadcasting Corporation is what pulled me out. When I worked in Phnom Penh I received a lot of teaching materials from the BBC. Two of the tapes were called "Stories from Asia." I remembered those stories by heart, which were mostly about animals, acceptable by the "new society." We were not allowed to tell stories about classes, imperialism, or wealthy people. But stories of animals, fine. And the good thing was, those stories made the teenage prison guards laugh.

I became their favorite storyteller. But not in daytime, only at night, because it was illegal. They forced me to tell them stories. And then they would send some of their friends to the kitchen to get me some leftover rice, illegally. These guards were twelve and thirteen years old. One of them, the son of the highest officer in the region— eleven years old. He was the most powerful guard. He can order anyone to do anything. And the M-16 rifle he carried was bigger than him.

I saw that the eleven-year-old boy was the most powerful. So I tried to tell him more and more stories that made him laugh, hoping to get favor.

One evening the decision was made to clear out the prison, in order to make room for the newcomers who would be much stronger than us. Because it was harvest time. And we were mostly sick.

That evening, we heard footsteps. Strange—not like the regular footsteps that would mean two or three soldiers would be coming. Either to change the guard shift or to take one or two of us out for execution. This type of execution was done nearly every evening.

But they didn't call out names, like for regular executions. They said, "Okay, one after another." And they began to tie a rope from the arms of one man to the neck of the next, all the way down the line. I heard the voice of my story-listener, the eleven-year-old kid. He said, "I need him." So two other guards, thirteen and fourteen years old, snuck in and pulled me out. They hid me in a little pond used by buffaloes. It was full of mud. And leeches. Oh! Hundreds of leeches. The guards told me, "Stay here. Don't move." So I stayed the whole night. You can't imagine how many leeches were on me.

Early in the morning I heard strange noises. More soldiers coming in. And then I heard a truck. Soldiers formed lines to keep security for fear that the new prisoners would run away. The prisoners were unloaded from the truck to the hut. And they counted, "One, two, three, four..." The night before there were thirty-seven, and thirty-six were taken out to execution. I was the only one to survive.

They now counted up to "Seventy, seventy-one." And the young soldier who saved me, came to me and said, "Hurry up! Out of the pond." He dragged my body out of the mud and pulled me into the line. He called out, "Seventy-two."

But the real Seventy-two was just out of the truck. This eleven-year-old soldier, having some power because of his father, said, "Seventy-two, that's enough. That one is unproductive, crazy." The real Number Seventy-two is sort of a sickly young man. He looked a little bit Chinese, and a little bit insane.

The eleven-year-old said, "We don't need him." So the other soldiers brought the insane boy to the back field and executed him. The plan was very well made. Thirty-seven executed. Seventy-two alive in the jail.

BERTA ROMERO: In 1977 I went back to Thailand to work in the newly formed Joint Voluntary Agency (JVA). The American Embassy had voluntary-agency people running the refugee program at that particular time. There were a few of us who had worked on the 1976 refugee program.

In the Cambodian refugee camps a lot of former Khmer military people had joined resistance groups. They left the camps and went back to fight the Khmer Rouge. But at that time I was assigned by JVA to work with the Laotian hill-tribe refugees in northern Thailand. The Hmong and Lao people were coming across the border in droves. It was very bad. They were suffering tremendously. We'd see the kids with swollen bellies from starvation. And their feet were all scarred because they had no shoes.

They had suffered so much persecution in their home villages. And then had to survive Vietnamese and Pathet Lao ambushes during their escape. And then I'd hear other types of horror stories from ethnic Lao, because I also worked in Ubon Refugee Camp.

The Ubon camp was exclusively for ethnic Lao. It was situated in the former American ammunition dump at Ubon Airfield. When the Americans pulled out, the ammo dump was empty. So the refugees were put into it. The area where Americans kept their military dogs was now the area for new Lao arrivals. The Lao had a saying, "The Americans knew how to treat dogs much better than they treat the Lao people." The ironies of the war's aftermath were very apparent. There was a lot of bitterness when the Americans pulled out of Laos and left them.

In the province where the camp was located, Thai corruption ran from local government all the way down to the camp level. A lot of rice was smuggled out and there was a lot of abuse by the paramilitary guards. The rapes were kept silent. We heard more about the beatings. We heard more about the rapes in the Cambodian camps.

There was an incredible black market going on in camp. In Ubon, the food was more expensive in the camp than in town. If a refugee had enough money, he could pay his way out of the camp. Some Lao were more ambitious than others and had enough money saved to have thriving businesses in camp and exploit people.

Ubon Camp is now closed. But it was one of the worst camps in the entire country. And a lot of visitors thought it was the best because it was the only camp with cement and paved roads. It's always been an illusion to see a camp with little gardens or looking relatively clean. People think it's a nice camp. But they don't know what goes on at night.

I worked with the Lao for about a year and a half.

Then, in 1979, I was assigned to Visitor Control, where I organized all of the visits by congressional delegations. My job was to sell them on the need for more refugee immigration numbers, and escort them on tours of the camps.

I did a tour of all the Southeast Asian camps with Joan Baez. She was one of the warmest, most sensitive people. She sat with a tape recorder and interviewed refugees. Lengthy discussions, writing explicit notes. She was overwhelmed with it all. This was when the Khmer were really decimated...just skin and bones.

We were right along the Thai-Cambodian border during a mortar attack during the Vietnamese invasion. There was a lot of shouting. And I managed to talk the Thai military into permitting us into the camp. They didn't want Joan around because she was a singer: "My God, she's not going to sing?" I convinced them to let us through as the living dead were staggering across the border. We could see the smoke from Vietnamese artillery in the background, people hitting the ground, and Thai military all around.

The press was the pits. They were there to get a statement from Joan Baez. And they were stepping over refugees who were dropping dead, suffocating in the mud. The Japanese press was the worst. I got to the point where I just started smacking some of the press people and their cameras. I said, "Get the hell out of here. Can't you see..." Joan got very furious with them and said that she wasn't going to make any statements. So they backed off. Cambodians dying of starvation were coming across in droves, with only the clothes on their backs. This was evening.

The next morning, I thought people were dead all over the field. They were lying still from exhaustion and hunger. Baez saw this and was extremely moved.

We traveled north and she saw a group of Hmong refugees coming across from Laos. She gave a concert in Ban Vinai Camp. Baez was fantastic in terms of spending time with the refugees. Her delegation wound up sponsoring a young Vietnamese woman whom they met on an Indonesian island. The Vietnamese were talking about reeducation camps in Vietnam and why they were fleeing in boats.

I returned from the Baez trip and was given twenty-four hours to prepare for a visit by the First Lady, Rosalynn Carter. It was an incredible experience, believe me. My job was to escort her around the Ubon Camp. She had just come from seeing the Khmer at Sakeo, which was a hellhole. And apparently very moving for Mrs. Carter.

Before she landed at Ubon Camp, the Thai did an incredible job. They cleaned it up in twenty-four hours. It became the cleanest camp I'd ever seen. Everything was organized. And the ethnic Lao are such that they arranged flowers and welcoming delegations. It seemed to me that Mrs. Carter was concerned not about talking with refugees, but getting her photograph taken by journalists.

We wanted to tell her about problems and things going on in the camp. But she wouldn't land her helicopter before the press arrived, so they could snap her photograph. We lost forty-five minutes of her time because she was circling in the air. She only had forty-five minutes to see the refugees once she landed before going back to Bangkok to visit with the royal family.

At one point I was walking and talking with Mrs. Carter. I'm telling her about the rice. And the desperate need to get more numbers to take some of the Lao to the U.S. She didn't say a single word. She just smiled. At one point, the Japanese press, who are very flamboyant and very pushy, were yowling for her to have her picture taken. I saw her step back onto a few kids, without really noticing. Stepping on their toes so she could pose. And that turned me off.

I had a very hard time dealing with that whole Mrs. Carter business. But then I had to bury my resentment, because after all, she did help. She sent out a White House plane with medical supplies that were badly needed. And admission numbers of the Lao were increased.

But after she left, we were so relieved. We all went out and got drunk.

KASSIE NEOU: I was released from the Khmer Rouge prison in April 1977. My storytelling to the soldiers had saved my life. I was delivered to a new village in Battambang Province, not far from Thailand. They still treated me like a prisoner, assigning much harder work than to regular people. But my mother, my children, and my sister's family were allowed to join me.

By 1978, though we were in a labor village controlled by the Khmer Rouge, we heard a lot about the fighting between the KR and the Vietnamese. During each educational meeting, the guards told us, "We must be strong to fight the Vietnamese." But they didn't tell us that the Vietnamese had attacked.

On January 7, 1979, the Khmer Rouge cadre disappeared from the village. We woke up and went to the food warehouse. No cadre were there. Some people took advantage of this and ran up to Battambang. Those are the ones who were killed. The Khmer Rouge were there. And that night the KR returned. They told us not to go anywhere. If someone is missing, the whole family will be executed.

Soon, we started seeing helicopters. We saw jet planes. On January 12 we heard shooting. The Vietnamese came on National Road 6, crossing Siem Reap. They attacked and the Khmer Rouge ran. But they took us with them. They shot anyone who was slow. They accused us of trying to join the Vietnamese: "If you are slow, you want to go to the Vietnamese? You want to join them to fight us?" So we had no choice but to go along with them until April. Four months in the woods, into the Cardamom Mountains.

The Vietnamese chased behind closer and closer. Until one day the Khmer Rouge ran out of supplies. The Vietnamese kept shelling, so we kept moving —to the left, to the right, forward, backward—away from the national road. Many sick people died and some of us were shot dead. My mother was not healthy, but I had a buffalo cart to carry her and the children.

We escaped through the woods to the Great Lake area. Out of the Khmer Rouge authority, we cautiously moved back toward Battambang. We stayed there for a while. And then we heard of the border crossing. That was our plan. We decided to cross the border to Thailand.

By May, the three hundred people in my group had arrived at the Thai refugee camp at Nong Chan. There were thousands and thousands of Cambodians there already. Everyone camped out in an open field. There were no United Nations people present, only Thai soldiers.

On the morning of June 8, the Thai closed the road. No Red Cross or international relief could enter the Nong Chan village, only big buses and soldiers. They forced us to load into the buses at gunpoint. One Thai soldier hit me on the head with a stick because I was too slow. And they did the same thing to anyone. You could not refuse. Children and women were crying and saluting: "Please, please, let me stay. I don't want to go."

After a twelve-hour ride on the buses, we were unloaded at night near Preah Vihear. Very early in the morning, a loudspeaker said that we had to go back to Cambodia. Anyone trying to make a detour back to Thailand would be shot dead. We had to climb down a very steep mountain. The Thai soldiers began to shoot from behind us.

As I climbed down the mountain with my mother and children, I saw the dead body of the wife of a man who was shot dead by Thai bandits on our way into Thailand. She had refused to go down the mountain. She saluted the Thai soldiers, saying, "Please pity me. I cannot go because I don't have any other relatives. Over there the Communists killed everyone except my husband and child. And he was killed when we came to Nong Chan. I cannot go. I have no one and nowhere to go." She was shot dead, in the head. Her baby crawled around for a while before the Thai soldiers forced someone to take him out. But as we climbed further down the mountain, I saw the dead body of the baby on a piece of rock. So this whole family had been made extinct... Extinct.

The Thai continued shooting in the air and shooting people. Anyone who refused to go. Thousands and thousands of people, not only from Nong Chan but Aranyaprathet and another camp east of us. All together I'd say forty thousand.

As my children and I climbed down, all day we kept hearing explosions. I didn't know what they were until we got midway down. Someone said, "We cannot go any further because of the minefields."

I walked over many dead bodies. In one spot... a whole family. Father, mother, grandmom, uncle, and babies, just piled all together. All dead. But most of the bodies belonged to the first group, who had been unloaded on the evening of June 8. I was in the third group, and not as many of us were killed because we saw that terrible scene and were very careful. We stepped on each other's footprints. So you can imagine, thousands of people walking in a single line. It took three days.

I spent two nights in the middle of the minefield. Some dead bodies on my left, some dead bodies on my right side. And it smelled horrible all around. The third day we saw an American-built helicopter. But from the Cambodian side of the border.

So people in the minefield said, "We will be rescued. The authorities have come to help us." But those helicopters were Vietnamese officers coming to block our exit. I didn't go out of the minefield through the Vietnamese checkpoint, because I knew it would be dangerous. So I decided to go out through the woods, risking my whole family. We were followed by other families to the central part of Cambodia.

We saw many dead bodies lying along the roadside. They had died of sickness and starvation. And without food, we ate a lot of wild bamboo shoots. My children were both very small and very sick. My son could barely walk and my daughter was five years old. We walked across the jungle for fifty-nine days. But God saved us. Many of my friends forgot that they were in trouble and tried to make contact with the Vietnamese officers. They were arrested, never to be heard from again.

A few years later in Khao I Dang Refugee Camp I met one man who had bribed his way out of one of the detention camps in Vietnam. He said, "Other Cambodian prisoners with me were those forcibly repatriated out of Thailand." They were put in prison in Vietnam and had to do slave labor like the Vietnamese prisoners. Three camps with thousands of Cambodian people doing hard labor.

At first the Vietnamese Communist occupation forces behaved in a very friendly manner. They said they had come to rescue us from Pol Pot. But later, I saw that they didn't come to help us, but to take our country. So in 1980, I decided to escape again to Thailand.

# THE COALITION GOVERNMENT

--------

## Dr. Yang Dao

*Political Council*
*Laos Coalition Government*
*Vientiane*

*April 1974—May 1975*


*Dr. Dao, a member of the Hmong hill tribe, returned to Laos after receiving his Ph.D. from the University of Paris in 1972.*

In April 1974, the Pathet Lao Communists signed an agreement with the Royal Lao Government to form a coalition government. I became a member of the Political Council, directed by Prince Souphanouvong, the "Red Prince." He was an older man who had been trained and supported by Ho Chi Minh since the 1940s.

There were forty-two members of the Political Council. Sixteen from the Vientiane [Royal Lao] side, sixteen from the Pathet Lao, and ten independents. The majority of the Vientiane members believed that we could negotiate with the Communists and have a successful coalition. But after four or five months, I realized that the Pathet Lao did not wish to cooperate.

According to the coalition agreement, any Lao could travel throughout the country. But in reality, the Pathet Lao soldiers and police prevented people from moving into territory that they controlled. The non-Communist Laotians allowed the Pathet Lao to travel into the areas they controlled. So the Communists infiltrated the Royal Government's territory. It was an unfair balance of power. The right to travel was only for Pathet Lao.

The North Vietnamese always had an important role with the Pathet Lao. In each Pathet Lao military unit, there was always a Vietnamese military officer. Even during the coalition period. In early 1975 I was returning from a conference up-country. There was a Pathet Lao military

260

post controlling the road from Van Vieng to Vientiane.

At this post, a Vietnamese in a Pathet Lao uniform stopped my car. He spoke to me in Lao, asking to see my papers. I had an identity card as a member of the Political Council. He couldn't read it—he turned the card in various ways to look at the Lao script. And his face got all red. Because I was looking at him, right in his eyes.

He walked back to the two Pathet Lao soldiers to check out the papers. They were Kha tribespeople who couldn't read. I said, "What about this, younger brothers? Can't you read? That's the signature of Prince Souphanouvong, your chief." So they took it back to the Vietnamese officer, then came back to me. They said, "Okay, you can go."

In May 1975 I had just returned to Laos from traveling in a delegation to Hanoi, Peking, East Berlin, and Moscow. Phnom Penh and Saigon had recently fallen. Suddenly the Pathet Lao made a complete turnabout and openly violated the Accords for National Reconciliation.

They had infiltrated their political cadre into all sectors of Laotian society: the army, the administration, the police, the students, and among the people. These agents organized large public demonstrations. They called for the removal of all non-Communist members of the coalition government.

The government was directed by Prince Souvanna Phouma, a non-Communist neutralist. The Pathet Lao demanded the resignation of the minister of defense, the leading generals of the non-Communist side, and government ministers. And they created an atmosphere of hatred against the Hmong hill-tribe people.

On May 9, 1975, the Pathet Lao newspaper put in black and white that it was necessary to exterminate the Meo [a derogatory name for the Hmong] "to the last root." When I saw this in the paper, I went to see the Pathet Lao members of the Political Council. They said, "We did not do that. It must have been a propaganda agent of the right wing who is trying to create discord." I replied, "But it is in your newspaper." And at that moment the Pathet Lao said that all the military regions of Laos had surrendered to the "government"—the Pathet Lao faction—except Military Region II, commanded by [Hmong] General Vang Pao. The Pathet Lao then said, "We must liberate the second Military Region by force."

At that moment I went directly to see Prince Souvanna Phouma. I asked him to resolve the conflict peacefully. Souvanna Phouma was sick, he was isolated, and just not aware of the situation.

He picked up his telephone to call the Pathet Lao to ask about this. But his telephone wouldn't work. And you can imagine—the leader of a country and his telephone wouldn't work! He and I were sitting face to face when he picked up the phone to call Phoumi Vongvichit, the Pathet Lao vice–prime minister of the coaliton. And after trying several times, Souvanna Phouma put down the phone and said, "Well, Mr. Yang Dao. My telephone doesn't work anymore."

He said, "Mr. Yang Dao, why don't you go to see Phoumi Vongvichit and tell him about the situation." So I went to see Phoumi to raise the issue. He acted very tough and said, "If General Vang Pao wants to fight a war, the Pathet Lao will fight a war." I said, "No, we don't want war. We want peace. Laos is made up of all the different ethnic groups [more than half of the population is hill-tribe]. We all must cooperate in a spirit of friendship to build national peace and reconciliation."

But after the fall of Phnom Penh and Saigon, the Pathet Lao became very stubborn and hard. Previously when the war was still going on in Vietnam and Cambodia, they were terribly friendly. They would bow and smile, hold their arms out to embrace you, and say, "We have to work together. We have to forget about the past. Together we can approach the future and bring about the construction of a wonderful country in Laos."

And at that time, I was a young Laotian. I had never fought in the war against them. I had spent my years studying, earning a Ph.D. in economics and sociology, preparing myself to be able to better serve my country. And I believed their sincerity. I spent all my energy to work for national unity—as did the other non-Communist Laotians in the coalition. That's why, in 1975, many of my associates either in the administration or the Political Council did not wish to leave the country.

The secretary of the Political Council convened a ses-

sion in Luang Prabang, the northern royal capital. I sensed
that the Pathet Lao would do something against the accords. So I arranged to secretly leave Vientiane.

When the members of the Political Council arrived at
Luang Prabang, they were told, "The meeting is not here,
but Prince Souphanouvong is at Sam Neua." This is a
traditional Pathet Lao stronghold on the North Vietnamese border. So the members were taken to Sam Neua.
That was forever. They've never returned.

The Pathet Lao sent members of the government, military, and all technicians off to reeducation "seminar
camps." And their families who remained in Vientiane or
in villages around Laos didn't count as people anymore.
The Pathet Lao said: "Please arrange your affairs so that
you can go for a week." And most non-Communist members of the government have been gone since 1975.

# SEMINAR CAMP
--------

**Prasith Sayaphon**

*Prisoner*
*Pathet Lao Seminar Camp*
*Laos-Vietnam Border*
*June 1975—May 1982*

In May 1982 I escaped from a seminar camp where I had been held prisoner for five years.

Before 1975, I had been a lieutenant in the Laotian air force, working in the supply and maintenance section. After the Pathet Lao took power, at first I thought that they, like myself, wanted to help build our country. They had a campaign to persuade former government officials and military to go to the seminar camps to learn about their good policies.

We were loaded into trucks and taken to a dense forest in the mountainous area on the Laos-Vietnam border. There were no houses or shelters. The Pathet Lao made us build everything from scratch with bamboo and grass roofs. The prisoners included civil servants, district chiefs, and military officers to the rank of captain. Higher government officials, military leaders, and religious persons were put in other camps.

There were five other camps in my area. Each camp held about six hundred prisoners. Most everyone in the camp wanted to escape, but we were in a difficult mountainous terrain and in a very weak physical state from malnutrition and disease. We were forced to do hard labor—cut logs and build roads. It was very dangerous to clear the wooded area because there were many unexploded bombs sunk part way into the ground. The Pathet Lao guards forced us to dismantle the bombs by hand. Some exploded, killing many prisoners.

The only food we received was old stale rice that the

Pathet Lao had left over from the war. Some of it was up to ten years old. And only a little more than half a handful each day. To survive, we had to search for food in the forests, such as bamboo shoots.

Because of the lack of nutrition and the type of food we ate, there was much disease. Dysentery was very common and other stomach ailments. I became very skinny and my skin turned pale yellow.

To maintain control in the camp, the Pathet Lao used prisoners as spies. They reported to the Pathet Lao the names of dissidents and conversations they heard among other prisoners. There were many executions by firing squad. Some people were sent to jails from which they never returned. Others were shot while trying to escape.

On one occasion, a group of thirty prisoners talked among themselves about conditions in the camp. A spy overheard this and told a Pathet Lao official. The thirty conversants were rounded up. The Pathet Lao accused twelve of them of being "radical rightists." They were tied with a rope and forced to sit.

The soldiers picked up big hammers that we used to break stones, and hit the prisoners on the head. They were lying in a pool of their own blood. But they were not dead. And the victims' eighteen friends stood around them, paralyzed with fear. The Pathet Lao ordered them to bury the twelve friends alive.

The eighteen protested strongly that these wounded men were still alive. They refused to bury them. The Pathet Lao became furious. They handed the prisoners the bloody hammers and ordered them to beat the men lying on the ground to make sure they were dead. Unfortunately, the men had no choice but to finish off their friends. They then buried them as the Pathet Lao ordered.

# PRISONERS OF CONSCIENCE

## Ginetta Sagan

*Human Rights Advocate*
*Indochina Involvement*

*1967—Present*

I was born in Italy. During World War II, I worked in the underground to help free prisoners being held by the Nazis. And we helped Allied POWs who were hiding in northern Italy. I became well acquainted with the institution of repression from my own arrest and interrogation by the Gestapo, and all that followed...I saw people executed. I was very lucky to survive.

I came to America after the war. And in 1967 I began working internationally with prisoners of conscience, whether they be held in a Fascist or Communist regime. Because just as I have survived, I would like for others to have the same opportunity.

I first became involved with Indochina because I had some Vietnamese friends when I went to the university at the Sorbonne in Paris, 1948–51. Many of them didn't want either French or Communist rule in Vietnam. In 1967–68, they were passing me some very accurate information about detainees of the Thieu regime [the South Vietnamese president, Nguyen Van Thieu, 1967–75] security forces and their interrogation methods. And they told me about the assassination of village chiefs and schoolteachers by the Viet Cong. They objected strongly to both.

These friends were distressed because they wanted the Americans out of Vietnam and an end to the war. That was their major concern. But at the same time they were troubled by the possibility that if the Hanoi regime conquered South Vietnam, the Communists would use the same repressive tactics they were using in the North.

I worked very hard for the release of prisoners of conscience being held by the Thieu regime. I visited representatives of the Hanoi regime and PRG [Viet Cong] in Paris on several occasions from 1968 to 1973, to bring to their attention my concern about the treatment of American POWs being held in North Vietnam. At that time the Communist representatives were guaranteeing personal and political freedoms the Vietnamese people would receive at the end of the war. And Article 11 of the Paris Peace Agreement stated:

"Immediately after the cease-fire, the two Vietnamese parties will achieve national reconciliation and concord, end hatred and enmity, and prohibit all acts of reprisal and discrimination against individuals or organizations that have collaborated with one side or the other."

But soon after May 1975 information began reaching the West that more than one million Vietnamese were being called to report to reeducation camps. European friends, knowing my long-standing concern for human rights violations in Vietnam during the war, began sending me specific reports of these massive new internments.

At first the people called were former military and political officials. But subsequently journalists, artists, doctors, lawyers, religious clergy, academicians, and students were also sent for. Members of the judiciary were at first sent to prisons and later moved to reeducation camps. Professionals, many with overseas training, also became inmates. Many of my Vietnamese friends who had been involved in the human rights movement against Diem and Thieu either escaped or died in Communist prisons.

In 1978 I began systematically interviewing former prisoners of these camps. I have spoken to some six hundred former prisoners. Coworkers interviewed another two hundred. Our aim is to bring to light the continued imprisonment of thousands of people in defiance of the United Nations Universal Declaration of Human Rights of December 1948 and the UN Covenant of Civil and Political Rights of 1966.

An unknown number of prisoners in these camps have died of substandard diet, labor accidents in the jungle, or lack of medical care. Others have died of malaria and dysentery. Some prisoners have been executed for attempting escape. Others died after severe beatings.

Before 1975 when I worked to release prisoners of the Thieu regime, the International Committee of the Red Cross (ICRC) was allowed to visit the prisons in South Vietnam. The ICRC made recommendations for the physical improvement of the facilities as well as the treatment of prisoners. But today in Vietnam, nearly ten years after the war ended, thousands of political prisoners are detained without charges or trial. And they are brutally punished for the slightest infraction of prison-camp rules.

And as when the American POWs were held in Hanoi during the war, once again the Red Cross has not been allowed to visit these camps. Underfed, overworked, and living in the most degrading conditions, many of these prisoners will not survive. The question I have often asked is why such massive human rights violations have had such scant attention from the media and the leadership of the U.S. peace movement?

Former antiwar leaders have been divided on the issue. Some joined Joan Baez in 1979 in a public plea for release of the prisoners. Others aggressively attempted to cast doubts on the accuracy of information provided to Baez. But there are many cases, such as the deaths of two prominent lawyers, Le Si Giai and Tran Van Tuyen, once the chairman of the opposition bloc in the Lower House of the South Vietnamese government and co-founder of the International League for Human Rights in Vietnam, that should have convinced even the most ardent supporters of the Hanoi regime.

Many former members of the peace movement have chosen to hide the ongoing tragedy in Vietnam, or to justify it in other ways. Some have made trips to Vietnam, often as guests of the Hanoi regime. One such invited guest (who testified before the U.S. Congress) described her impression of a reeducation camp in 1977. She said it was a place that "looked as though it could have been a tropical resort." And she described the daily routine of the inmates as "training in skills for nonmilitary jobs, manual labor in vegetable and animal production, as well as cultural and sporting activities." She was told by her guides that there was no restriction on family visits and no punishment for would-be escapees.

Her account reminded me of the German-American Friendship Society during World War II, which went to visit a model camp in Germany when allegations of abuses against the Jews came out. Those people came back with glowing reports.

I thought, "Hasn't this woman learned from World War II that dictators will go to any length to hide what's happening within the police state, within the camps?"

# THE STUBBORN GUY

## Doan Van Toai

*Political Prisoner*
*Ho Chi Minh City*

*June 1975–October 1977*

During the war years, in 1970, I was one of the Saigon student leaders. I organized demonstrations against the Thieu regime and against American interventionism in Vietnam. At the end of 1970 into January 1971, I came to the United States to speak at Stanford Unversity and Berkeley, sponsored by some professors in the antiwar student groups.

Because of my activities against the government, I was jailed twice in Saigon. And I was expelled from the university. I found a job in a private bank in Saigon. During this time, I helped some people in the NLF write financial reports on the economic situation in South Vietnam.

When the Communists took over in April 1975, they asked me to work with the financial committee. In June 1975 this committee asked me to submit ideas for a program on how to confiscate all the property of all the people. I disagreed with that. I proposed a program to confiscate the property of those made rich through the war and the corrupt generals.

The Communists said that my proposal is only appropriate in a democratic revolution. But in a socialist revolution, as Marxist-Leninists we don't tolerate any private property. I told them that under the circumstances I could not cooperate with them. I wanted to resign. But they don't let me do that. A few days later, when I was attending a concert in Saigon, they arrested me and put me in jail for twenty-eight months. They did not charge me with anything or give me a reason. It was because they thought that I was a stubborn guy.

The conditions in the Communist jail were terrible . . . much worse than in the "tiger cages" of Thieu. The difference is that in the Thieu regime they only tortured your body. The Communists not only torture you physically, but in a very clever manner they torture your spirit.

Previously, when I heard that there was "brainwashing" I think, "A man cannot be brainwashed." But when I was in the Communist prison I understand. For instance, they put you in a very isolated cell for a few days. You become very thirsty for talking with somebody. And you want to read, anything. After a couple of months, they give you a lot of Communist papers. So when you first read it, you remember it. And this makes little changes in your mind.

They asked everything about my life since I was eight years old. They treated me friendly during the questioning. I told them the truth because I believed that I had not done anything against them. But their tone changed. They chained me—right wrist to left ankle; left wrist to right ankle. And for three weeks they only released me twice a day for about five minutes to eat. I protested. They answered, "This is because you tell lies." I asked, "What lies?" They said, "That's what you must think about."

After two months in solitary, because of the large amount of new prisoners, they moved me into a collective cell. In this cell were many kinds of people: former politicans, writers, intellectuals and former Viet Cong fighters. I met many people who were Viet Cong members. Through these special prisoners I learned a lot about Communism. One old man had been arrested by the French, the Diem government, the Thieu government, and then by the Communists. In other words, they arrested any nationalist who was perceived to be a threat to the Hanoi government.

These nationalists, maybe leftists, are the real enemies of the Communists. Because they are the free-thinkers. They are the real revolutionaries.

Also, two hundred thousand Viet Cong deserted the Communists' ranks during the war and joined the Republic side. Where are they now? The Communists did not consider them to be people. They were executed, eliminated in 1975.

Buddhists were the strongest force against the Diem

and Thieu regimes. But they were one of the first targets of the Communist reprisal. The Hanoi regime fear that they will again organize an antigovernment movement. Pagodas were not closed down. The Communists are more clever than that. They let them remain open, but they expelled the very stubborn Buddhist leaders. And replaced them with puppet venerables who support Communist control of religion.

In the crowded Ho Chi Minh City jail cells there were monks, Catholic priests, lawyers, journalists. Between sixty and one hundred people were crushed into a collective cell, five meters by eight meters. With the heat of Vietnam, many could not survive.

Every night, every day, I watched friends die at my feet, especially the old people. We did not have room to sleep lying down. The young men had to sleep by sitting up and left floor room for the older men. I met prisoners more than eighty years old. Even babies and children were in jail. Because when the cadres arrest the mother and father, they also arrest the children.

While I was in prison in 1976, one Western delegation visited my jail. Three days before that, the Communists moved all the prisoners out to another prison. And we were replaced by soldiers and officials from the government. And they showcased some generals of the Thieu regime who are cowards and will say anything to get favors from the jailers.

# JUGÉS ET CONDAMNÉS

--------

## Al Santoli

*Journalist & Vietnam Veteran*
*Southeast Asia*
*1968–1969, 1983–1984*

I have now interviewed a large number of Vietnamese who have been in reeducation camps. I am deeply concerned because if you study the structure of the early Nazi concentration camps—the overwork, underfeeding, lack of medical treatment, and severe punishment—the similarity is stunning.

I am not talking about Auschwitz. Rather, Mathausen, for example, during 1933–40, when the Nazis were incarcerating Germans from all walks of life: trade unionists, professors, students, priests, and Protestant ministers. I have seen a deposition from a Protestant minister arrested in Vietnam. If you compare it to a deposition of a Protestant minister from Nazi Germany, there is no difference.

After April 1975, instead of truly unifying and rebuilding the country after the war, the Communist regime continued a policy of military dominance and escalation, so that Vietnam now has the third or fourth largest standing army in the world. And to guarantee a socialist society, the government has jailed or forced into exile all of its best-trained people who could have improved the economic conditions of the country.

I have found with many former Vietnamese reeducation camp prisoners that the threat of reprisal if they speak out about their experiences is very great. While I was in Europe interviewing a number of former Viet Cong and North Vietnamese who are now refugees, a friend of mine had a terrifying experience in Paris after interviewing former reeducation camp prisoners.

Still shaken by the experience, my friend told me: "I had just finished conducting the interviews. And as I was preparing to leave Paris, the phone rang. I was staying in a place that nobody should have known about. A voice in French said that if I made public the information that I had learned from these former prisoners, '*Serons jugés et condamnés*.' It was a threat: 'They will be judged, and they will be condemned.' This meant reprisals against their families still living in Vietnam."

During the past few years, I have spoken with human rights activists and government officials who have worked with former prisoners of many countries. Never have they found stark terror like that in the former prisoners of Communist Vietnam. The fear is for their relatives.

# THE CONCERT

--------

## Doan Van Toai

*Political Prisoner*
*Ho Chi Minh City*

*June 1975–October 1977*

After April 1975, the northerners saw the reality in the South, which was the opposite of everything Hanoi had said.

One colonel from the North came to see his son in Saigon. He brought a small can of milk and a kilo of sugar. He told his son, "I thought you would be hungry and have no sugar, so I reserve my ration for two months to buy this for you. But why do you work for the CIA?"

The son was very surprised. He asked, "Why do you say that I am working for the CIA?" And the father said, "If you are not working for the CIA, then why is your house big like this? You have enough to eat, a car, everything." The son said, "I am a garage man. I repair cars. I never work for the CIA. I didn't know any Americans here. Father, most people here in Saigon live like this." And the father woke up.

During the war years I supported Hanoi because I thought, "No opposition in the North. That's a good regime." But I asked a friend of mine from the North after April 'seventy-five, "Why did you come south?" In private he complained about everything. But in public he would always support the government. I asked, "How can you people live under that Hanoi regime for twenty years with no opposition?" And he told me:

"In a Communist society, like in a music concert, all the musicians must be in the same voice. If one of them is a little bit different, he will be automatically eliminated. And they don't do it to yourself only. They do it to your relatives to blackmail you."

When I was put into the political prison in 1975, the first day I was incarcerated the Communists told me, "If you try to escape from prison or you are suspected to escape, your wife and your relatives will be arrested immediately." So in front of the prison there is no barbed wire. And no need for many soldiers or policemen.

# THE DISCIPLINE HOUSE

--------

## Tran Tri Vu

*Political Prisoner*
*Reeducation Camps*
*Vietnam*

*1975–1979*

In 1975, shortly after the Communists took over, they asked all the previous officers of the former regime to register for ten days of classes. I had been a press officer in Saigon and signed up for the classes with some trepidation. They brought us into the forest, where we remained for years and years.

There are countless camps throughout Vietnam. For example, in Saigon there are eleven districts. In each district there were assembly points to gather and transport prisoners to eleven regions of camps. In any case, it was Thu Duc Camp.

The Thu Duc camp had many subcamps. [Women prisoners were kept in a separate area of the camps.] And the Communists opened more camps in ten other regions. Most were in Ham Tan, near Phan Thiet. But they called all of these camps "Thu Duc Camp." So in reality, there may be a dozen camps all under one name, to give the appearance that there are less camps and less prisoners than there really are.

Your family might try to send a letter to you at Thu Duc Camp, thinking that you were near Saigon. But you could be in Ham Tan, eighty miles northeast, or in Song Be, eighty miles northwest on the Cambodian border. Prisoners were used to construct other camps to receive more and more new prisoners. Throughout the five years I was held prisoner, I constructed more and more camps.

In my last camp there were only around a thousand prisoners. But we constructed another camp to receive another thousand from Saigon. And when I was leaving in 1979, we were constructing a third camp to receive another large number. We used cement donated by Western countries supposedly as humanitarian aid. For instance, I read on a food package, "Donated by the people of France for the humanitarian society." This food was used to feed the Communist soldiers, not the prisoners or local civilians. And we were forced to carry the bags of food from trucks to the warehouse where it is stored.

A day in reeducation camp would be something like this: In the morning we get a small portion of food—not rice but some cereal that is usually for feeding pigs. When we eat this cereal we have many stomach problems. As we couldn't eat the food given in camp, we dug into the ground to find roots and wild potatoes. Many people died in the camps from starvation and we did not have enough medicine.

From 7:00 A.M. until 4:00 P.M. we worked in the forest. And in the evening we had political indoctrination. The cadre would read to us from a Communist text and ask if we had any questions. If you asked questions, that would show that you had the "wrong view." So they kept the period of study going very late into the evening. We were exhausted from working in the forest and wanted to rest. If we agreed with their doctrinal explanations, we could end the study period.

If a prisoner offended a Communist officer, they would be taken away to a special camp, even old men. And in our camp, if you didn't listen to the guards, if you stand up against them, you must live in the "discipline house." Here, you are put in chains for many months and not permitted to see the sunlight, you are always in darkness. A very respected Vietnamese sculptor was kept in the discipline house for more than eight months.

Even well-behaved prisoners were forced to work like slaves. If we resisted, the guards would take away our portion of food. They controlled our lives with the threat of starvation. Also, a special form of punishment was to hold back letters from our families.

The way that the Communists fool international opinion is that when Western journalists visit reeducation camps, they are tricked. On one occasion, the Communists had the prisoners from my camp build another camp, very very beautiful. We could not figure out why we had to construct this beautiful camp in an artistic way: a meeting hall for the cinema or theater, tennis court, a volleyball court. Afterwards they brought many units of their soldiers to live here. They are all very healthy and very gay, with guitars and songs. We were very angry that we had to build this camp for them.

Afterwards, many international delegations came to visit this camp. And the Communists told them that this was a typical reeducation camp. We realized that all of these delegations had proposed to see us.

In the dry season we would burn wooded areas. The ashes become good fertilizer and after a couple weeks of rain, this land will produce a very good rice crop. But this kind of agriculture is very bad for the soil. Because after two rainy seasons, all the topsoil is washed away. The Communists organized us to do this type of slash-and-burn agriculture. They continue to do this to get a quick good crop. But they are destroying the land in the process. And the Communists then tell visiting Western delegations that it was American defoliation that did this.

I saw many previous agents of the National Liberation Front who were now prisoners. These men were tortured and forced to sign statements saying that they had collaborated with the previous regime. I think that many of the former Viet Cong, as well as the majority of the South Vietnamese ... nobody in their hearts wants to collaborate with the Hanoi regime.

In the five years I was held prisoner, I thought of escaping many times. But my family sent me letters to convince me that they could buy my freedom in Saigon. My wife tried to offer all that we had, including our house, to a high-ranking Communist's wife. And I had parents in France who asked the French government to arrange my release. But it was a very special occasion when I was released in 1979.

At this time there was a conference in Geneva about Vietnamese refugees. And the Communists promised the Red Cross to release a number of prisoners, to show their goodwill. So in my camp, two or three people were allowed to leave the country. This was after Joan Baez and the group in the West had the petition about political prisoners. The Communists wanted to make propaganda to show that the boat people are not their responsibility.

But in reality, only a few people were allowed to leave legally—and they had to pay an extraordinary amount of money. In my case, my family gave up all that we had in exchange for my exit visa.

# THE VIGIL

## Mrs. Lu Thi Duc

*Wife of Reeducation Prisoner*
*Saigon*

*1975–Present*

My husband was put into reeducation in 1975. Like all former civil servants, he presented himself voluntarily for what the Communists publicly promised would be a ten-day study period. I kept waiting and he did not return. So I made a request to see Mr. Cao Dang Chiem, who was in charge of police and intelligence force in the Saigon-Cholon area.

Chiem said he could not give me permission to see my husband. I said, "If my husband will be executed, please let me have a last chance to talk with him."

Previously a number of other wives made requests to visit their husbands and asked why they had not returned. Frustrated by the authorities' negative responses, the wives became desperate. One day they gathered outside the police station to make a public demonstration.

That night, the Communist police sent a truck out to arrest each of these women at their homes. They were never seen again. And their children were left parentless, without hope. Instead, they were encouraged to leave Saigon and go into the jungle to the New Economic Zones.

# NEW ECONOMIC ZONE

---------

**Tran Thanh Son**

*Collective Laborer*
*New Economic Zone*
*Bac Lieu Province*

*1976–1982*

When I returned to Saigon from reeducation camp in 1976, the authorities forced my family and I to go to a New Economic Zone. We were trucked to the jungle in the Vinh My area of Bac Lieu Province. Around two thousand people from Saigon were sent to this zone. We all were unhappy because we had lived in the city all of our lives and knew nothing about farming.

We had to clear the forest by hand with primitive tools that we created. The Communist soldiers watched over us and graded our efforts. If the work was to their satisfaction, our reward was a little rice . . . barely enough to subsist on.

By 1978 there were many tombs in the area. The main cause of death was malaria and malnutrition. Mostly grandparents and young children were the first to perish. My six children were very sick. My wife and I feared that they would not survive. We foraged for manioc leaves and wild vegetation.

By 1980 many young people were escaping from the New Economic Zones in our area. Some returned to the city. Other people tried to reach the seaside to escape by boat. Because they could no longer endure the suffering.

# WINNERS AND LOSERS

--------

## Col. Harry Summers

*Historian*
*Strategic Studies Institute*
*U.S. Army War College*
*Carlisle, Pennsylvania*

The entire focus of America's Asian policy from the Korean War period until the end of the Vietnam War had been the containment of China. Once the opening was made to China, we lost the entire focus of our strategy. And we're still having some problems in that part of the world focusing on what our strategy is. What are we trying to do in Asia?

It's funny that the Soviets have come in, and they've accomplished what we tried to do for so long. They have encircled China.

You could make the point that the great strategic loser of the Vietnam War was not the United States, but China. That is one of the ironies. In the Korean War we fought the Chinese army and both of us won: China now has a buffer state [North Korea] on one of its most sensitive borders. And the United States still has an ally in South Korea.

In the Vietnam War we avoided a fight with China, and we both lost. China now has an enemy on its southern border. And South Vietnam has disappeared.

The other great loser of the war was the Viet Cong. Those poor bastards lost to everyone. They lost to the Americans, they lost to the South Vietnamese. And most conclusively of all, they lost to the North Vietnamese.

# PROMISES

## Nguyen Cong Hoan

*Representative*
*National Assembly*
*Socialist Republic of Vietnam*
*Ho Chi Minh City—Hanoi*

*1976–1977*

During my youth, in high school and as a university student, I worked in peace groups opposing the Ngo Dinh
Diem and Nguyen Van Thieu regimes. In 1971, I won a
National Assembly seat representing Phu Yen, my native
province in South Vietnam. I became a member of the
opposition bloc led by Representative Tran Van Tuyen.
And in 1974, I joined the National Reconciliation Force
in an attempt to set up a viable third force.

Our main objective was to oust the Thieu regime. We
would have liked to have anyone from the reform parties—Tran Van Tuyen, Vu Van Mau or Nguyen Van Huyen—become president, and then play a central role in
a neutral postwar Vietnam. The leaders of North Vietnam
always talked about independence and neutrality. They
never talked about Communism and called themselves
the "Workers Party." We believed that unification with
North Vietnam would evolve gradually over a period of
time. And all elements of the population would have a
fair, equal place in society and prosper.

In April 1975, I was at my home in Phu Yen, four hundred
miles northeast of Saigon. When the Communists took
over, they said, "Stay here. Don't go anywhere." So I
became a teacher in the local high school. Within days
the North Vietnamese *bo-doi* [soldiers] ordered me to
disband the National Reconciliation Force chapter in my
province.

Although no major bloodbath took place in the major
cities after the Communist victory, in the provinces where

284

there were no outside observers, eliminations and killings were widespread and took many forms. In Phu Yen, directly after the Communist takeover, around five hundred people were killed en masse in a forested area near Hoa Quang village. Others personally known to me who were victims of the authorities' policy of revenge were:

Venerable Thich Dieu Bon, of the Unified Buddhist Church in Phu Yen, was suspected of being a CIA agent, simply because he had a certificate of appreciation from the U.S. government for helping to search for MIAs. He was killed.

Mr. Tran Pho, a teacher in Song Cau and uncle of my private secretary, was killed with a machete at Le Uyen.

Mr. Nguyen Huu Tri, a Dai Viet Party member from Song Cau, was buried alive.

Mr. Truong Tu Thien, a Dai Viet Party leader, was arrested in Saigon, then brought back to Nha Trang. He had undergone extremely atrocious tortures.

Many others died in concentration camps. Victims of overwork, malnutrition, and unhealthy conditions.

In early 1976, I was chosen to be a member of the National Assembly of the Socialist Republic [SRV]. In reality, the National Assembly had no actual function. All decisions were made by the Party in Hanoi and dictated to the South. We had no right to talk against Party policies.

I participated in two sessions of the National Assembly in Hanoi, in June 1976 and January 1977. As a member of the Committee on Culture, I had access to many reports and discussions dealing with national objectives, long-term projections, and official policies of the government.

At the 1976 Party Congress, they talked about the coming fights against China and Cambodia, due to Russian influence on the Vietnamese leaders and policies of the regime. The Party leaders expressed their closeness with the Soviets and intentions to let them use Cam Ranh Bay for their navy.

By 1976 there was already a little dissension in the National Liberation Front because they were given such little responsibility by the northerners. By early 1977, the Communist Party began arresting a number of NLF people because they began openly expressing their disillusionment. At that time, I'd estimate more than three hundred thousand people were in jail. In Phu Yen Province, the province chief was NLF. But in 1977 he was kicked out by the Party and his property confiscated. They replaced him with a Party member from the North.

In 1977 when I was in Hanoi for the second assembly session, I had a chance to visit some pagodas. The present state of religious life in Hanoi and the rest of Vietnam is quite sad. People do not have time to visit pagodas or worship the Buddha because of the burden placed on them by the Communists. And on Sundays and Christian holy days, the government enforces collective labor to dig ditches or patch roads, to prevent people from going to church. Or they force people to attend mandatory political classes on Party line. However, when certain Westerners visit, the government allows people to go to church or temple.

The Communists control and repress religions through associations that carry out the Party policy toward religions. Priests and monks who obey the Party blindly are appointed to lead these associations.

The propaganda machinery of the government openly slanders the major faiths. A film, *All Saints' Day*, defamed Catholics through the image of a girl raped by a priest during her confession on All Saints' Day. This film was strongly opposed by people, who left the theater refusing to see the rest. However, the film was shown again to teachers during a ceremony to promote the charter of the Patriotic Teachers' Association.

The Hoa Hao Buddhists have remained fiercely anti-Communist in the western Mekong Delta. When the Communists took over, they arrested and killed the Hoa Hao leaders who they thought would be dangerous for them. But the Hoa Hao have never forgotten the Communist murder of their prophet, Huynh Phu So [1947], and continue to resist today.

During the war, many of the highland tribes helped the Communists because they were promised a better life. Instead, the Communists tried to put them in flatland reservations, so they could be observed and easily controlled. Many of the Montagnard people left these labor camps. And they also continue to fight the Communists. A high-level Communist leader in Hanoi told me that in response, Party policy was to arrest some tribal leaders and use the yellow chemical weapons on the tribes. This is to break their traditional structure and prevent them from living on their ancestral land.

Throughout Vietnam, resistance continues. By 1977 I knew of some courageous youth groups in various parts of Vietnam who were spreading leaflets against the Communist regime.

The economy is in shambles. Thousands of people have been press-ganged into nonpaying "voluntary" labor brigades, and many families shipped off to desolate New Economic Zones.

The authorities rule by force and terror. The An Ninh secret police are feared worse than any previous regime. All large family gatherings, even weddings and funerals, must have previous permission by authorities, who send public security officers to attend. Any meeting involving more than two or three persons outside the family is immediately suspect. Those involved can be requested to give a report on what they have talked about or are immediately arrested.

Everywhere is fear. An indiscreet remark can mean instant arrest and an indefinite prison term. A Gulag Archipelago has been instituted in Vietnam.

But the Party does not want to stop there. During the first session of the unified National Assembly held in Hanoi in June 1976, we were given a copy of a document entitled *Vietnam—Southeast Asia*, which was subsequently taken back because of its sensitive nature. At this same session, Mr. Tran Quynh, private secretary to Le Duan [the Party leader], told me, "The liberation of Thailand will be next. It is a historical necessity and a responsibility of ours."

# TIGERS

## Hoang Van Chi

*Resistance Operative*
*Viet Minh*
*North Vietnam*
*1945–1954*

While in the resistance, I met Ho Chi Minh three or four times at various stages of the revolution. Basically he was always the same—dogmatic, expressing blind faith in Marxism.

He made a statement in the Soviet newspaper *Pravda* in 1960. He said that in the beginning, he was a nationalist. But by working in the Soviet Comintern and studying Marxism, he came to realize that Communism is not only a compass, but a "magic bag." What was very unfortunate for Ho and Vietnam is that he vaguely knew about the myth of the magic bag. But he did not know that this myth came from India, as a most significant anecdote.

According to the story, there was a small, weak kingdom in North India that bordered on a very powerful one. And the king of the small kingdom was very concerned. He didn't know what to do if one day the big kingdom attacked him. So he shared his concern with his ministers.

The king's Supreme Counselor, an astrologer, suggested that short of magic power there was no way to defeat the larger army. But in a faraway city called Takasila, there was a wise man who knew many wonderful magic tricks. He suggested that the king ask this wise man for some magic. The king decided to go in person. He brought with him four cabinet ministers, four military ministers, the astrologer, and the queen. The trip took many days by horse.

The wise man welcomed them. He was very kind and gave the king a magic bag. He told the King, "Keep this bag with you. Any time you are faced with danger, open it and you will see a piece of paper giving you instructions."

The king thanked the wise man, and the group went home. But unfortunately, on the long journey home they became lost in the jungle. For many days they went around and around, but could not find their way out. The king was very concerned. But the astrologer reminded him of this magic bag.

The king opened the bag and found a piece of paper with an inscription. The instructions said that the ministers stand at the four corners of a rectangle, the queen in the center, and the astrologer and the king on each end. And in a chorus they had to recite, "I become a tiger."

Suddenly the whole group became a tiger. They were no longer afraid of starving. Because the tiger can catch any small animals to eat. But they could no longer recover human nature. They forgot about finding a solution for their country and they lost their human conscience.

That is exactly the case of Ho Chi Minh. He used Communism as a means to an end, and he got caught within that means. He lost the feeling of nationalism and sacrificed his own country for the cause of international Communism.

# NEW SOCIALIST MAN

## Nguyen Tuong Lai

*Security Official*
*Socialist Republic of Vietnam*
*Southern Vietnam*

*1975–1978*

After the liberation in 1975, after twenty-one years of fighting, I believed that peace had finally come and the new life would begin.

During the long war, the southern Party members dreamed of reunification of our country. We did not realize that after 1975 things would get worse.

During the war, there were two groups within the NLF. The first were Party members, led by Pham Hung and Nguyen Huu Tho. The second group were those not belonging to the Party, led by people such as Trinh Dinh Thao, Lam Van Thiet, and Truong Nhu Tang. After the war, a small number of the second group were encouraged by the Party to become members of the National Assembly, which did not have any power.

During the war, we used two magic words. The first word was "nationalism," to get monks, priests, students, and all social classes to join our front. The second word is "democracy," promising land reform and political equality for all South Vietnamese.

In retrospect, the propaganda tactics of the liberation front were the political means of the Communist Party to grab power. The PRG [Provisional Revolutionary Government] was established to gain international support.

Many high-ranking cadre from the South had relatives in the deposed regime. I had a brother-in-law who had been in the South Vietnamese army. A friend of mine had a brother who was a landowner. We wanted to contact our families and have good relations. But the northern Party members were against this.

In self-criticism sessions, northern cadre belittled us for visiting our relatives. They accused myself and others of not following Party directives to make distinctions between capitalists and ourselves. But I didn't agree with the socialist way of developing the country. Originally, I had heard the way that Ho Chi Minh talked about communism, which sounded fantastic. But I had been to Russia and Eastern Europe and realized that the Communist way was not the best. Especially in comparing the standard of living with what had been in South Vietnam.

After 1975, most enterprise was nationalized and run by Party cadre. This has failed. Because people refuse to produce without economic incentives. And the economy has deteriorated rapidly because of inadequate industrial planning by the Soviet-trained northern cadre. And while people go hungry, rice grown in Vietnam is shipped to the Soviet Union.

In 1975, I was put in charge of planning how to deal with former GVN officials who failed to register for reeducation camps. I visited reeducation camps in my area and taught classes on creating the "New Socialist Man."

I was then put in charge of Long Tan Reeducation Camp, which was formerly a large orphanage built by the Americans. This was a temporary camp for former high-ranking civil servants. They received one to three months' indoctrination. Then many people in Long Tan Camp were transferred to harsh camps in North Vietnam or in the jungles of South Vietnam, where discipline is more severe.

Reeducation camps differ from jails for Party dissidents. I knew many southern Party members who were imprisoned. And most of the world never realized that immediately after liberation, in the districts and provinces, public courts sentenced many people to death. Main targets were the Hoi Chanh [two hundred thousand former Viet Cong who had rallied to the GVN during the war] and GVN intelligence and security forces working with the Americans. Also, officials like Mr. Ho Ngoc Can, of Chuong Thien Province, were sentenced to death.

These unfortunate people were killed and nobody knows where. Because Party policy was very clear: Every death sentence should be public, to enhance the hatred of the people for the Party's enemies and to gain support for the revolution. But the executions must be done in secret, so the people would not have pity for the victims.

The socialism carried out in Vietnam now is the same as in Russia. The relationship between the Party, the Congress, and the people is based on the Leninist-Stalinist model. In Party meetings many of us asked, "What is the reason for accepting this Soviet model? We fought the French and the Americans. Why do we now accept a Soviet system?"

The only answer we received from the Central Committee was, "If there was no October Revolution in Russia, there would not be a socialist revolution now in Eastern Europe and the Third World. And who made the October Revolution? It was Marx, Lenin, and Stalin. This is the only valuable model."

In 1978, Vietnam began to attack Cambodia. At first the Politburo wanted to test the Chinese reaction. The Central Committee had planned the attack long before. At that time I received orders from Cambodia.

I am not afraid to sacrifice and die for my country. But I was against the mission in Cambodia. As a Party member, I was obliged to obey my orders. But many southern members questioned the reasons and merits for going into Cambodia. Many of us felt that it was because of Cambodia's alliance with China and our own Party's obedience to Soviet dictates.

After twenty-one years of war, now another front, another war, was beginning that will never finish. I felt that it would not be good for the reconstruction of Vietnam. So even though I was unsure how my former enemies would accept me, in November 1978 I decided to leave.

# VIETNAMIZATION OF CAMBODIA

## Prak Savath

*District Chief*
*Battambang Province, Cambodia*

*1980–1983*

## Oung Chumnet

*Railroad Official*
*Phnom Penh*

*1979–1983*

## Mrs. Keo Vey

*Farm Wife*
*Nong Samet Refugee Camp,*
*Cambodia*

*1983–*

PRAK SAVATH: After the Pol Pot forces were driven from my area, I was assigned district chief for Tmor Puok in 1980. The order was not given to me directly by the Vietnamese. But the Vietnamese told the Heng Samrin government [Samrin, a former Khmer Rouge, is president of the Vietnamese-surrogate Cambodian government] to assign me because I was a well-known militiaman. And I could speak Vietnamese.

Under the Pol Pot regime, many people died in my village. And since the people were afraid of the Khmer Rouge, we thought the Vietnamese might be an alternative. But now we know there is no hope. The Khmer Rouge and Vietnamese are both Communists. So the same system—all collectivity, no liberty.

In my district, the people work hard to grow food, but still go hungry. We have to sell our crop to the state. So we sell our rice to Heng Samrin officials who are under direct orders of the Vietnamese soldiers.

We sell the rice to the state, one kilo for eight cents. But to buy back our ration, they charge sixteen cents for a kilo. And even that is only for their sympathizers. They control people by starvation.

Today, people are being arrested in many villages. Many men and women have been tortured, some have died. That's why I reported to the Vietnamese 5th Division headquarters at Svay Chek. I asked the Vietnamese authorities, "Why do you do these terrible things?" And each time I reported, I was beaten by them. They told me, "You serve us."

In June 1983, I was arrested in Svay Chek and sent to a jail in Sisophon, twenty-five miles away. More than one hundred prisoners were there, especially village and district chiefs. There were new people coming in all the time. There were a few Heng Samrin people working as jailers, but mostly Vietnamese. And they would conduct the torture.

If I tried to defend my village, I was accused of all sorts of things. The first question was, "Why do you help the people?" That means, "You are in connection with the non-Communist resistance forces." At each question they grabbed my hair and pulled it out. They hung me up on the wall and beat me until I passed out. Sometimes they beat me three times in one day. They knocked all of my front teeth out. They said, "You must confess..."

When I was in Sisophon district, I saw many Vietnamese civilians, men, women, and children, come in two or three big trucks to buy cloth and supplies. Where they went back to, I don't know.

In recent months [1982–83] there have been many high and special meetings conducted by the Vietnamese for district and province leaders. They say that now Vietnamese civilians—farmers, fishermen, and others—are moving into Cambodia. The Cambodian people in the interior are concerned about this growing Vietnamese presence. Whenever Vietnamese civilians are seen, we all feel that our country is being taken over. I discussed this with people in my village.

We understand well what the Vietnamese would like to do to our country. That's why so many people are here in this border [refugee] camp. From my village, one hundred five families have fled to Ampil Camp.

OUNG CHUMNET: I left Phnom Penh on September 9, 1983. I was working as a government official on the railroad. There is only one railroad, which belongs to the state. In the Cambodian government in Phnom Penh we suffer more and more pressure from the Vietnamese.

In the administration you see a Cambodian name, but all has been decided by the Vietnamese. And the percentage of Vietnamese now living in areas of Phnom Penh now numbers more than Cambodians, around sixty percent. Some are officials and wounded soldiers. But most are civilians who come to work, simple people. They don't feel that they have come to another country. Now they act like it's home.

In 1979 and 1980 in Phnom Penh there was a lot of humanitarian aid delivered by international agencies. If this aid went to the population, in one or two years we would have been sufficiently helped. But we never received this aid. It went to Vietnam at night by truck.

In 1979–80 many Western relief workers in Phnom Penh wanted to talk with Cambodian residents. But the Vietnamese told us, "You have no right to talk with the foreigners." Add to this, all the offices of the ministries have spies working for the Vietnamese.

Many Westerners, especially people from church groups and the international aid groups, go to Phnom Penh, and they will be given Cambodian people to talk with. These people will give the impression that we are happy with the way things are since the Vietnamese came. But even if they wanted to tell the truth, they couldn't. Because they know that someone will report them to the authorities. There are many people in political jails, including government officials who have disagreed with the Vietnamese.

Today, while people go hungry, the Vietnamese and Soviets take much of the Cambodian-grown rice and other natural resources. In return, what we receive from the Soviets is not really aid—only military weapons. They take much more than they give—our rubber, rice, and our liberty.

The past few months, I saw many big guns and tanks being delivered by the Soviets to the port of Kompong Som, and then transported to other parts of the country.

\* \* \*

MRS. KEO VEY: My home village is named after a revered pagoda. My family and I escaped because we have suffered so much under the Vietnamese occupation of our country.

The people in my village are forced to do hard labor for the Vietnamese soldiers, with no time to grow food to feed our families or earn a living. Working in the woods, many days' walk from our homes, some people were crippled or killed by land-mine explosions.

Some girls were raped, even married women, and some killed by the Vietnamese soldiers. And Vietnamese families have moved onto our land. They have brought many household items. Including water pots so big that you cannot lift one alone.

When we saw so many Vietnamese residents moving onto our land, we became frightened and decided to leave. We think that there will be no more Cambodia. We escaped at night with twenty-seven other families. Some men could only let wives and children go because they were conscripted by the Vietnamese. Even children under the age of ten have been drafted.

I am thirty-four years old and have an infant daughter. My mother is sixty-five. I thought that she was going to die on the journey because we had to walk so quickly in the dark woods. And she moves so slowly. Vietnamese and Heng Samrin soldiers were everywhere to prevent people from escaping. So we walked only at night. We were shot at and some families were captured. I was just praying to get safely to the border. We were very afraid to die.

We thought our lives were over. But we were found by a group of Sereika [the non-Communist Khmer People's National Liberation Front], who fought off the Communists and guided us to this border camp. I didn't know anything about the Sereika before we came here. I only came to the border because I wanted to survive and live with my family. Now my only hope is this border camp. And I will die here if necessary.

My husband arrived with me. But now he has joined the guerillas in the forest. I will wait for him here until Cambodia is liberated. Then I will return. Now we must try to survive on the border.

# SECTION V

# VALUES

# THE PICNIC

## Jim Noonan

*Communications*
*1st Shore Party Battalion*
*Chu Lai*

September 1966 – October 1967

A few years ago, a friend of my wife was having a picnic at her parents' house in Connecticut. So we all went up for the day. One of her friends was a student at NYU, a young Vietnamese woman, who rode with us. I had been in Danang in 1967, this woman's hometown. And I was at a bit of a loss, because here was this woman in America. And her family was still in Vietnam. I couldn't help thinking that I had played some role in the disruption of this woman's life. I experienced some real guilt, and was very quiet with her.

Halfway through the day, I went over to a table on the side, away from the volleyball court. It had all the hamburgers and food. I went over to get something to eat. And this Vietnamese woman came over and sat next to me. She said, "So when were you there, Jim?" She sensed it.

We sat down and talked. She sought to cleanse me of some guilt. I thought this was pretty impressive, given her situation. We talked about the war. I told her how terrible I thought it was for the Vietnamese people. I talked about relocation centers and orphanages I had seen. The children's hospital where there wasn't even mosquito netting, flies on open wounds . . . just horrible conditions for children.

She talked a little bit about how young American boys were pawns. How we were used the same way the Vietnamese people were. She made an association between the guys in America who were willing to go to Vietnam, and the Vietnamese—who are still the victims.

I felt pretty relieved after that discussion. It eased my mind about a number of matters. It was like she sensed, "I can help this person." And went to it. I was pretty impressed by her concern.

I had been always a little biased about the Vietnamese that came here. I always thought of them as the rich people who benefited from corruption in the Vietnamese government. And that's just not the case.

The sad thing is, the same way that Vietnam vets were stigmatized, the South Vietnamese were stigmatized, too. Because of a few corrupt or bad people.

# THE WOMEN'S CENTER

## Eve Burton

*Director*
*Center for Unaccompanied Women*
*Songkhla Refugee Camp*
*Thailand*

*1979–1980*

I grew up in New York City during the Vietnam War. I remember painting antiwar signs and walking around Columbia University with all the students.

In 1977, during my sophomore year in college, I took a course on "America's Peoples: Immigrants and Exiles." We discussed Southeast Asian refugees. And what really struck me was that this was an urgent problem that no one really talked about.

In the summer of 1979 I took a job at the United Nations High Commission for Refugees in Geneva, Switzerland. They wanted me to organize a library. One day I walked into the office and there was a telex from Thailand: "Khmer crossing border. Please advise." And I thought to myself, "Lord, what am I doing here? I've got to go to Asia."

I took my money and bought a one-way ticket to Thailand. In Bangkok I pounded the pavement looking for work.

Save the Children had an opening at their Women's Center in Songkhla Refugee Camp. Located on the Thai-Malaysian border, eight hundred miles south of Bangkok, Songkhla was the refugee camp for Vietnamese boat people. The camp was smaller than a football field. But the number of refugees living there was between four thousand and nine thousand, depending on the rainy season.

Even though the Thai and Vietnamese are traditional enemies, the Americans said, "We accept you." So no matter how hurt they were, no matter how much it had cost emotionally, physically, financially to go from Viet-

301

nam to Songkhla Camp, they were now nine-tenths on their way to America. That was both the greatness and the sadness of what I saw.

The greatness being that there was a future for these people. The sadness was that they did not understand where they were going, for the most part. They understood very well why they were going. But they didn't speak English and had no idea of how to find a house or a job.

My job was separate from the rest of the camp, running the Center for Unaccompanied Women, half funded by the UN and half by Save the Children. In reality, it was a center for women who had been battered and raped on the seas. And these women had greater apprehension about where they were going than the rest of the camp. Especially being single, without family, and badly hurt. They didn't know that Americans have a different view on rape than the Vietnamese.

Most of these women wouldn't say what had happened unless they arrived battered on a beach with no clothes on. I'm talking about women who had been held by pirates for weeks on islands. Or who had been taken to a village and kept hostage . . .

Their biggest goal was just to be able to melt into a camp population where no one was going to notice them. I'm not sure that those who came into the Women's Center were even honest with me after months and months. Some of them hid it because they didn't want to think about it. Others had fear of never being eligible for marriage in the Vietnamese community.

A constant number of thirty to forty lived in the center. The idea was to take care of each other. Our youngest was an eight-year-old whose mother and brother had been killed. She had been abducted by pirates. They had abused her. I'll never forget when she arrived.

She had a little friend with her, an eleven-year-old girl. They sat together on a bamboo platform that our women had built. They wouldn't eat, they wouldn't talk. No emotion, no hunger, no conversation the first two weeks. They would only shake their heads. These two girls had no family outside of Vietnam. But they had gone through this whole ordeal together. They were the only thing each other had in this whole world.

The resettlement system is such that the French wanted children under ten years old, so they could place them in French homes and have them become beautiful French citizens. So the eight-year-old was whisked away to France. The eleven-year-old went to Australia. Because the Aussies want young women because they don't have enough to get married and have babies.

The day they left, I sat there and watched them go off— the eight-year-old girl on one bus and the eleven-year-old on another. Their lives just scattered to the wind.

By the time I arrived back in the United States, in November 1980, I knew one hundred of these women very well. Over a period of the following year I heard from all of them. And today, I'm still closely in touch with thirty or forty. Most of them are either adolescent or don't have family. They call me "Chi," their big sister. I don't think any of them realized when they left Vietnam that they were crossing over a horizon where there's no way back.

Lyn is now twenty years old. She left Vietnam when she was fifteen. She was in Songkhla Camp for almost a whole year because she was an unaccompanied minor. She had been held by pirates on Kra Island for ten or twelve days. The only reason she survived Kra was at that time the UNHCR had large boats. And one of the fishermen, after he had raped a whole lot of women on the island, in return for amnesty told UNHCR where these women were.

For women like Lyn, to live, survive, get to Thailand, is worth celebrating. Lyn went twelve days with no water, no food. One-hundred-degree heat on a small island surrounded by salt water. Caves . . . I finally understood what Kra Island was after Lyn arrived in the U.S.

We went to see the movie that had no words, *Quest for Fire*, about the Stone Age. I thought, "Oh, superb movie. No English, no problem, we can all go to the film. We can all understand." Well, Lyn absolutely flipped out. It reminded her of Kra. She was in absolute terror. We were with some other Vietnamese, so she didn't want to leave. But she was in tears, shaking, upset. All of a sudden I had an understanding of what Kra Island was—savage.

I'd say that Lyn is a pretty average case. An unaccompanied teenager sent off by her parents to have a better life. She arrived in Thailand raped, beaten, everything stolen. I don't mean just gold, I mean clothes. You name it.

And this one fishermen who told the UNHCR that these women were on the island . . . she called him "the kind man." I never got over that. Lyn said, "He screwed me, hurt me, twenty times. I'm alive. He's the reason, he gave me water."

Lyn arrived in the Women's Center wearing a CARE T-shirt. There was a group of about five fifteen- and sixteen-year-olds who all slept together. They ate very, very little. They said nothing, just huddled together.

I'll never forget the first time I saw Lyn laugh. When you don't see someone talk for three weeks and rarely smile, a giggle is beautiful. One morning I asked someone to bring us water. And Vietnamese is a five-tone language. I put the tones a little bit wrong and it came out, "My grandmother had just been put in the grave." When they figured out I had made this mistake, Lyn exploded into laughter. She thought it was so funny to see this entertaining American trying to speak Vietnamese.

Her attitude became, "I'm going to make it wherever I go. I want to get a high-school diploma. I want to be like any other American. I want to go to the best university or college. And I want to be an architect."

So the American world views her as a star student. I went to Houston to visit her. Her teacher said, "Oh, this amazing girl. Look what she's done. But she never talks much about Asia. She tells us how long it took her to get from there. But she never really talks about it."

Lyn fits into the crowd with her Levi's blue jeans. Her spiffy white windbreaker, perfect haircut . . . everything fits. You certainly would never know her out of any other teenager walking down the hall in Houston. She gets beautiful report cards and the whole thing. I'm probably the only person in the world who knows how she feels.

I received a letter from Lyn about a week ago. She was taking her SAT tests to get into college. This letter represents how she is when she goes out every day and how she really is:

*Dear Eve,*
*I'm a bad test taker. I can never take my mind off*

*what happened on the boat, and concentrate on the test. I was so sensitive about pregnancy, birth, abortion, death. That makes my flesh creep. Two years ago I thought I would make my life in the U.S. new and clean. But I was wrong, Eve. I always feel guilty. My inferiority complex begins since that. I'm not as strong as you think. It is just my mask.*

*A lot of times I wake up at midnight. I thought I was in that damn cold and stinky cave with my heart almost stopped because of the rattle sound from the man. It obsess me. I can hear it. Feel it so vividly whenever I close my eyes. But I think it was my problem, my fault, so I don't want to talk. I don't want people to feel sorry for me or despise me.*

*Sometimes I am just like a wild animal. I want to tear all the books, break the walls around me. But I have to control it somehow. Then I sob. I look to the invisible space. It always listens and never says anything, just satisfy me. I'm so confused when I talk about this experience.*

*Eve, I'm sorry to bother you. You're right. I must stay busy.*

This is the same person who goes out every day and her teacher says, "This girl is amazing." But the teachers are never going to understand, never going to know. And she's not an isolated example.

I live two miles from Arlington. I can drive across the bridge to the Vietnamese community. And I would certainly not think that it was a radical statement to say there's fifty to a hundred single women there similar to Lyn. I'm working with some of them now. Trying to get them organized into a cleaning co-op, to get their minds off what happened on their journey.

# AMERICA
--------
## Kassie Neou
*Cambodian Survivor*
*1975–1981*

I arrived in the U.S. on March 20, 1981. Los Angeles, our first sight in the Western world, was a real heaven to us. We feel that we were reborn in the New World. We were with smiles and hope . . . I cannot find a word to say how much joy I have.

An American family who belonged to the Lutheran Church in Silver Spring, Maryland, sponsored my family. We lived with this American family for a while, before they could find us an apartment. It was okay for me, but my children were shy at first to be with American kids. But after a couple of days, they are better adjusted than me.

When we arrived, according to the government program, I was on welfare for a while. Even though we had nothing, I felt ashamed of living on welfare. So after three months I found a job teaching English in a refugee program in Washington. I worked there for fourteen months. Then I got a job at Saint George College in Maryland, teaching Khmer. I quit that job because the pay was not enough. While I taught, I drove a taxicab at night at the D.C. airport. This means I worked more than twelve hours, sometimes fifteen hours a day, just to make ends meet.

My family is thirteen members: my two children, my mother, my sister and her husband and daughter, my fiancée and her three children. That's the Khmer extended family. But the American family is my fiancée and the five kids.

Being Cambodian, I still dream of going back to a free Cambodia. A Cambodia like now, I will never go back to. I don't think my kids would go—they are Americans now.

I now own a gas station. It's a new experience owning a business. Sometimes it shocks me, too. I hired a man off the street who said that he needed a job to pay rent and buy food for his children. That made me recall my past experience in Cambodia when I needed help so desperately. That's why I offered him the job. It was not proper to do that, but it's deep in my heart when somebody says, "Please, I need food." I could hear more than that. Because I experienced a thousand times worse.

So I felt sorry for him and gave him the job. Two and a half hours later, he walked off with seven hundred dollars. I made a report to the police. That shocked me. But now I hired a good young man to help pump gas and another young man from Pennsylvania who is a good mechanic. We work long hours—thirteen to fifteen hours, six days a week.

My fiancée is now working at the Department of Commerce. Her income is only six hundred dollars a month. We don't want to live in a crowded situation, but we have no choice. Yet, when we think back to our past experience, this is still heaven to us.

# THE DOCTOR FROM HONDURAS

## Dr. Erwin Parson

*Medic*
*8th Field Hospital*
*Nha Trang*
*May 1966–April 1967*

I was born in the Republic of Honduras in Central America. I came to New York in 1958 at the age of fifteen. First we lived in Harlem before moving to Jamaica, Queens.

I went to a vocational high school, studying woodworking. I grew up around carpentry, but I saw that my dad was killing himself. And I knew that was not something I wanted to do for the rest of my life. My mother and my aunt were pressuring me to be a minister. So I thought, "I ought to be a minister. That's college." So in the fall of 'sixty-two I took two courses at Queens College.

I couldn't pass an SAT exam. There was no way I could get into college through the front door. So I took two matriculating courses. One was psychology, the other sociology. Report cards came out and I received a D in sociology and an F in psychology. I was utterly hurt by that. I always felt that I wasn't college material. And the D and F confirmed that sensation gnawing inside of me: "That's not what you're about."

I was drafted in 1965. I had registered as a conscientious objector—before it was popular. But I received orders for Vietnam. I was trained in Company D3, the only one of its kind in the military, for people who refuse to use weapons.

Just before going to Vietnam, the executive officer of the medical detachment said to me, "Parson, I know you don't use weapons. But we're going to the range today to practice before we go to Vietnam. You don't have to come if you don't want to. I understand."

I thought of all the cynical comments people I trained with in the medical company had made to me a month before: "You're a medic. But if you are in the field and VC are coming after you and your patient with weapons, what are you going to do?" Those thoughts came back to me. I said, "Yeah, I think I should learn how to use a weapon."

When I first arrived in Vietnam, I was assigned to be an ambulance driver. I had to drive out to rescue people in remote areas. I had some very close calls. The roads blowing up and grenades being thrown into the van—which happened four times.

I served at the 8th Field Hospital in Nha Trang as a medical specialist. I tended wounded people brought in by medevac helicopters. There were other soldiers who had medical problems not as severe, who needed shots or had small wounds that I could clean up and suture.

I decided I wanted to go to college. I was still in Vietnam when I applied. It was not an easy decision based on my academic history. I think it had to do with coming so close to death. Being terrorized and having my life pass in front of me. I said, "If I get out of this alive, I want to really do something with my life."

I did it out of anger, as well. And determination: "This is something that I want to do and that I should do. And by golly, I'm going to do it."

My previous school failure had plagued me so much. That past was really painful—failing, getting the D and F. It had been devastating. One of the things that helped build my confidence was having gone through the Medical Training Center at Fort Sam Houston. It made me feel, "I can learn things. I can think. I can put facts together." That was helpful. Plus the good work I was doing in Vietnam. I was a damned good medic.

I don't know if coming from another country or being black had anything to do with it. I came to realize that in order to have control over one's life and destiny, education was extremely important. Being in Vietnam, feeling that, "My life is cheap over here. People are dying like flies. I mean, it could be me." And saying to myself, "If I get out of here, I'm going to make sure that I get control over my life. So this will never happen to me again."

I came home from Vietnam in May 1967. It was close to a year before I was accepted by the University of Massachusetts. I had applied there because it was the school that my sister was going to. And even today, I don't know how I got in. I didn't have any SATs, it was like a miracle.

I received my acceptance letter on a Friday and was told to report Sunday morning. I had no money. My mother gave me the last three hundred dollars she had. She went to the bank and took it out. I'll never forget that.

I was told very clearly by the dean, "You're in, but you have many deficiencies to take care of. Otherwise, we'll kick you out." I was deficient in math, no science, no language. One of the most humiliating experiences of my life was sitting down in high school classes with kids. Here I was, a soldier coming back from Vietnam, a man. I didn't know a thing about algebra. I felt very self-conscious. I was the only black person, the only adult. But I completed my requirements.

When I first started college, it was to be a physical therapist. But I happened to take an introductory psychology course, and that's the direction I went in. Now, I'm talking about myself, but I think I speak for a lot of veterans. What we want more than anything is to be able to serve. More than monuments.

Monuments are important in some ways, but most Vietnam vets want to do something constructive. Here I was, really terrified of failing in college. But I decided to work a full-time job while going to school. I had the GI Bill from the government that was helpful. But there were times that the checks did not come on time. And it wasn't enough money to pay for tuition. So I had to borrow money.

I'd never had a lot of money. I thought, "The most important thing now is school. Drop everything else. Sell your car, put everything you've got into school." But I didn't want to do that. I said to myself, "I'm tired of sacrificing, after all I've been through in Vietnam."

I graduated from the University of Massachusetts psychology program in 1972. I got married and two years later earned my master of science degree. And two years after that I had my Ph.D. I found that once I got into a groove in school, I just kind of breezed right through. I learned the necessary discipline in Vietnam and the military. And if I hadn't gone to Vietnam, I probably wouldn't be a psychologist today. No doubt in my mind. I wouldn't have had the guts, the courage to try.

In 1979 I was working in the clinical program at Queens Hospital Medical Center. This is where I started to work with Vietnam vets. I was a Vietnam vet who was very successful in obliterating Vietnam from my mind. I stayed very, very busy and didn't have time to think about the past.

But shortly after I began working with veterans, I was invited to do a local television program. That morning, I was sitting at the breakfast table with my wife. I began reflecting on Vietnam. All of a sudden I started feeling very anxious and tearful. I couldn't understand it. Because it had been thirteen years at that point. I felt tears coming into my eyes, and I didn't want my wife to see me like this.

So I walked up to the bathroom. Tears came rushing out of me like two rivers. I had been bottling a lot of stuff inside me. The terror . . . that came back. I sat down with my wife and told her what happened. I told her I was just so damned scared of this terror.

That was something I thought was over . . . there weren't any battles or heavy stuff, but there was a lot of dying around me. I saw the aftermath of the shooting. I had people die on me . . . mangled bodies, headless bodies . . . I thought it was all in perspective. I thought I had outgrown it. But I still remember moments.

# MIAs
--------
## Dan Pitzer

*Prisoner of War*
*U Minh Forest*
*October 1963–November 1967*

If Americans are still alive as prisoners in Vietnam now, twelve years after all the prisoners were supposed to have been released, I'd say that psychologically they'd be more like a zombie. More like a person who has just given up and accepted the fact that he is there.

The only way I can explain it—In the short time that I was a prisoner, four years, I learned to live with pain and the threat of death. It's the feeling of abandonment that destroys you.

When I was first captured, it was a dream. This could not be real. Reality was back in the United States—my family, my past. Within a year and a half, I did a 180-degree change on that. Being a prisoner was reality. The good stuff back in the United States became the dream.

So, these prisoners who may still be held, somewhere along the line have made this same transition. Vaguely remembering their families, vaguely remembering life in the United States.

In the prison camp, an older man, Mr. Hai, was our first interrogator. Every once in a while he'd sit down and tell us stories about the French. This one French outfit, over a hundred men, were wiped out. Some killed, some of them captured. And the Viet Minh kept them as prisoners. They kept them in the villages and let them marry Vietnamese women after ten or fifteen years. And I believed it. Because some of my guards were almost six feet tall, some had curly hair, not all of them were one hundred percent Vietnamese. And we were offered, "You come over to our side. We'll let you live in our villages. You can eat anything you want. Just work with us." People like Robert Garwood [the defector who returned to the U.S. from Vietnam in 1979] were swayed over. And they also threatened us if we didn't cooperate, "The war might end tomorrow. But we can keep you here forever."

We know there's bodies being held. They always come up with bodies when they are trying to get something from us or are looking for publicity.

# ACCEPTABLE LEVEL OF CASUALTY

## Kay Bosiljevac

*Wife of an American MIA*
*Omaha, Nebraska*

*September 1972–Present*

My husband Mike was an air force pilot shot down over North Vietnam on September 29, 1972. Both he and his flying partner, Lieutenant Colonel James O'Neill, ejected from their F-105 after it was hit by a SAM missile. That day, Hanoi Radio announced the capture of the two pilots.

Other pilots in the squadron watched their parachutes, had radio contact with them, and knew exactly where they were. It was one o'clock in the afternoon. Red Crown [the electronic countermeasures aircraft] had contact with them on the ground. Two days later, the CBS evening news flashed a picture of Jim O'Neill being paraded in front of the cameras for propaganda in Hanoi.

At the time, Mike Junior was nine months old and my daughter Susan was two and a half. They were pretty tiny. In fact, when the air force chaplain came to notify me, I was trying to soothe Michael's little gums that were just beginning to teethe.

The kids were too young to understand, but they knew that I was very upset. The only way I can describe it is that I was in a state of shock for two or three weeks. The only thing that I could do during that time was wait for any kind of information.

In 1973, Hanoi began releasing the prisoners. In April, Jim O'Neill was released. He told me that the biggest shock in his life, worse than being shot down, was to look around the airport in Hanoi. He searched through the group of prisoners that was being released to give Mike the "thumbs-up" signal. And Mike wasn't there.

Jim told me that on the fifth day of his confinement, a

314

guard who spoke fluent English asked him, "Is there anything that you want?" And Jim wrotes Mike's name and said,
"Yes, I'd like to know about Mike Bosiljevac." The guard
went away for about ten minutes. When he returned, he
told Jim, "He's alive and well and uninjured. And luckier
than you."

Months before, I'd met Mike for his R and R in Hawaii.
As we were sitting on the beach, I stupidly asked him, "What
would you do if I died?" He looked at me and said, "What
you're asking me is what will you do if something happens
to me. Well, I must be honest, the combat missions are very
heavy. We've been hit a couple of times. I'm not afraid. The
only thing I'm shook up about is to go down and become
missing. The facts of life are that the Vietnamese are using
Soviet intelligence. They know everything about me. They
informed me over Radio Hanoi when Michael John, our son,
was born."

Usually Radio Hanoi would talk to the pilots, saying
things like, "Your wife is out with another guy." But Radio
Hanoi had informed him of our son's birth even before the
Red Cross did. This fact becomes important years later,
when the packages I continued to send Mike were always
precisely returned to me on our son's birthday. And letters
would be returned without photos that I had enclosed, on
Mike's birthday. The last one I received, in 1981, came back
with an East German postmark . . . on my son's birthday.

In October 1973, six months after the last American was
released by Hanoi, I went to Vientiane, Laos. I visited the
North Vietnamese Embassy. They went into a twenty-five-
minute harangue about "the U.S. is an imperialist war-
monger" and all the usual stuff. Then the chargé said to me,
"You have two children." And I said, "Yes." He said, "You
have one son who is now in Manhattan Beach, California.
And your daughter is in Colorado Springs." (I had each of
them staying with a different friend's family.) And without
displaying shock or anything, I said, "Yes." And the only
question I asked was, "What is my husband's condition?"

The chargé said to me, "Your husband is alive. He will
be released contingent upon fifteen conditions that we have
put to your government." Things like: removing the U.S.
airplanes from Thailand; removing the mines from Haiphong; reparations; and he kept going on and on and on.

Then he talked about American prisoners in Laos, saying that there were Americans still being held. I asked him how many. And he said, "If I told you that, I would have thirteen hundred families knocking at my door." That was the number of how many people were still missing.

When I returned to Thailand, an American who was attached to MACTHAI [Military Assistance Command, Thailand] took me aside and said, "I want to talk to you." We walked away from the building and he said, "I found Mike's name on a list with thirty-six others. It was a 'possibles' list." Mike could have been moved to a third country.

A while later, I received a copy of the Geneva Accords and its addendums. The North Vietnamese, North Koreans, Russians, and Chinese added a clause regarding prisoners of war that refers to "holding countries"—in which they reserve the right to transfer prisoners to other fraternal countries.

Mike had specialized training that made him valuable. His ECM [electronics countermeasures] training was considered the best anywhere. He had also gone through an Atomic Energy Commission fellowship to get a master's degree in radiation shielding. But his ECM expertise was most valuable to the Communists—the super stuff that makes airplanes disappear and appear where they aren't. And the ability to jam enemy radar. What struck me about what the man at MACTHAI said was that it was a list of technicians.

The air force tried to discourage me from the beginning. But in 1976, I went to Paris. I went to the American Embassy to see a consular officer whose photo I had seen many times at the Paris peace negotiations. He was a very knowledgeable person, a distinguished diplomatic man. He took me upstairs to his office and closed the door.

He said that they were having difficulties making inquiries through the French. Because in the past, Henry Kissinger would not allow any activity to go on anywhere without being personally involved. I told him what I had heard about Mike being on a third-country list. His response was, "It's more likely Russia than China." I made an inquiry to the government about this, but nothing ever became of it.

At first, the U.S. government said that all of the MIAs

would be declared dead a year and a day from May 1973. All the families knew that once the government declared them all dead, that would be the end. By August 1973 we had a court order to stop them. Or to slow them down until we could find out more information. Because they had stories of so many different missing men on file that they couldn't possibly check them all out in that short period of time.

When the military was in the process of trying to make the "status change" they always told us, "Do yourself a favor. You're young women. You have needs of your own. It would be better for your children if you went on with your life. You owe yourself this."

Some of us would just pop right back at them, "What about our husbands' rights? Don't you feel a little shabby about this?"

I did a *60 Minutes* program in 1974 which really set the air force off. But there were memos coming out of Vietnam at that time that reported prisoners or defectors talking about live Americans still being held. And there was reporting coming out from intelligence agents. I obtained documents through the Freedom of Information Act in 1978 or 1979, showing that there was reporting of live prisoners still going on.

My kids have grown up with the situation and have done well. I've never pulled any punches with them. I've always told them what the truth is: "We don't really know." They ask a lot of questions about their dad. And they ask a lot of questions about patriotism and commitment.

There was an occasion when a kid teased Susan that her father was dead. She came home and did not make a big deal out of it. She did cry. And I told her, "What you've got to learn in your life is to forgive. Because some people don't understand what they are saying. They know they are hurting you. But in your life, one thing that you're going to be blessed with is the capacity to understand other kids' hurt. Just store this in your book of memories and remember what it's like to be hurt. And don't do it to anyone else."

Last Christmas, Susan danced in *The Nutcracker*. And there was an older man with an agonized look on his face who kept staring at me. And I thought, "What's wrong with this guy?" I vaguely remembered that his kids had been in

*The Nutcracker* the previous year, but I didn't know what it was about him.

Then one day I had to do a shuttle run from way across town to pick up Susan from rehearsal. I stopped for a cup of coffee and got Michael a glass of milk and a donut. And here was this same man also in the donut shop. The place was kind of packed and there were about four feet of snow on the ground outside. In the middle of this packed place he looked at me and said, "Do you remember me?" It sort of scared me. I said, "No. I'm sorry, I don't." And he said, "I came to your house at four-thirty on a Friday afternoon." What he meant was that he was the air force officer sent to notify me that they had declared Mike "presumed dead."

He broke down crying. I felt so bad that here's this man suffering, thinking somehow I hated him. At the time of notification I made it very clear how I felt. But I wasn't offensive nor did I blame the people sent to tell me. I had asked the air force not to make a personal notification visit. Rather, to simply notify my attorney. Because I felt the impact on the kids would not be good. And it wasn't.

I had just come home from work. I was tired and sitting in the recreation room. Michael opened the door and let the officers in. The families knew the Carter administration was going to do this. We fought it in court. This was 1979.

Michael told me that someone was at the door. And I thought they were from a local store making a delivery. But he came back and said, "There's two air force officers here to see you." I looked up and said, "Michael, you're such a sweetheart, you would let the devil in. Wouldn't you?" He was eight years old and was being very polite: "Yes, sir; no, sir." I came in and saw the men standing at the door in uniform but with a horrified look on their faces. I said, "Gentlemen, would you go sit down on the couch, please." And I phoned my attorney. I said, "Now what should I do?"

Susan began to cry and ran upstairs. So I talked with her and said, "Look, Susan, I want you to understand something. This has been coming for a long time. We knew they were going to do this. Those two men down there are bleeding from every pore in their body, because they are hurting to have to do this. For the sake of all of us, calm down. And when you compose yourself, come down. A piece of paper is not going to make any real difference. But don't hate those men, please."

This memory came into my mind during that strange little encounter in the donut shop, as all the people sat there with their mouths gaping open as this man began to cry. Ever since that time, he and his wife have always made a special point of saying "Hi." And we have become very good friends. But he thought I hated him. You can't diminish the impact on people who have had to work with this.

Among our 2,500 MIAs, the status of Category 1 means men who were known to have been captured alive but never returned by Hanoi. The U.S. government has repeatedly given Hanoi files on these men: their names, ranks, and serial numbers. Hanoi knows everything about them. Plus they have Soviet intelligence on them. There are 166 men classified as Category 1. And 1,100 are classified Category 2, which means suspected of being captured alive.

From 1973 through 1980, the U.S. government position was to wear the families down and eliminate us through frustration and attrition. So they wouldn't ever have to deal with the problem. The "presumptions of death" are a pretty good example. Those men unaccounted for were labeled by the Pentagon "a reasonable level of casualty." I've seen it in print.

There was one man on the POW task force who at least was honest about it. He was the only one who had the guts to sit there and say it to your face.

We'd sit there and I'd say, "You son of a bitch." He'd say, "It's not my words, Kay. This is the way it is. If it were 20,000 men it would be different. But it's only 2,500. That's all they're looking at—numbers. Acceptable level of casualty."

My gut feeling is that Mike could still be alive. But I just don't know. I love my husband. And if he had to die in Vietnam or a Soviet . . . wherever they took him, the best memorial to him would be to get the rest of the live men out. But if he's not dead . . .

I don't know how he would react or what state of mind he would be in after so many years of captivity. But he does have two beautiful kids.

# THE MONUMENT

## Jim Noonan

Communications
1st Shore Party Battalion
Chu Lai

September 1966–October 1967

The Vietnam Memorial in New York City grew out of a task force that the mayor put together. Many people felt that there had never been the recognition of Vietnam veterans that they deserved. That they served their country with all the dignity, valor, and honor that this country had come to expect of our soldiers.

A monument is nothing more than bricks and mortar, it's nothing more than a symbol. But it is very important for those guys who between 1965 and 1973 came home and experienced disparaging remarks, perhaps were spit on, perhaps were called "baby-killers."

In my experience in Vietnam, I never saw anybody shoot a kid indiscriminately, or any of that kind of stuff. If anything, quite the opposite. We'd go out to the orphanages all the time. Because the kids were a source of sanity.

The monument will provide very tangible evidence that now people understand that we were honorable men attempting to do a very difficult job. And we did it to the best of our ability.

I believed that it was my duty to go to Vietnam. And that has to do with the values my parents instilled in me. I'd like to think that I have maintained those values, because they are good ones. I'm very proud of my family. They're all honest, hardworking, caring people who would go out of their way for another human being if it would help that person. Of those values that I see as my best points now, Vietnam was part of their forming stages.

320

I got through high school by the skin of my teeth. But after Vietnam, I went through college in three years on the dean's list. Yet, it's hard to reflect upon a situation where so many have suffered and think about it in terms of what you personally have gained. But I do think that as a result of my military experience I am a stronger and more confident person. I also doubt that I'll ever be that scared again. I can always think, "No matter what comes up, I'll know I've been more scared."

One of the reasons I joined the Marine Corps was their tradition: You don't leave your dead, you don't leave your wounded. You don't leave your brothers out on the battlefield. And in Vietnam, there were a lot of guys who put their life on the line for their brothers, for principle, for whatever reasons they thought it was important. And it's in the moment when a person makes that decision that the effort really stands out.

We have gone through our dark night following the war. And we have had the courage to face up to those sometimes very painful memories. One comment Vietnam veterans make is, "I'm not going to fight another war unless you're going to let me win it." And that is probably going to have a serious impact on the military. Because the young officers who served in Vietnam are going to be generals very soon. They might not be quite there yet. But they are on the verge of assuming some very real responsibility. And the lessons they learned in Vietnam will be reflected in the judgments they make throughout their careers.

# HORATIO AT THE BRIDGE

--------

## Lt. Col. Michael Andrews

*Platoon Leader*
*25th Infantry Division*
*Dau Tieng*
*June 1968–June 1969*

The Gulf of Tonkin incident happened in 1964, my sophomore year at West Point. For the next three years, the specter of Vietnam overshadowed everything: our relationship with women, our studies, our friendships. Vietnam emerged as the reason for being.

It seemed that every sergeant would begin every class by saying, "If you don't pay attention to this class, you're going to die in Vietnam." I went to Ranger School. There were leadership classes telling us how to do everything. But it was all academic and in theory.

The thing that impressed me most when I got to Vietnam was that I looked into the faces and the eyes of the soldiers who were there. I began to realize that I was responsible for these people. Their very safety could depend on how well I did my job.

I had somehow thought that the soldiers of my first unit would be seasoned, hardened troops who mechanically knew how to do things. But they were young people, who were doing the best they could.

My first firefight was on the nineteenth of September, 1968. I was ordered to take my platoon across an open field and move into the tree line. About halfway across, I knew something was wrong. I turned and asked a young soldier who was carrying a machine gun to come forward. And in the next couple of seconds, an ambush was sprung. The first round hit this boy in the head, whom I had just told to come up. The boy on the other side of me was hit in the head also.

The kid with the machine gun died instantly. The firefight intensified and everyone did what we had to do. I went over to the other boy who was hit in the head. I was holding him. He was crying. I could see the brains . . . the top of his head opened up. And he was just delirious.

We were right in front of the VC machine gun and I was trying to hold him down. He was thrashing around. I decided that we better just get out of there. So I put his arm around my neck and lifted him, trying to get him to safety. We drew fire and he was hit again.

So I lay there with him for a while, just trying to hold him down. During those few minutes, he was crying and praying—asking for God and Jesus—for his mother. And at the end of that stream, he asked for Two-Six. That was my radio call sign.

After it was over, that boy, and the other boy that died, just devastated me. I carried the body back that night. I sat and looked at that boy, absolutely appalled that it happened. That was the turning point.

I would look at the soldiers and ruminate about who was going to take care of them and train them. I honestly felt that I cared about them. And I thought, "There will always be another time when we will be sending young people into desperate situations. The contribution I can make is to be there with them."

I had never intended to stay in the army. I went to West Point to get an education. Didn't know anything about the army. Didn't know what officers did. Through four years of West Point I never thought about it. But I could remember this almost horror of responsibility evolving.

I very much disliked some of the tactics that I saw in Vietnam. I thought that in our area, we approached the problem wrong—our operations were too big and we disrupted civilian people. While back in the brigade base camp, there was a swimming pool and air-conditioned offices.

I saw some very poor lieutenants and captains, who I did not think did a good job or cared whether they did a good job. And with regard to integrity, there probably is no profession that depends upon it more.

I went to graduate school at Duke University in the early seventies. I can remember vividly young coeds calling me a baby-killer and mindless military robot. That is a dreadful misconception of the kind of guy that is in the military. We're just like most other people. We have frailties and wives and children.

So it was a vicious circle for me, with this rumination that I had in Vietnam. But I began to realize that the most important time of all for a soldier is not during a war, but in between wars. Between wars you don't have the public support or the resources or money and soldiers are forgotten. But at this time, politicians must think and soldiers train to be ready. You don't train during a war, you experience things one after another at a mind-boggling rate. It is absolutely essential to be well trained and prepared to deal on a level of crises. So instead of getting out of the army and joining the reserves, egotistically coming back in if there happened to be a war, I stayed in like Horatio at the bridge.

I talked with my wife about it. Just as before Vietnam, I thought about perhaps myself being in danger. But it might have been after that first firefight that I started worrying more about the people I was responsible for being in danger or hurt. I still think about that . . . the guy who was hit. That's worse than being hit yourself.

I believe that soldiers, professional soldiers, do become exhilarated with the tactics of it all. During training, I have experienced it on terrain boards, becoming wrapped up in the chase and the intensity and wanting to play again. But those blocks on the terrain board are not people. And in training exercises, when things are going well and the radios are working, the tracks [armed personnel carriers] are going thirty miles an hour and the wind is in my face, I feel exhilarated. But I can't imagine that feeling extending to wanting the real thing. Because it becomes horrible very fast.

There's a misconception in the civilian community to think that a career soldier, professional soldier, has a craving for war. Among my peers, I don't think that any of them feel that way. As MacArthur said in his farewell address to West Point, "A soldier, above all others, wants peace. He wants to avoid war because he experiences it. He's the one who is separated from his family and endangered."

Always through history there's been a danger that a society will regard its military as a protective monster that is pulled out of the closet to attend to some problem, then is put back in. Being in the military is perceived as being some kind of embarrassment: "Nobody would really want to do that for a living."

And there is and probably always will be a real gulf between the civilian community and the military community. But there is a supreme danger in that. If the military becomes isolated from the civilian community, it is no longer representative of the society.

# THE TWILIGHT ZONE
--------

## Eddie Adams

*Photographer*
Time *and* Parade *magazines*
*Vietnam*
*1983*

I went back to Vietnam in 1983. It was spooky. I never did want to go back, but I had to. Because *Time* said, "Go." I often felt that I didn't leave anything there. But I was wrong. Man, was I wrong.

The weirdest thing was to see the Russians in Saigon, in the little shops on Tu Do Street. They're everything a cartoonist would dream of. Like little Khrushchevs running around. My feeling was, "This is my country, man. What the hell are you doing here?"

When I came into Saigon from the airport, I went to where the AP and embassy office used to be, near the place where they sold all the flowers. AP and NBC shared part of the German Embassy on the second floor. And I lived right near there. I just wanted to walk, to reminisce and think. All of a sudden, where these flowers are, I see Cung.

I never knew Cung's full name. But I knew he was Viet Cong, even at the time. I remember Cung had very rich black hair and a black mustache. Looking at this man, I thought it was Cung. But his hair and mustache were white. So I shouted across the street at him. It was like an island of flowers. And he shouted back at me.

He came over and grabbed me, and I embraced him. As soon as he did that, it was really funny ... he let me go real quick. He jumped back and looked over his shoulders. So I said, "Well, let's just cut it off. I don't want to get you in any trouble."

There was a coffee shop below the old AP office where I used to go all the time. It always had good coffee. So I went in and was looking around for familiar faces. I didn't recognize anyone. So I asked one guy how long he had worked there. He said, "Ever since the Liberation." I was telling him that I used to come in there all the time and what it was like. But he was different. And the people . . .

One of the things that really bothered me was these little Amerasian kids. They look more like Americans than they do Vietnamese. And they consider themselves Americans. They speak English—pretty damned good. I was walking out of the Majestic Hotel, and one of these kids approached me. An older boy, about sixteen years old. He said, "Where are you going?" I said, "Oh, I'm looking for someplace for coffee." He said, "Just follow me. I'll show you a good place."

He brings me down a couple of streets, to a little side street and into a tiny little coffee shop, like a bar. So I went in and the kid left me at the door and walked away. I walked over to the counter. And this Vietnamese woman came towards me. She's looking at me, eyeing me all over. I sat down, and she said, "Do you mind if I sit here?" I said, "Go right ahead." And she said, "What are you doing here?" And she got a little bit nervous and said, "Could you come in the back room?"

When we got in the back, she asked, "Are you really an American?" She started laughing, and then she started to cry. I was sitting there thinking, "Holy shit." She started telling me, "They're following you. Don't go out at night." And she seemed to be very concerned for me.

Then she told me her story. During the war she had lived with an American from USAID, and they had a daughter. He wanted to marry her. But her mother wouldn't allow her to marry an American. Then the evacuation took place. Afterwards, he tried to get in touch with her, but there was no way out.

She told me his name, where they lived, and how rotten Vietnam was now. She really hated it. And she was really concerned about my safety. It was really sad. She had tears and grabbed ahold of my hand. She told me that the thing that really bothered her was the lack of education for her kids. They were treated badly by the Communists because she had lived with an American. It was one of the saddest scenes.

So I took her name. And when I left Vietnam, I turned it over to the embassy in Bangkok because the U.S. has representatives going into Vietnam to take out some of these American kids. But she can't get out unless they contact the USAID guy or something. A bunch of bullshit. I really got pissed off. She had worked for USAID for several years. I was getting very upset—I had cried with her. And I said to the U.S. officials, "Goddamn it!"

She had given me her address and said she could receive mail. But I had seen the Communists go through every package that comes into the country—they rip them all open. I went to the area where they do it, where people go to claim packages sent by relatives overseas.

The people line up in long rows. They sit there for days waiting for their packages. The cadre look at every one. It's an unreal scene. Like a big bus or train station where all these people come with their chits. And they wait while the police rip open all their packages.

Another very spooky thing happened when I was down in Can Tho. I'm always drinking coffee. So I went to one of these outdoor coffee stands. It was in the market, right on the river. I sat down. And a group of kids surrounded my table. They didn't say anything, they just stood there. There was this little black American girl, thirteen or four-teen years old. She sat there and just kept staring at me. Didn't say a word. None of them said a word. They were all ages up to maybe nineteen. And this little black girl sat all by herself just really staring. Looking at like I was from outer space. There was like this warm feeling, yet a cold distance. Jesus, it sent chills...

In Saigon, I had this little kid that became my mascot. He had red hair—Vietnamese—blue eyes, freckles. He drove a cyclo and followed me everyplace I went. I was taking pictures on a lawn near the palace in Saigon of students practicing with rifles. And there were some Com-munist instructors. They have little red stars on the uni-form. It was wrong—there's something wrong there. The whole trip was like Rod Serling. It was like a *Twilight Zone* for me. And for the Vietnamese in the South, it's like a *Twilight Zone*, too. There are still a lot of boat people. Being there I can understand it.

During the war, even with heavy fighting going on and

civilians being killed, they still would try to go back to their villages. They did not want to leave their homes. Somebody who doesn't understand the Vietnamese wouldn't understand what it means that today they put their families in boats just to get out of there. Something's got to be wrong. The so-called peace there now.

# THE DREAM
--------
## Nguyen Cong Hoan

*Representative*
*National Assembly*
*Socialist Republic of Vietnam*
*Ho Chi Minh City—Hanoi*
*1976—1977*

In April 1977, after the second assembly session in Hanoi, I left by boat from Nha Trang with thirty-three other people. Two other assemblymen were with me, among many different types of people in our boat, captained by a fisherman.

Our engine broke down on the high seas. We drifted for two days aimlessly. A Japanese ship rescued us and gave us passage to Tokyo.

Today, it's ironic to live in America, whose presence in my country I opposed for so many years. When I first arrived, I went to Washington and talked with congressmen. They had their own concerns and did not want to think about Vietnam. So I came to California to take care of my family, working in an electronics firm.

America has been good to us and offered many opportunities. But we Vietnamese have different customs. The young adapt more quickly than the old. To the Vietnamese, family cohesiveness is the most important thing in life. Vietnamese children are brought up with respect for their parents. But in the U.S., children have their own lives at seventeen or eighteen years old. They don't want to listen to their parents or stay at home.

Now, our children grow up without knowing their homeland, the customs, the scenery. They only hear the older people talk about it. Even though I now live well, I only think and dream to someday go back home.

I am very regretful that I did not understand the Communists before. The Communists always speak in lofty terms that appeal to the better part of people. Then they are used for a tragic end. I believed them, I was wrong. And now I can never be happy until I return to my country.

# FULL CIRCLE

**Ken Moorefield**

*Military and Foreign Service Officer*
*South Vietnam*
*1967–1975*

From 1975 until around 1980 it seemed that everyone was trying to forget Vietnam. During that time, I decided to change my focus and try to get away from the Indochina issue. I managed to do that successfully until 1979, when I was asked by a Hollywood screenwriter to help with a script called *The Last Days of Saigon*. This reawakened old memories and refocused my thinking.

Through the years I've had recurring dreams, usually of battlefield action. I'm engaged in a pitched battle with North Vietnamese and Viet Cong forces. Always the same haunting scenario of thousands of Communist soldiers moving back and forth without a fixed battle line. The sense that they could be behind any corner or any rice paddy. Always that sense of being infiltrated. Not knowing whom to trust.

There's great intensity in these dreams because the excitement and fear are so real and vivid. Similar to the intensity that I experienced in battles that we actually fought in the middle of the night. We were literally nose to nose with the enemy. I have vivid memories of the uniforms, the AK-47s—the flashes of their rifles. The feel of the battlefield . . . I guess that lives with me.

The final days of Saigon are more like a dream. I can remember very vividly events that flowed during that final period. But there was so much life lived during the final ten days, with the country literally crashing down around our ears. The speed, the rapidity, of the events during that experience makes it, in retrospect, almost as if a movie were being run in front of me at a very fast speed.

I'm sure that Vietnam will always live with me. And I don't want it not to be there. Vietnam veterans experienced something that transcended ourselves. Despite the fact that we suffered a political defeat, the values for which we fought are larger than each of us and the fundamental reason for our willingness to give and to serve.

I went back to Southeast Asia in the summer of 1983, to film the Indochina refugee experience. Seeing thousands of Cambodians, Laotians, and Vietnamese still pouring out of those countries brought me back in touch again. I'd come full circle. I became aware that the struggle for the values that we fought for in Vietnam still continues in Indochina today, as it does in other parts of the world. And as long as people are living without freedom and basic human liberties, that struggle will never, never be over.

# CHRONOLOGY OF EVENTS

1930   *February 10:* The Yen Bay uprising, led by the non-Communist VNQDD Nationalist Movement (formed in 1927) marks the beginning of the modern Vietnamese struggle against the French. The same year the Vietnamese (later Indochinese) Communist Party is formed in Hong Kong, mostly by Soviet-trained Comintern agents. Nguyen Ai Quoc (later named Ho Chi Minh) had been head of the Comintern's Far Eastern Bureau (under Mikhail Borodin) in Shanghai, acting as liaison for Moscow. In 1939 the non-Communist Dai Viet Party is formed by Truong Tu Anh, and begins organizing in northern and central Vietnam. During this period a number of nationalist organizations are also active in the South, including the Cao Dai and Hoa Hao political/religious sects, Trotskyite Communists, and a variety of older non-Communist groups.

1940   *Sept. 22:* Following the German occupation of France, the French sign a treaty with Japan allowing Japanese military presence in Indochina.

1941   *May:* The Viet Minh (Viet Minh Doc Lap Dong Minh Hoi) is formed during the 8th Session of the Indochina Communist Party Central Committee. Simultaneously, numerous Viet Minh support groups, led by ICP cadre, are formed in the large Vietnamese communities in Laos and northeast Thailand.

Early   Nationalist Chinese general Siao Wen (secret member of
1943   Mao's Communist Party and political advisor to Chiang Kai-shek's commanding general in southern China, Fa-Kwei) convinces the non-Communist Vietnamese Revolutionary League to ask for Ho Chi Minh's release from a Chinese

prison to join their organization against the Japanese. Siao Wen then subsidizes Ho to go into north Vietnam to join other Communist Party members, who are collaborating with the French. This gives the ICP the opportunity to reorganize and leads to contact with the Allies in southern China. At this time Vietnamese non-Communist revolutionary groups are playing off relationships with the Chinese and Japanese to maneuver for eventual independence from colonial rule.

1945    *March 9–13:* Japanese depose French rule in Indochina and declare Cambodia, Laos, and Vietnam (under Emperor Bao Dai) independent countries.

*May 8:* V-E Day; Germany surrenders.

*July:* At Potsdam Conference, Allied leaders assign British to disarm Japanese in southern Vietnam and Chinese Nationalists to disarm Japanese in northern Vietnam.

*August 15:* V-J Day; Japan capitulates after Hiroshima and Nagasaki are hit with atomic bombs.

*August 20:* Emperor Bao Dai writes to President Truman requesting Vietnam's independence. Having received no answer and believing that the Viet Minh are the Allies' choice, he abdicates his power to the Viet Minh on August 25. At the same time, non-Communist nationalists attempting to reach Hanoi before the Viet Minh are stopped by monsoon floods. Other nationalists still operating out of China do not arrive in time to give Bao Dai the correct information about the Allies' views.

*September 2:* Ho Chi Minh proclaims the Democratic Republic of Vietnam in Hanoi. The Viet Minh begin using their power to co-opt or eliminate non-Communist nationalist rivals.

*September 13:* British General Douglas Gracey arrives in Saigon and prepares to return power to French. On September 22 the French return to Vietnam. From October to February 1946 they conduct a military campaign, reconquering southern Vietnam and Cambodia.

*October:* Ho Chi Minh orders Laotian Prince Souphanouvong, one of the youngest of twenty Lao princes, back to Laos accompanied by twelve Viet Minh operatives wearing Lao uniforms. They began to organize the Pathet Lao Army, supported by the Vietnamese business community in Laos. Souphanouvong is made commander, with Vietnamese bodyguards and advisors. The Vietnamese control every department of the Pathet Lao through advisors; most of the original soldiers are ethnic Vietnamese.

1946    *March 6:* Ho Chi Minh signs agreement with France allowing French soldiers to return to northern and central Vietnam in return for France's recognizing Ho's government. Ho uses this respite with France to eliminate political opponents, in collaboration with the French. By November, with the nationalist factions weakened, the French turn on Ho's Communists.

*December 19:* The Viet Minh launch attacks on French garrisons in the Hanoi area, then retreat to rural areas. The Indochina War begins. The non-Communist nationalists, the Trotskyites, and Cao Dai and Hoa Hao religious sects are caught between the French and Viet Minh crossfire. By 1948–49, many of these groups are either decimated or integrated into the French-supported Bao Dai government to fight the Communists.

1948    *April:* Soviets blockade Berlin. U.S.-British stage a massive airlift of supplies.

1949    *July 1:* In agreement with the French, Bao Dai forms the first government of the state of Vietnam.

*October 1:* Communists achieve victory in China under Mao Tse-tung.

1950    *January:* The People's Republic of China and the Soviet Union recognize the Viet Minh government. In February, China begins sending large quantities of weapons, supplies, and advisors to aid Ho's forces. The Viet Minh begin successfully stepping up attacks on French outposts.

*Feb. 7:* The state of Vietnam is recognized by Great Britain, the United States, and the Vatican.

*May 8:* President Truman reacts to Mao's victory and to Chinese support of the Viet Minh by announcing economic and military aid to the French forces in Indochina.

*June 25:* North Korean Communists invade South Korea. Korean War begins. President Truman commits U.S. troops under United Nations auspices.

*June 27:* President Truman announces thirty-eight-member military mission to Vietnam. On July 26, Truman signs legislation for $15 million military aid to French in Indochina.

*October 7:* Chinese launch invasion of Tibet.

1951    *February:* Strengthened by China's influence and support, the Vietnamese Communist Party officially resurfaces as the Lao Dong (Workers') Party, with Ho Chi Minh as Chairman and Troung Chinh as Secretary-General. The Viet Minh begin a policy of hostility toward intellectuals, landowners, and influential village leaders, including nondogmatic members of the Communist Party.

*September 7:* Aid treaty signed between U.S. and state of Vietnam.

1953    *February:* Viet Minh, with Chinese advisors, begin first phase of Thought and Land Reform terror campaigns in north Vietnam, based on Mao's tactics, which lead to gradual communization of countryside. Thousands are sentenced to death and imprisoned.

*July 27:* Armistice ends Korean War, dividing Korea.

*October–November:* France grants independence to Laos and Cambodia.

*November 12:* The French government, shocked by the Bao Dai government's request for independence outside of the French union, and facing domestic opposition to the seven-year war, announces it will negotiate with the Viet Minh to resolve the Indochina conflict.

*November 20:* The Viet Minh step up attacks against the Royal Lao government. French forces respond by occupying the Laos–Vietnam border outpost at Dien Bien Phu.

1954    *April:* The Geneva Conference on Korea and Indochina begins. The Viet Minh raise the stakes by launching an offensive in already independent Cambodia, trying to gain a foothold on territory for negotiation purposes.

*May 7:* French surrender at Dien Bien Phu, breaking morale to continue fighting. In June, Pierre Mendes-France begins private negotiations with China's Chou En-lai to end war.

*June 16:* Emperor Bao Dai selects former nationalist prime minister Ngo Dinh Diem as Vietnam's new prime minister.

*July 21:* Geneva Accords proclaimed to end hostilities in Indochina. Provisions divide Vietnam at 17th Parallel and guarantee independence of Laos and Cambodia. Laos is divided, with two provinces on Vietnam's border given to Pathet Lao. The Viet Minh demand that Cambodia also be divided, but China's Chou En-lai convinces them to remove all forces from Cambodia. The Viet Minh withdraw, taking with them the small number of Khmer Communists and force-marching 5,000 peasants for military and political training in North Vietnam. The agreement is not signed by the South Vietnamese or Americans, who cite unfair advantages given to the Communists.

The provisions of the agreement also call for 300 days of free movement between North and South. Nearly one million refugees, mostly Catholic peasants, will flee to South Vietnam in 1954 and 1955, despite Viet Minh intimidation and controls. Many Viet Minh lesser cadre remain in South Vietnam to organize and agitate against the southern government.

*September 8:* SEATO pact established in Manila for defense of Southeast Asia. Signed by United States, Britain, Philippines, Thailand, Australia, New Zealand, France, and Pakistan.

*October 9:* French forces leave Hanoi.

*October 23:* President Eisenhower, in a letter to President Diem, promises that the U.S. will provide aid directly to South Vietnam, rather than through the French.

1955    *March–September:* President Diem's forces defeat the Binh Xuyen gangsters, who had controlled the Saigon police and underworld, and neutralize the powerful Cao Dai and Hoa Hao sects, temporarily stabilizing South Vietnam.

*July 20:* Talks called for by the Geneva Accords to pave the way for reunification elections in 1956 are scheduled to begin, but President Diem refuses North Vietnam's invitation to participate until Hanoi puts an end to terrorism and guarantees free elections and political liberties.

*October 26:* The Republic of Vietnam is proclaimed in the South by Ngo Dinh Diem, after a national referendum ousts Bao Dai as chief of state.

1956    *February 21:* The French government announces that Diem has requested the withdrawal of remaining French forces in Vietnam and that his request will be honored.

*June:* The Vietnamese Communist Political Bureau in Hanoi implements a resolution calling for an armed struggle in the South to win political power. Party policy includes the buildup of armed forces and base areas combined with the formation of a broad political front.

*October–November:* In Hungary, the Soviet crushing of a popular revolt overshadows a peasant uprising against Communist rule in Nghe An Province in North Vietnam, Ho Chi Minh's birthplace.

1957    *January 3:* The United Nations–appointed International Control Commission declares that neither North nor South Vietnam has complied with the Geneva Accords.

*October:* Communist insurgent activity begins in accordance with the Hanoi resolution. Thirty-seven armed companies are operating in the Mekong Delta. Viet Cong units in South Vietnam mount a campaign of terrorism, assassination, and propaganda. In North Vietnam, the military is continuing a buildup in preparation for war.

1959    *January 1:* Fidel Castro assumes power in Cuba.

*January–March:* China crushes uprising in Tibet; Dalai Lama flees.

*May:* At the fifteenth Party Plenum in Hanoi, the decision is made to reunify North and South Vietnam by force. Unit 559 is established to transport troops and supplies to South Vietnam through Laos and Cambodia on the Ho Chi Minh Trail. During the next few years some 20,000 to 40,000 soldiers and political cadre are sent south to establish the Viet Cong.

*July 8:* Major Dale Buis and Sergeant Chester Ovnand, killed by guerillas in Bien Hoa, are the first official American casualties of the war.

*September:* The North Vietnamese Army forms Unit 959 to advise, supply, and organize the Pathet Lao and directly command North Vietnamese forces operating throughout Laos.

1960    *April:* North Vietnam imposes universal military conscription.

*May:* President Eisenhower announces an increase in the number of U.S. military advisors, to 685.

*September:* The 3rd Communist Party Congress in Hanoi calls for unification of South Vietnam by force, and the formation of the National Liberation Front and army in the South.

*December:* The National Liberation Front is officially formed in Tay Ninh Province, on the Cambodian border.

1961 *March 19:* The NLF decides to mount an offensive to prevent presidential elections in the South.

*April 17:* The U.S.–backed Bay of Pigs invasion of Cuba by anti-Castro exiles fails.

*May:* Viet Cong operatives in the Mekong Delta attempt to choke flow of food into Saigon. For the first time VC units of up to 1,000 troops are used in attacks in the central and northerly provinces. On May 13, 100 U.S. Special Forces are sent to Vietnam. U.S. advisors begin accompanying ARVN units into combat.

*Mid-August:* The Berlin Wall is imposed by Soviet and East German soldiers to divide the city.

*November 14:* With Communist attacks in South Vietnam mounting, John Kennedy informs Saigon that he is increasing the number of U.S. advisors from 900 to 16,000 over a two-year period.

*December 11:* The first U.S. combat support unit—two helicopter companies—arrives in South Vietnam.

1962 *February 8:* The U.S. Military Assistance Command (MACV) is established in Saigon.

*February 27:* President Diem's presidential palace is bombed by two South Vietnamese Air Force pilots. A substantial number of South Vietnamese are disenchanted with the Diem family's rule, especially with Diem's brother Nhu and his outspoken wife.

*July 23:* A Geneva treaty calling for the removal of all foreign forces from Laos ends a two-year civil war.

*October 7:* The U.S. withdraws its 666 military advisors from Laos, but North Vietnam disregards the treaty and maintains at least 10,000 troops in support of the Pathet Lao and continues developing the Ho Chi Minh Trail, infiltrating larger amounts of supplies and troops into South Vietnam.

*October 16–28:* The Soviet buildup of nuclear missiles in Cuba is met with a U.S. naval and air blockade that brings both countries to the brink of war. By November 1 the Soviets began dismantling the missiles.

1963 *May 8:* Buddhist demonstrations, violently dealt with by police in Hue, lead to nationwide demonstrations including

the self-immolation of monks. U.S. officials begin to agree
with South Vietnamese military that Diem must be removed
from power.

*November 1:* A military coup overthrows the Diem government. It is replaced by a military junta led by General Big
Minh, and begins a four-year period of political chaos in
South Vietnam. Later in the month Prince Sihanouk de-
nounces U.S. aid and orders the closing of the U.S. Embassy
in Cambodia. Sihanouk later agrees to allow the North
Vietnamese and the Viet Cong to let their troops stage in
Cambodian sanctuaries and use the port of Sihanoukville as
a supply base.

*November 22:* President Kennedy is assassinated and succeeded by Lyndon Johnson.

*December 31:* U.S. forces in Vietnam total 16,300.

1964    *August 2:* North Vietnamese torpedo boats attack U.S. Navy
destroyer *Maddox* in the Gulf of Tonkin.

*August 7:* The Tonkin Gulf Resolution of the U.S. Congress
authorizes President Johnson to use necessary force in Vietnam to deter North Vietnamese aggression.

*October 14:* Nikita Khruschev is ousted as head of Soviet
Communist Party. His successor is Leonid Brezhnev.

*October 16:* China explodes its first atomic bomb.

1965    *February 7:* A Viet Cong attack on Pleiku base kills eight
Americans.

*February 13:* President Johnson authorizes Operation Rolling Thunder, aerial bombardment of selected military targets
in North Vietnam.

*March 8:* The first American infantry unit, the 9th Marine
Brigade, with 3,500 men, arrives in Danang.

*April 7:* President Johnson proposes negotiations to Hanoi
to end the war, offering $1 billion in developmental aid. The
offer is denounced by Hanoi, who by 1969 (by General Giap's
own admission) will have lost more than 500,000 soldiers in
the South.

*June:* Nguyen Cao Ky becomes Premier of South Vietnam,
the ninth government since the Diem coup 19 months earlier.

*July 28:* President Johnson announces his decision to increase U.S. combat forces in Vietnam to 100,000.

*August 18–21:* The U.S. Marines conduct Operation Starlight, south of Chu Lai. The first major ground action fought solely by U.S. troops, it produces 600 known enemy casualties on the body-count scorecard that comes to dominate the U.S. government's perception of progress of the war.

*October:* The first battle between regular North Vietnamese and U.S. forces (the 1st Cavalry Division) in Ia Drang Valley blunts an attempt by the North Vietnamese to isolate southern Vietnam from the central highlands.

1967  *January 8–May 14:* Operations Cedar Falls and Junction City, conducted by U.S. Army and ARVN in the Communist strongholds in War Zone C and the Iron Triangle, inflict an estimated several thousand enemy casualties and help to establish the "light at the end of the tunnel" theory in Washington.

*September 3:* Nguyen Van Thieu elected president of South Vietnam.

*November 17:* The National Liberation Front radio (Radio Giai Phong) announces a seven-day cease-fire for the January Tet Lunar New Year.

1968  *January 23:* The crew of the U.S. Navy ship *Pueblo* are captured by North Korea, which refuses to release them.

*January 30:* Communist forces launch Tet Offensive at Nha Trang. Within twenty-four hours, attacks take place in thirty-six of South Vietnam's forty-four provincial capitals. Most cities are cleared of Communist forces by February 4, but prolonged fighting takes place in some cities like Saigon and Dalat. Hue is not completely recaptured until February 25, after fierce fighting. There, 2,800 bodies of civilian families executed by the Communists, some buried alive, are found in mass graves. Though an overwhelming military victory by the Americans and South Vietnamese, it is portrayed as a defeat in the United States.

*March 31:* President Johnson announces he will not seek reelection, and also announces a partial bombing halt over North Vietnam.

*May 13:* First formal session of U.S. and North Vietnamese negotiators at Paris peace talks.

*June 10:* General William Westmoreland is appointed Army Chief of Staff. His replacement as Commander of U.S. Forces in Vietnam is Army General Creighton Abrams.

*August 20:* Soviet and Warsaw Pact troops invade Czechoslovakia.

*October 31:* President Johnson announces the halt of all bombing of North Vietnam.

1969  *June 8:* President Richard Nixon announces first phase of withdrawal of U.S. troops from Vietnam.

*November:* The public learns of the massacre in My Lai, a village in Vietnam, in 1968.

1970  *March 18:* Prince Norodom Sihanouk is deposed as ruler of Cambodia. New government is led by Sihanouk's prime minister, General Lon Nol. By March 23, Sihanouk announces in Peking a United Front with the Khmer Rouge to oppose the Lon Nol government.

*April 29–June 30:* U.S. and South Vietnamese soldiers invade North Vietnamese and Viet Cong sanctuaries in Cambodia to stall an offensive against the new Cambodian government and secure the safety of the adjoining Vietnamese provinces before the main withdrawal of U.S. troops from Vietnam. Confined to a limit of thirty kilometers into Cambodia, large quantities of small arms and ammunition are captured. The reaction in the United States to the invasion is intensified by the killing of four protesting students at Kent State University on May 4.

*December:* The U.S. Senate rejects the Tonkin Gulf Resolution; approves the Cooper-Church Amendment preventing further military operations in Cambodia and placing tight Congressional restrictions on aid to the Cambodian government.

1971  *June 13: The New York Times* begins printing the Pentagon Papers on U.S. involvement in Southeast Asia.

*October 25:* The People's Republic of China is admitted to the United Nations, ousting Taiwan.

1972  *February 21–28:* President Nixon's historic trip to China opens door to normalizing relations with that country.

*March 30:* The North Vietnamese launch the Easter Offensive from the DMZ and sanctuaries in Cambodia and Laos.

After initial gains, the NVA are repulsed in the populated areas by ARVN troops supported by U.S. air power. Nevertheless the North Vietnamese succeed in establishing themselves in some wilderness areas on South Vietnamese soil, where 145,000–200,000 of their troops will be allowed to remain after the 1973 Paris Peace Agreement.

*May 8:* President Nixon orders the mining of Haiphong and other North Vietnamese harbors.

*December 18:* After the Paris peace negotiations break down because of North Vietnamese obstinacy, President Nixon orders the eleven-day bombing of Hanoi and Haiphong, which brings Hanoi back to the bargaining table.

1973   *January 27:* The Peace Agreement is signed in Paris by Henry Kissinger and Hanoi's Le Duc Tho. The cease-fire begins on January 28. South Vietnam's leadership, which earlier denounced the terms of the agreement as a sell-out by the Americans, unwillingly agrees to comply, due to promises by President Nixon of continued support.

*March 29:* Last U.S. combat troops leave Vietnam, MACV is deactivated.

*May 10:* U.S. House of Representatives blocks use of funds for continued bombing of Cambodia.

*August 14:* American bombing in Indochina is terminated. With North Vietnam transporting record amounts of Soviet bloc and Chinese armaments to South Vietnam and the Khmer Rouge advancing on urban centers of Cambodia, all U.S. military actions in Indochina end.

*October:* The Communist Party Central Committee's 21st Plenum in Hanoi, encouraged by the U.S. withdrawal, issues a resolution caling for a fierce war that will defeat South Vietnam completely. The resolution calls for drastically increasing supplies to the battlefield in the South and resolves to help the Khmer Rouge and Pathet Lao win victories.

*October 6:* The Yom Kippur Arab–Israeli War begins with armored attack across the Suez by Egypt. On October 25 the U.S. puts all forces on worldwide alert in response to signs of Soviet intervention in the Middle East.

1974   *August 9:* Nixon resigns as President in Watergate scandal.

*December:* North Vietnamese troop strength in the South

rises to 285,000 men. The North Vietnamese Army begins the Spring Offensive with an attack on An Loc, 75 miles northwest of Saigon.

1975   *February:* North Vietnamese launch major attacks in Central Highlands. Ban Me Thuot falls on March 13, Kontum and Pleiku on March 16. A panic ensues in the northern provinces. Hue and Danang fall by March 29, as the ARVN are routed and the NVA begins its advances on Saigon. The ARVN make heroic stands at Go Dau Ha and Xuan Loc, but lacking supplies and overwhelmed by unlimited NVA forces, they begin to pull back toward Saigon around April 15.

*April 17:* The Khmer Rouge capture Phnom Penh, and immediately begin to force-evacuate the city of all residents. A 3½-year reign of terror begins that eliminates up to one-third of Cambodia's 1975 population.

*April 30:* Saigon falls. North Vietnam conquers the South.

*May 15:* Communists hold Victory Parade in Ho Chi Minh City (Saigon). Hanoi begins imposing communism on the South.

*Late May–August:* The Hanoi-backed Pathet Lao begin to eliminate non-Communist members of the 1973 Coalition, imprisoning most in desolate "seminar camps" (an estimated 40,000–60,000 people are eventually imprisoned, out of a population of three million). Pathet Lao and North Vietnamese troops begin attacks on hill tribes (who form majority of Lao population), especially against Hmong, that continue under such operations as "Extinct Destruction" and "Razing Entirely." In December the Pathet Lao establish the People's Democratic Republic of Laos.

1976   *July 2:* Vietnam is officially unified as the Socialist Republic of Vietnam (SRV). The National Liberation Front is disbanded in the South, while Northern Party members dominate administration, embittering many former Viet Cong.

1978   *March–May:* The Communist government launches a program to confiscate all private businesses in southern Vietnam. In May, a currency reform wipes out most private savings; the dispossessed are encouraged to move out to rural labor camps, New Economic Zones. Simultaneously, hostility by the Communists toward the 1.5 million ethnic Chinese in Vietnam intensifies.

*November 3:* Vietnam and the Soviet Union sign a Friendship Treaty, granting Soviet forces free access to Vietnam's harbors and rivers.

*November:* The boat-person exodus dramatically increases from 15,600 in 1977 to 21,505 in the month of November 1978 alone. For all of 1978, more than 205,000 refugees survive the escape to asylum countries.

*December 25:* Vietnam invades Cambodia, capturing Phnom Penh by January 7. Pol Pot's Khmer Rouge are forced into the jungle and mountains near the Thailand border. The Vietnamese install a puppet regime, the People's Republic of Kampuchea (PRK), led by former Khmer Rouge general Heng Samrin.

1979     *February–March:* China attacks Vietnam, but pulls back following heavy casualties on both sides. Tension remains along the border as both sides build up their forces.

*March:* Soviet warships enter Cam Ranh Bay, which the Americans had previously spent two billion dollars to build up before 1975.

*Mid-1979:* 260,000 Sino-Vietnamese are forced to flee overland into China. Refugees become Vietnam's main industry. Government offices are set up to collect exit fees and bribes and to confiscate property.

*October:* The non-Communist Khmer People's National Liberation Front (KPNLF), under the leadership of former neutralist Prime Minister Son Sann, unites disparate resistance groups along the Thai–Cambodian border to fight both the Vietnamese and Khmer Rouge.

*December:* Members of the French Parliament return to Paris from Cambodia and report that the Vietnamese are attempting to starve the Cambodian population and that international aid to Cambodia is being diverted by the Vietnamese. The U.S. estimates that 350,000 Cambodian civilians died from starvation in 1979.

1981     *September:* Vietnam's one-million-man military is the fourth largest in the world. Colonel Bui Tin, deputy editor of the *People's Army Daily News* in Hanoi, says that a strong Vietnam is good for Soviet strategy to help develop revolutionary movements in Southeast Asia and throughout the world. Colonel Tin confirms that Vietnam is sending weapons left behind by the U.S. in Vietnam to guerillas in El Salvador.

1982   *February:* Two of Vietnam's most important Buddhist leaders, Thich Quang Do and Thich Huyen Quang, are arrested in Ho Chi Minh City and sent into exile by authorities. A national directive calls for a crackdown on all Catholic priests and their activities. Catholic leaders like Bishop Phan Ngoc Chi of Danang and Monsignor Nguyen Van Thuan, former archbishop of Nha Trang, have been placed under house arrest or sent into exile, and a number of Catholic priests, like Jesuit Superior Nguyen Cong Doan, and evangelical Protestant ministers have been imprisoned. Temples, churches, and seminaries remain closed, replaced by religious organizations set up by the government.

*June 22:* Unable to obtain support from the West for their resistance war against the Vietnamese occupation and Khmer Rouge in Cambodia, Prince Sihanouk and Son Sann's non-Communist resistance organizations join in a coalition government with the Khmer Rouge in order to receive aid from China and the ASEAN countries to fight the Vietnamese colonization of Cambodia. Provisions of the Coalition Agreement guarantee that each faction maintain its own organization's integrity and receive aid separately, which allows China to continue to favor the Khmer Rouge.

*September–October:* The Vietnamese-controlled People's Republic of Kampuchea (PRK) issues circulars authorizing the settlement of hundreds of thousands of Vietnamese civilians into Cambodia. Besides Vietnamese who previously lived in Cambodia, the circulars specifically call for new Vietnamese and "relatives and friends of Vietnamese settlers" to come to work in farming, fishing, lumber, handicrafts, and related areas. These settlers are added to 180,000 occupation soldiers, thousands of political cadre, and illegal entry by settlers who enter by river.

1983   *January–March:* Thai officials report eleven incidents of chemical weapons drifting into Chantaburi Province during Vietnamese air force and artillery attacks on the Cambodian border.

*June:* Rep. Stephen Solarz (Dem.-NY) reports that beyond a reasonable doubt, Vietnam has been using some kind of chemical weapons in Southeast Asia. Hanoi domestic radio service reports that all branches of the armed services and schools undergo annual chemical weapons training.

*July:* The PRK signs an agreement with Hanoi granting Vietnam legal annexation of border territories and Cambodian islands, in violation of the 1954 Geneva Accords that granted Cambodia's independence.

*December 16:* Laos and Kampuchea sign an agreement with Vietnam to link the banking and economic systems of the three countries.

1984    By 1984 the non-Communist Cambodian KPNLF has grown to a force of 12,000 armed men and another 8,000 needing equipment, protecting the majority of refugee camps along the Thai-Cambodian border and operating in many of Cambodia's provinces.

*March–May:* A new wave of persecution and repression of cultural and religious leaders is conducted in southern Vietnam. Large numbers are arrested, including the popular novelists Doan Quoc Si and Hoang Hai Thuy; poet Quach Tan; journalist Duong Hung Cuong and singer Duy Trac. In Ho Chi Minh City, police raid Gia Lam Pagoda and Van Hanh Monastery, arresting a dozen leading monks and nuns. On April 2, Buddhist venerable Thich Tri Thu dies following a day of police interrogation. Government media launch a denunciation campaign against Catholic leaders, including Bishop Nguyen Kim Dien of Hue.

*April:* Hanoi announces that nearly 100,000 people were sent to New Economic Zone labor camps during the first three months of 1984, equal to the number sent during the first nine months of 1983. Communist Party policy calls for a total of one million people to be living in the Zones by the end of 1985 to produce agriculture, primarily for export to the Soviet bloc.

*April:* Soviet troops stage an amphibious landing exercise on the coast of central Vietnam. The Soviet naval and air force buildup at Danang and Cam Ranh Bay continues. At Cam Ranh between twenty and thirty Soviet warships are operating out of the base, ten Badger bombers are at the airfield and an electronic intelligence complex monitors U.S. naval movement and transmissions between the Philippines and the Indian Ocean. Cam Ranh has dramatically reduced Soviet naval travel time to the Straits of Malacca, where the vast majority of strategic materials used by the West must pass.

*June:* A strategic road linking Dong Ha in central Vietnam to Savannakhet, Laos, on Thailand's border is completed. Since the 1977 Treaty of Friendship and Co-operation, an estimated 100,000 Vietnamese have settled in central and southern Laos, and approximately 60,000 Vietnamese soldiers and advisors secure Pathet Lao rule against sporadic resistance activity.

*June–September:* During the rainy season that began in May, the population of refugees living in makeshift camps on Thailand's border rises from 230,000 to 252,000, as Vietnamese repression continues inside Cambodia. Vietnamese troops continue artillery shelling of border refugee camps, forcing 85,000 refugees to remain in temporary shelters in Thailand. Inside Cambodia, the three resistance factions continue guerilla activities.

*September:* Secretary of State George Shultz announces that the U.S. is willing to take 10,000 political prisoners and their families from Vietnam's reeducation camps, above the 50,000 Indochina refugees sanctioned for the fiscal year 1984–85.

*September:* Nearly ten years after the fall of Indochina, two million refugees have survived; by lowest estimates 200,000 Vietnamese have died at sea. Thousands continue to flee each month. During the first six months of 1984, 10,000 Lao refugees arrive in Thailand; around 22,000 Cambodians arrive on the Thai border; and through orderly departure and escape by boat or overland, an average 4,000 Vietnamese (including orderly departure refugees) arrive in foreign lands each month.

# GLOSSARY

Advance Guard Youth: a Vietnamese student social and sports organization that evolved into a non-Communist nationalistic movement by 1945.

AID: Agency for International Development.

Airborne: refers to soldiers who are qualified as parachutists.

air cav: air cavalry; helicopter-borne infantry. Helicopter gunship assault teams.

AK-47: the standard rifle used by the North Vietnamese and Viet Cong.

amtrack: amphibious armored vehicle used to transport troops and supplies, used by marines.

AO: area of operations for a military unit.

APC: armored personnel carrier; used by army to transport troops and supplies.

arc light: B-52 bomber strike, shaking earth for ten miles away from target area.

ARVN: the Army of the Republic of South Vietnam, or a member of the army.

base camp: brigade- or division-size headquarters.

B-40 rocket: a shoulder-held rocket-propelled grenade (RPG) launcher.

Binh Xuyen: the organized-crime syndicate that controlled much of the Vietnamese underworld and Saigon police until deposed by Ngo Dinh Diem's forces in 1955.

bird: any aircraft, usually referring to helicopters.

body bag: plastic bag used for retrieval of dead bodies on the battlefield.

C and C: Command and Control helicopter used by reconnaissance or unit commanders.

Can Lao Party: the powerful semisecret political party of the Diem government headed by Ngo Dinh Nhu, Diem's brother. It per-

meated the entire administrative, intelligence, and defense structures of South Vietnam.

Cao Dai: a religious and political sect formed in the 1920s by a group
of South Vietnamese intellectuals, combining the three major
religions of Vietnam—Buddhism, Confucianism, and Christianity—with the worship of Vietnamese and Western heroes. Today with a strength of more than 1,500,000 followers, groups of
Cao Dai are still fighting a stubborn resistance war against the
Communists, especially in Tay Ninh Province.

Charlie: Viet Cong.

Chieu Hoi: the "open arms" amnesty program to encourage surrender
by VC and NVA soldiers and cadres. Around 200,000 came over
to the South Vietnamese side.

chinook: a supply and transport helicopter.

chopper: helicopter.

CIB: Combat Infantry Badge; awarded to army infantrymen who
have been under fire in a combat zone. Worn on both fatigues
and dress uniforms.

CIDG: Civilian Irregular Defense Groups. Ethnic minorities trained
by U.S. Special Forces for village defense or commando operations.

CINCPAC: Commander in Chief of all American forces in the Pacific
region.

claymore: antipersonnel mine carried by infantry.

clearance: permission from both military and politicians to engage
enemy in a particular area.

CO: commanding officer.

Cochin-china: the French name for its southern Vietnam colony,
encompassing the III Corps and Mekong Delta rice-producing
lowlands, which earlier was part of Cambodia.

Code of Conduct: military rules for U.S. soldiers taken prisoner.

compound: a fortified military installation.

connex container: corrugated metal packing crate, approximately
six feet in length.

contact: firing on or being fired upon by the enemy.

CORDS: Civil Operations and Revolutionary Development Support;
created by civilian administration, MACV, and CIA to coordinate
American pacification efforts.

COSVN: (Central Office of South Vietnam) Communist headquarters for military and political action in South Vietnam.

counterinsurgency: antiguerilla warfare.

C-ration: box of canned food used in military operations.

Dai Doan Ket Party: Party of Great Solidarity. Organized in 1954
to unify the non-Communist nationalist organizations in South
Vietnam in the period before Ngo Dinh Diem came to full power.
Headed by Diem's brother, Ngo Dinh Nhu, this was the fore-
runner of the Can Lao Party.

Dai Viet Party: formed in 1930 as a non-Communist revolutionary and political organization throughout Vietnam. Though more widespread and with a larger membership than Ho Chi Minh's Viet Minh or Lao Dong [Communist] Party, the Dai Viets were fragmented into regional factions. The assassination of Truong Tu Anh, the Dai Viet leader, in 1946 by Ho's agents further fragmented the Dai Viets. By the mid-1960s the Dai Viets had evolved into two major parties that both played key roles in opposing or supporting the various South Vietnamese governments. Since 1975, there has been severe repression against Dai Viet members, some of whom still carry on resistance to the Communist government.

DMZ: demilitarized zone; the seventeenth parallel area that divided the two Vietnams.

doc: a medic or corpsman.

dust off: medical evacuation helicopters.

elephant grass: tall, sharp-edged grass found in the highlands of Vietnam.

fatigues: standard combat uniform, green in color.

fire base: a temporary artillery encampment used for fire support of forward ground operations.

firefight: exchange of small-arms fire with the enemy.

flak jacket: heavy fiberglass-filled vest worn for protection from shrapnel.

flare: illumination projectile; hand-fired or shot from artillery, mortars, or air.

FULRO: United Front for the Struggle of Oppressed Races; resistance organization in the highlands of Vietnam made up of Montagnards, Cham, and ethnic Khmer. FULRO is still conducting fierce resistance against Communist operations to subjugate the indigenous tribal peoples.

FUNCINPEC: National United Front for an Independent, Neutral, Peaceful, and Cooperative Cambodia; Prince Sihanouk's current non-Communist political and military organization that is attempting to help drive the Vietnamese occupation forces out of Cambodia and reestablish independence. In 1982 FUNCINPEC joined the Cambodian Coalition Government (CGDK) and shares the seat at the United Nations.

gunship: attack helicopter armed with machine guns and rockets.

GVN: Government of South Vietnam.

hamlet: a small rural village.

hammer and anvil: an infantry tactic of surrounding an enemy base area, then sending in other units to drive the enemy out of hiding.

Hmong: A dominant Laotian hill tribe, around sixty percent of whom opposed the North Vietnamese and Pathet Lao, in alliance with the Americans and Royal Lao government. After 1975 the Communists stepped up repression against the Hmong, who refused to be collectivized. Massive numbers of Hmong have been slaughtered or driven into Thailand.

Hoa Hao: A Buddhist sect of two million faithful in the western Mekong Delta, founded in the 1930s. Since the assassination of the founder and prophet, Huynh Phu So, by Ho Chi Minh's Communists, the Hoa Hao have been fiercely anti-Communist. They are continuing stiff resistance to the present regime.

Hoi Chanh: Vietnamese Communist soldiers and cadre who rallied to the South Vietnamese government under the Chieu Hoi amnesty program.

hootch: a simply constructed dwelling, either military or civilian.

hot: an area under fire.

I Corps: the northernmost military region in South Vietnam.

II Corps: the Central Highlands military region in South Vietnam.

III Corps: the densely populated, fertile military region between Saigon and the highlands.

IV Corps: The marshy Mekong Delta southernmost military region.

KIA: killed in action.

KPNLF: Khmer People's National Liberation Front; the major non-Communist Cambodian political and resistance organization currently fighting against the Vietnamese occupation forces. Formed in 1979 by former prime minister Son Sann, the KPNLF is responsible for caring for and protecting nearly two-thirds of the 250,000 Cambodian refugees on the Thailand border from attacks by both the Khmer Rouge and the Vietnamese. Also called the Sereika [free men] by Cambodians, the KPNLF joined the resistance coalition government [CGDK] in 1982 and shares Cambodia's seat at the United Nations.

LCM: a mechanized landing craft used in harbors and inland waterways.

LP: (1) listening post; forward observation post of two or three men; (2) amphibious landing platform; used by infantry for storming beaches from the sea.

LST: troop landing ship.

LZ: landing zone for helicopters, usually a clearing in a rural area.

MACV: Military Assistance Command Vietnam; U.S. Army military advisors to the Vietnamese.

Mat Tran: the National Liberation Front.

medevac: medical evacuation helicopter used for fast evacuation of wounded.

Mike Forces: ethnic minority troops trained by U.S. Special Forces for rescue operations and reinforcement.

M-1: World War II–vintage American rifle.

M-14: wood-stock rifle used in early portion of Vietnam conflict.

M-16: the standard American rifle used in Vietnam after 1966.

M-79: single-barreled grenade launcher used by infantry.

Montagnards: aboriginal tribespeople inhabiting the hills and mountains of central and northern Vietnam, seventy-five percent of the total land mass.

NCO: noncommissioned officer. Usually a squad leader or platoon sergeant.

New Socialist Man: the Orwellian concept used by the Communists of the ideal collectivized citizen.

Nung: tribespeople of Chinese origin from the highlands of North Vietnam; some who moved south worked with U.S. Special Forces.

NVA: North Vietnamese Army.

Pathet Lao: the Laotian Communists, who from their inception have been under the control of the Vietnamese Communist Party.

point: the forward man or element on a combat mission.

poncho liner: nylon insert to the military rain poncho, used as a blanket.

province chief: governor of a state-sized administrative territory in South Vietnam, usually a high-ranking military officer.

Rangers: elite infantry and commandos.

reeducation camps: political prisons and labor camps of varying degrees of severity and size that comprise the Soviet-style gulag system throughout Vietnam.

RF/PF: Regional and Popular Forces. The South Vietnamese National Guard–type units. Regional Forces were company-size and protected district areas; Popular Forces were platoon-size and guarded their home villages.

Rules of Engagement: the political and military restrictions that dominated American military tactics in Vietnam.

sampan: a Vietnamese peasant's boat.

sapper: a VC or NVA commando, usually armed with explosives.

seminar camp: the Laotian Communist version of the reeducation camp for political prisoners.

Sereika (Khmer Serei): the non-Communist Cambodian resistance forces.

short-timer: soldier nearing the end of his tour in Vietnam.

sky crane: huge double-engine helicopter used for lifting and transporting heavy equipment.

starlight scope: a night observation device that uses reflected light from the stars and moon.

strategic hamlet program: a controversial pacification and village self-defense program implemented by the Diem government that attempted to turn all sixteen thousand South Vietnamese hamlets into fortified compounds.

USARV: U.S. Army Republic of Vietnam; command of operations unit for all U.S. military forces in Vietnam, based in Long Binh.

USOM: U.S. Operations Mission, which funded U.S. programs during the early American involvement in Vietnam.

VC: Viet Cong.

Viet Cong: the Communist-led forces fighting the South Vietnamese government. (*Cong* is short for *Cong-san*, which means "Communist.") The political wing was known as the National Liberation Front, and the military was called the People's Liberation Armed Forces. Both the NLF and PLAF were directed by the People's Revolutionary Party (PRP), the southern branch of the Vietnamese Community Party, which received direction from Hanoi through COSVN, which was located in III Corps on the Cambodian border. After 1968, as negotiations began in Paris, the NLF established the Provisional Revolutionary Government to appear politically legitimate.

Viet Minh: Viet Nam Doc Lap Dong Minh Hoi, or the Vietnamese Allied Independence League. A political and resistance organization established by Ho Chi Minh before the end of World War II, dominated by the Community Party. Though at first smaller and less famous than the non-Communist nationalist movements, the Viet Minh seized power through superior organizational skill, ruthless tactics, and foreign support.

Vietnamization: President Nixon's program to gradually turn the war over to the South Vietnamese while phasing out American troops.

VNQDD: Viet Nam Quoc Dan Dang, or Nationalist Party of Vietnam. A non-Communist movement formed in 1926, based on the doctrines of Sun Yat-sen. The VNQDD conducted the Yen Bai uprising in 1930, which began the modern struggle for Vietnamese independence. During World War II, the VNQDD staged in southern China and were instrumental in gaining Ho Chi Minh's release from a Chinese prison to help with the resistance fight against the Japanese. They were later betrayed by Ho, whose forces collaborated with the French to attack and assassinate VNQDD members in northern and central Vietnam after 1945. By 1950, having lost their bases in southern China when Mao came to power, the VNQDD ceased to exist as an effective organization.

wasted: killed.

White Mice: South Vietnamese police. The nickname came from their uniform white helmets and gloves.

WIA: wounded in action.

the world: the GIs' term for the United States.

# BIOGRAPHIES

EDDIE ADAMS is a native of New Kensington, Pennsylvania. He is one of the premier news photographers, and has received over five hundred national and international awards for his pictures, including the Pulitzer for the 1968 Tet photo. He is currently on the staffs of *Parade* and *Time* magazines. He lives in New York City.

CHUCK ALLEN is a native of Fort Lee, New Jersey. After twenty-four years in the army—twenty in Special Forces—he is now editor and publisher of the *National Vietnam Veterans Review* newspaper and founder of the Veterans Press Syndicate. He lives in Fayetteville, North Carolina, with his wife, Nita, and their children.

LT. COL. MICHAEL ANDREWS is a native of North Carolina. Following a tour of duty at the headquarters of the Department of the Army in Washington, he is now stationed in West Germany. He lives with his wife, Linda, and son, Michael.

MARK BERENT is a native of the Twin Cities, Minnesota. A retired fighter pilot, with four tours in Southeast Asia, he is currently a test pilot and reporter for various international defense journals. He has coauthored three flying novels under the pen name of Berent Sandberg. He lives with his wife, Mary Bess, on a horse farm in Remington, Virginia.

KAY BOSILJEVAC is a native of Omaha, Nebraska. She has been actively involved with the National League of POW/MIA Families, based in Washington, D.C., to resolve the MIA question. She lives in Omaha with her two children, Susan and Michael, Jr.

EDWARD BRADY is currently vice-president of a federal contract research center supporting the Defense Department in Washington, D.C. He lives in the Washington area with his wife, Kathy, and two children, Alex and Christine.

PETER BRAESTRUP has had a distinguished career as a journalist for *The New York Times* and the *Washington Post*. He is currently the editor of the *Wilson Quarterly*, published by the Woodrow Wilson International Center for Scholars at the Smithsonian Institution in Washington, D.C. He is the author of *Big Story*, which examines the role of the media in Vietnam during the Tet period of 1968.

EVE BURTON is a native of New York City. Presently she is a program evaluator for the General Accounting Office, the investigative branch of the U.S. Congress. She has worked with the Refugee Research Group at Smith College. Her writings on refugee affairs have appeared in several publications. She is currently completing a Fulbright Fellowship in Thailand.

CHHANG SONG was born in a Cambodian farm community. He is the founder and director of Save Cambodia, a refugee-assistance organization in Arlington, Virginia. He is the publisher of *Cambodia Today*. He lives with his wife and two children in the Washington area.

DOAN VAN TOAI was released from political prison in Ho Chi Minh City in 1977. He is currently a research fellow at the Institute of East Asian Studies at the University of California, Berkeley. His articles on the current situation in Vietnam have appeared in several publications. He is the author of *The Vietnamese Gulag* and coauthor of *A Viet Cong Memoir*. He lives with his family in the Los Angeles area.

JANIS DODGE OTIS has recently remarried, two years after waiting fourteen years for Hanoi to reveal the fate of her former husband. The impact of finally receiving his body from North Vietnam made her realize the importance of remains of loved ones being returned to the families who still wait. She lives in San Diego with her husband, Paul.

HA THUC KY was born in Thua Thien Province in central Vietnam. He has fought for Vietnam's independence since 1939, and has been chairman of the Revolutionary Dai Viet Party since 1965. He lives with his wife and seven children in Silver Spring, Maryland.

HOANG VAN CHI was born in Thanh Hoa Province in North Vietnam. A descendent of a long line of Confucian scholars, he holds university degrees in mathematics, physics, biology, and chemistry. Active in various revolutionary movements since 1936, he was director of the National Mint and a military chemist for Ho Chi Minh's forces in the war against France. He fled Vietnam in 1954. He is the author of *From Colonialism to Communism*, and has lectured at many universities.

KASSIE NEOU is secretary general of the Association of Cambodian Survivors. He currently owns a gas station in Washington, D.C., and lives with his family in McLean, Virginia.

MRS. KEO VEY was born in western Cambodia. She and her family escaped from Vietnamese occupation forces in 1983. She currently resides in Nong Samet (Rithisen) Refugee Camp on the Thailand–Cambodia border.

COL. DENNISON LANE has spent most of his twenty-year military career in Asia. He is currently working at the Department of Defense in Washington, where he lives with his wife, Malein, and two children.

GEN. EDWARD LANSDALE is a native of Detroit, Michigan. Since his retirement from the Air Force and government service, he has given many lectures on counter-insurgency and written articles on revolutionary wars, and is the author of *In the Midst of Wars*. He lives with his wife, Pat, in the Washington, D.C., area.

MRS. LE THI ANH is a native of Sadec Province in southern Vietnam. She is the director of the Vietnam Information Office, a refugee organization. Since 1977 she has worked with the National League of POW/MIA Families and the Forget Me Not organization to help resolve the fate of Americans still missing in Southeast Asia. She is the editor of the *Vietnam News* newsletter. She lives in Cheverly, Maryland.

GEN. LU MONG LAN is a native of Quang Tri Province in central Vietnam. He was commandant of the National Defense College in Saigon when South Vietnam collapsed in 1975. He is currently working as a building engineer and lives with his wife, Minh Duc, and six children in Falls Church, Virginia.

MRS. LU THI DUC was a hospital nurse in Saigon before escaping from Vietnam by boat in 1979. She currently lives in Belgium with her children.

FRANK McCARTHY is a native of the Philadelphia area. He is president of Agent Orange Victims International. His tireless efforts have been instrumental in bringing assistance to countless Vietnam veterans and their families. He currently lives in New York City with Aileen Blum.

ANNE MILLER was born in Clarksburg, West Virginia. She had a long career as a journalist and writer for many local publications, Associated Press, and a children's radio program on Mutual Broadcasting. She performed government service for the Voice of America and U.S. Information Service in the Philippines, Hong Kong, and throughout Southeast Asia. She is the author of an unpublished biography of Ngo Dinh Diem. Since retiring, she has worked as a volunteer for the Folger Library and the Smithsonian Museum of American History. She lives with her husband, Hank, in McLean, Virginia.

KEN MOOREFIELD spent his childhood traveling around the world in a military family. He is a graduate of West Point, with two combat tours in Vietnam. After working in the State Department as a foreign service officer in Vietnam, the Middle East, and Venezuela, he became director of the Vietnam Veterans Leadership Program. He is now a representative of the Department of Commerce in South America where he lives with his wife, Geraldine, and their first child.

NGUYEN CONG HOAN was born in Phu Yen Province in central Vietnam. He is currently involved in the Vietnamese Buddhist community and is working in an electronics firm in California, where he lives with his family.

NGUYEN TUONG LAI (ALIAS) was born in Bac Lieu Province in southern Vietnam. He is currently a factory worker in Europe, where he has resettled with his family.

JIM NOONAN is a native of Brooklyn, New York. He is an issues management consultant for the Edelman international public relations firm's New York office. He lives in Brooklyn with his wife, Peggy, and son, Bran.

RON NORRIS is a native of Greenville, South Carolina. He holds a degree in history from Bob Jones University. He is currently working in veterans' affairs in Greenville.

OUNG CHUMNET escaped from Phnom Penh, Cambodia, where he was a government railroad official, in 1983. He is currently living in Ban Sangae (Ampil) Refugee Camp on the Thailand–Cambodia border.

DR. ERWIN PARSON is a native of Honduras. He is a clinical psychologist and psychoanalyst and is co-author of *Vietnam Veterans: The Road to Recovery*. He has been northeast regional director of the federal Vietnam Veterans Outreach Center program. He lives in Uniondale, New York, with his wife, Jane, and two children.

PENN NOUTH was an architect of Cambodia's independence in 1953. He served as prime minister and advisor to the president, Prince Sihanouk, on numerous oc-

casions, until 1975. He currently lives with his wife in
Paris.

RUFUS PHILLIPS is president of Airways Engineering Corporation in Rosslyn, Virginia. He lives with his wife
and four children in McLean, Virginia.

DAN PITZER is a native of West Virginia. He spent twenty-
seven years in the army—fifteen in Special Forces.
Since retiring, he has worked in the U.S. Navy Survival Training School in San Diego. He and his wife
are currently dividing their time between a farm in West
Virginia and Fayetteville, North Carolina.

JONATHAN POLANSKY is a bartender, actor, and playwright.
He is the author of the play *In Pursuit of Liberty*. He
lives in New York City.

PRAK SAVATH was a district chief in Battambang Province
in western Cambodia before fleeing the Vietnamese
occupation in 1983. He currently resides in Ban Sangae
(Ampil) Refugee Camp on the Thailand–Cambodia
border.

PRASITH SAYAPHON escaped from a political prison "seminar" camp in Laos in 1982. Temporarily he is residing
in Panat Nikhom Refugee Camp in Thailand with his
family.

BERTA ROMERO is a native of Encinada, New Mexico. She
was a founding member of the U.S. Refugee Program
in Thailand. Currently she is coordinator of programs
at the National Immigration and Citizenship Forum in
Washington, D.C.

GINETTA SAGAN is a native of Italy. A member of the Italian
Resistance against the Nazis and Fascists in World War
II, she has been a lifelong human rights activist. She
is executive director of the Aurora Foundation and is
serving on the board of directors of Amnesty International. She lives in the San Francisco area with her
husband, Leonard, and three sons.

DAVID SCIACCHITANO is a native of Chicago. He is currently
working in the Office of Panamanian Affairs at the
State Department. He lives in Arlington, Virginia, with
his wife, Portia, and son, Maro.

ADOLPHUS STUART is a native of Staten Island, New York.
He is a free-lance writer working on a book about his
experiences with the Marines in Vietnam. He is also
an executive board member of the Veterans' Action
Coalition and creative consultant to Fama II Produc-
tions, a Vietnam veteran–owned video company. He
lives in Staten Island with his wife, Phyllis, and their
children.

COL. HARRY SUMMERS is a native of Ohio. He is a veteran
of both the Korean and Vietnam wars, and is now on
the faculty of the U.S. Army War College. He has
written many articles on military affairs and is author
of the acclaimed *On Strategy: A Critical Analysis of
the Vietnam War* and the *Vietnam War Almanac*. He
lives with his wife, Eloise, in Carlisle Barracks, Pennsylvania.

TRAN THANH SON is a native of Saigon and a former sergeant in the South Vietnamese Special Forces. After
a year's imprisonment in a reeducation camp, he and
his family were sent to be forced laborers in a New
Economic Zone in the Mekong Delta. They escaped
in late 1982 and fled across Cambodia to the Thailand
border, where they now reside in Dangrek Refugee
Camp.

TRAN TRI VU (ALIAS) lives with his wife in the Washington,
D.C., area. He is currently finishing a manuscript on
Vietnam under Communist rule and his reeducation
camp experiences.

TRAN VAN LUU was born in the Hue area in central Vietnam. A journalist in Saigon before the Communist
takeover, he escaped with his family by boat in 1977.
He is a graduate of the paralegal program at the Uni-

versity of San Diego and is currently an employment counselor for refugees with the International Rescue Committee. He lives with his family in San Diego.

TRUONG MEALY is a native of Soc Trang Province in southern Vietnam. He is a founding member of the Cambodian Buddhist Association in Paris and the Khmer-Lao-Vietnamese Association for Human Rights. He is now working in Bangkok, Thailand, in charge of humanitarian aid and social affairs for Prince Norodom Sihanouk's FUNCINPEC organization to assist Cambodian refugees on the Thailand border and to work for the independence of Cambodia.

TRUONG NHU TANG is a native of South Vietnam. He was a founder of the National Liberation Front and justice minister of the Provisional Revolutionary Government. He fled Vietnam by boat in 1979. His book, *A Viet Cong Memoir*, was recently published in the United States. He currently lives with his wife in Paris, France.

DR. YANG DAO was born in a Hmong tribal village in Xiang Thuong Province in Laos. He received his doctorate in sociology from the University of Paris in 1972. He is now a teaching and research specialist at the University of Minnesota and is writing a book on recent Laotian history. He lives in Minneapolis with his wife, Ly Mo, and five children.

STEPHEN YOUNG was born into a Washington diplomatic family. His father was an Asia specialist and ambassador to Thailand during the Kennedy administration. A fluent Vietnamese linguist, Stephen served for three years in Vietnam for the Agency for International Development. He has written many articles on the Vietnamese and assisted Ambassador Ellsworth Bunker in writing his Vietnam memoirs. He has been associate dean for student affairs at Harvard University and is currently dean of Hamline University Law School in Minnesota. He lives with his wife, Hoa, and three children in St. Paul.

# ABOUT THE AUTHOR

Born in Cleveland, Ohio, Al Santoli served in Vietnam with the 25th Infantry Division and received three Purple Hearts and a Bronze Star for valor. His first Book, *Everything We Had*, was nominated for the 1983 American Book Award. He now lives in New York with his wife, Phuong, and contributes regularly to *Parade*. His articles have also appeared in the *Atlantic*, *The New Republic*, and *Reader's Digest*.